THE BEST OF
NAUTICAL QUARTERLY

VOLUME I: THE LURE OF SAIL

EDITED BY REESE PALLEY AND ANTHONY DALTON

MBI

Dedication

To all seafarers:
The last truly free people on Earth

This edition first published in 2004 by MBI Publishing Company, Galtier Plaza, Suite 200, 380 Jackson Street, St. Paul, MN 55101-3885 USA

MBI Publishing Company titles are also available at discounts in bulk quantity for industrial or sales-promotional use. For details write to Special Sales Manager at Motorbooks International Wholesalers & Distributors, Galtier Plaza, Suite 200, 380 Jackson Street, St. Paul, MN 55101-3885 USA.

ISBN 0-7603-1820-4

Acquisition Editor: Dennis Pernu
Layout: Kou Lor

Printed in China

NAUTICAL QUARTERLY

FOREWORD
TWO BOOKENDS

BY JIM GILBERT

The life and times of the *Nautical Quarterly* really is the story of two people. In the abstract, it would be difficult to find a pair of individuals more different from one another than Joe Gribbins, the publication's illustrious but humble editor, and publishing impresario Don McGraw, the generous benefactor who financed the magazine for the entire, unprofitable, decade-and-a-half of its exquisite existence.

Don is charmingly outspoken and bigger than life. While it's not quite fair to describe him as a throwback to the Golden Era of yachting, without question he is a New York Yacht Club blueblood through and through. A captain of industry and silver spoon member of one of the world's biggest publishing empires, he is ambitious in business, and omnivorous in his yachting pursuits.

I was his invited guest at the launching of his last yacht, *Rainbow,* a stunning 124-foot motorboat completed at Delta Marine in Seattle in 1996, six years after the demise of *Nautical Quarterly*. *Rainbow* is an exquisitely finished boat with elaborate joinery. The staterooms, named after famous sailing boats, are decorated with lovely historical marine paintings, ship models, and half-models. In the middle of the tour, I congratulated Don on the way the yacht reflected his love for boats and the sea. Intending the comment to be the highest of compliments, I said, "You know, Don, the beauty and richness of everything on *Rainbow* reminds me so much of your old quarterly."

Don paused and for a brief second a wave of sadness swept over his broad, typically cheery face. "That was the second-nicest thing I ever made," he sighed.

Joe, on the other hand, was quiet and reserved. He was a man of the people who, though gregarious and well-spoken, was more at ease in an archive, library, or at the helm of a small sailboat than at a black-tie function. While he was no less ambitious than his chairman, his sense of accomplishment was measured on a macro scale, in the eclectic harmony of his subject matter for each issue, in the fine crafting of each article, in the judicious juxtaposition of images and text. Joe savored life no less, but his was a simpler pleasure that is

reflected in the many publications that long will be enjoyed and admired by fellow connoisseurs.

Even before I met Joe, I admired him and his craftsmanship as a writer and editor. I remember meeting in 1985 with Englishman George Nicholson, who many regard as one of the founding fathers of the modern mega-yacht industry. Joe had just interviewed Nicholson, at the time the premier yacht broker in the world, for a *Quarterly* article. An accomplished sailor and a member of one of the world's most venerable yachting families, Nicholson had been awestruck by Joe's depth of knowledge, as well as by his journalistic skills.

"We must have spoken for three hours," Nicholson said. "I didn't even know he was actually interviewing me for a story, because he never took a single note." Nicholson was surprised when, a few months later, he received his copy of the *Nautical Quarterly* containing a full feature on him.

"He got every quote absolutely, perfectly right," Nicholson said.

What Don and Joe shared in common made their differences pale in comparison. They both loved boats. Big, small, wood, metal, plastic; for sailing, for fishing, for rowing, for cruising; fancy, archaic, imaginative, plain; fast, slow; commercial, or pleasure: If it floated and moved they were enthralled. They loved the history, the traditions, and the artisanship surrounding boats and yachting. From their far different vantage points in life, they were the ultimate enthusiasts, and those of us who stand at every edge of the watery world are far, far better off for their unusual, if not incongruous, partnership.

In fact, it reasonably can be argued that it was the very nature of their differences that made the publication such an overwhelming artistic success, for between their different tastes and sensibilities there was little in the maritime world that was not covered. But the success of *Nautical Quarterly* was due only partly to the subject matter.

I remember meeting Joe in the *Quarterly*'s Connecticut offices during the publication's heyday. I was publishing nautical books at the time, and hoping to develop a joint publishing venture with the *Quarterly*. It was a luxuriously leisurely meeting, something I remember vividly because I was returning from a series of business meetings in New York, in which invariably I had felt rushed and harried. It was a breath of fresh air, I remember, to be talking to someone about the substance of a publishing project without immediately talking about whether it made any economic sense.

The *Quarterly*'s office was open with desks in the corners—Joe's of course cluttered with books, manuscripts, and page proofs—and large tables with ample room to spread out photo shoots and work on editorial spreads. It was a workshop more than an office. Everything moved at a sure, unhurried pace, not unlike wooden boat shops I've seen from Maine to Holland. It was a place for meticulous craftsmanship, not assembly-line production.

It was, in fact, exactly the romantic, intimate kind of space that you could imagine as the birthplace of the *Quarterly*'s distinctive look—that unique, iron-clad format which distinguished it from virtually every other publication in the world. As every *Quarterly* aficionado knows, there was something about that look which, like the compelling lines of a beautiful yacht, pulled both the eye and the heart of the reader.

The look of the *Quarterly* was perfect. It was elegant and refined. Not unlike the personalities of its creators, the book was simultaneously clean and modern, and yet the presentation still exuded an air of traditional elegance. It was a design that lent itself to all its widely divergent subject matter. Thanks to the *Quarterly*'s stunning editorial environment, a bit of the Old World seemed to rub off on every shiny new motor yacht it covered, and the oldest classics somehow seemed more hip and relevant to our fast-paced world.

As a person who has spent the last two decades in nautical publishing, I've often considered what influence the *Quarterly* had on both yachting and publishing. Perhaps another way of asking the same question is to reflect on what we miss most by the magazine's passing.

Without question, Joe and Don and their *Quarterly* still continue to exert profound influence. In its wake, several nautical titles have borrowed heavily from the publication's strengths, particularly its design. Many writers who rose to prominence in the *Quarterly*'s pages are still writing today. Perhaps the best measure of its enduring influence is the fact that every former subscriber treasures their collection. I've seen copies of *Bowdich, Chapman's Piloting,* and John Rousmaniere's *Annapolis Book of Seamanship* on discount shelves, but I've never seen a single copy of the *Quarterly* offered up at a yard sale. If anyone wants to test the long-term impact and influence of the publication, just try to borrow an issue out of its owner's office or library.

Perhaps no small measure of its critical acclaim, as well as its ultimate financial failure, was because the *Quarterly* appeared on the scene at a time when most nautical magazine publishing was beginning a steep, downward spiral of providing exposure for its advertisers, rather than stimulating the interest of its readers. It served—and still serves—as a constant reminder that the only true criterion for a good magazine is the quality of the substance it offers to its readers. Sadly, *Nautical Quarterly* is also a reminder that in today's publishing world, critical acclaim puts joy in one's heart and a smile on many faces, but it doesn't pay the bills.

To this day I believe that if the *Quarterly* could have been published monthly, or at least six times a year, it might have been possible for it to serve the ever-famished appetites of its readers. Then again, if Joe had had to crank out issues on an assembly-line basis, it might have changed the very hand-crafted soul that made each and every edition the beautiful jewel of a magazine that it was.

And though Don is as much a dyed-in-the-wool capitalist as any blazer-clad member of the New York Yacht Club, I suspect that he has never truly lamented a single penny of his generous patronage of the *Quarterly*.

Different as they were, I can't think of Joe and Don as anything but a pair of matching bookends surrounding their shared love for boating. Thankfully, their respective contributions continue to stir our appreciation for the water, and whet our appetites for messing around on boats.

INTRODUCTION
THE BOOKS IN BETWEEN

BY ANTHONY DALTON

When London-born printer Andrew Bradford published the first U.S. magazine in Philadelphia on February 13, 1741, he could hardly have foreseen the eventual results of his vision. Unfortunately, Bradford's venture was far ahead of its time. His publication only lasted three months, and it took another 152 years before the first mass-circulation magazines began to appear in 1893. From then until well into the 1930s a growing cadre of publishers competed for readerships with low-cost magazines. Those years, often considered the Golden Age of American publishing, spawned increasing numbers of cheap weekly reads and more than a few monthly titles. The sudden boom of television in the 1950s, with its huge capacity for advertising, was, to some extent, responsible for a marked decline in the number of available magazines.

During the twentieth century, magazine publishers increasingly targeted clearly defined audiences with dedicated subject matter. Not surprisingly, recreational boating, in its many forms, has proved a popular subject, as evidenced by the fact that both *Yachting* and *Motor Boating* (later *Motor Boating & Sailing*) have been around since the early 1900s. Many, including the two mentioned, were fine publications with enthusiastic followings. All of them, however, paled in comparison to *Nautical Quarterly*, which came on the scene in 1977.

Nautical Quarterly was, as my co-editor Reese Palley once stated, "the best damn looking magazine ever produced," either in the United States or abroad. Inside and out, it had no parallel. No other publication, maritime flavored or otherwise, came close for style. Where other magazines shouted their achievements, *Nautical Quarterly* quietly boasted the highest artistic standards and whispered its editorial magnificence. Its eventual physical appearance alone, a square, hardcover format, made a subtle, yet bold and definitive, statement: "This is the best."

Nautical Quarterly was the brainchild of the late Joseph Gribbins and art designer Martin Pederson. Gribbins, a man who had loved boats since his boyhood summers on the Delaware River, and who had a passion for books about boats, was the son of a successful freelance political journalist. He grew up surrounded by books, magazines, and newspapers. His father's work, and the piles of publications stacked about the house, instilled in Joe an enormous respect for the written word and the beauty of the English language. Not surprisingly, Joe Gribbins went on to earn a degree in English literature from Fordham University in 1961.

After graduation Gribbins joined the editorial staff of *Motor Boating*. In 1969 he moved to *The American Way* (an in-flight publication for American Airlines), where he worked with and learned from Don Moffitt, whose credits included a tenure as editor of *The Wall Street Journal*. There he also met Martin Pederson, who would feature largely in Joe's future publishing career. For a few years Joe wandered among editorial positions at airline and boating magazines, in addition to freelancing. After a second stint at *Motor Boating* and a brief interlude as editor of another short-lived boating publication, 1975 saw him briefly in the position of assistant publisher at *Automobile Quarterly,* an expensive hardcover, full-color magazine with a square trim size and no advertising content. When he left *AQ,* Joe retained the basics of its stylish formula in his mind. Another sojourn at *Motor Boating,* this time as senior editor, led him inexorably to his destiny. Early in 1977, Joe and Martin Pederson developed the concept for *Nautical Quarterly*—a boating magazine with a style above and beyond those that had gone before it and, indeed, those then in circulation. The planned magazine would differ from other boating and yachting magazines of the 1970s in several respects, arguably the most important of which was freedom from advertising—with no advertisers dictating content, editorial and art would reign supreme.

Of course, without advertising revenue, the embryonic publication would have to rely solely on circulation for income: a tall order for a magazine with no track record. Joe Gribbins had a small inheritance left him by his father. He used that, in part, to keep himself afloat while preparing the first issue of *Nautical Quarterly*. Income from Pederson's design studio provided the initial overhead. Gribbins and Pederson, with Michael Levitt as managing editor, worked on that premier edition in Pederson's New York studio. Lacking adequate funds, they dropped the idea of a hard cover but retained the book concept. Though they were in business, they still urgently required a financial sponsor of sorts—a great leap of faith by someone as yet unknown.

Because *Nautical Quarterly* No. 1 featured the America's Cup, it needed to be available by mid-August. Pederson arranged with the printer to extend credit for some months, and a beautiful publication rolled off the press and into tasteful slipcovers. Gribbins showed his entrepreneurial spirit—and his confidence in the magazine—when he loaded up his station wagon with as many copies as he could carry and set off for Newport, Rhode Island, site of that year's Cup races. He spent late August and most of September selling his stock to consumers and to shops. Rumor has it that *Nautical Quarterly* sold more copies in Newport that September than the highly respected and eminently better known *Yachting*. While the trio was promoting that first issue they met with Donald C. McGraw Jr. over lunch at a French restaurant in Manhattan. McGraw, a man with his own passion for boats, agreed to finance the magazine.

"We could never have done it without McGraw," Joe is reported to have admitted later. In truth, *Nautical Quarterly* could not have survived as long as it did without its dedicated core group of professionals: most importantly publisher McGraw, editor Joseph Gribbins, art director Martin Pederson (1977 to 1982), managing editor Michael Levitt, managing director C. S. Lovelace (early 1980 onward), and many others along the way.

In a 2001 tribute to Gribbins, noted marine writer Peter H. Spectre wrote: "*NQ* from the beginning was a critical success, the talk of the waterfront. A melding of history, literature, art, legend, biography, criticism, appreciation, and more, it wasn't just about yachting, after all, but about all aspects of the sea that are endlessly fascinating."

The second issue carried a short editorial, signed by McGraw, Gribbins, and Pederson, in which they expressed their vision: "We see it as a medium for the discovery and appreciation of the best in boats and boating experience rather than a medium for advertising . . . . We are working toward the most perfect boating magazine possible . . . ." High ideals, indeed, and exceedingly difficult to maintain.

Content ideas were spawned in-house, primarily. Gribbins and Pederson, plus Michael Levitt and a small staff, planned each issue and then went out and hustled the required photography, illustrations, and text without having to rely heavily on freelance submissions. If an article worked better with black-and-white photographs rather than color, it was published that way. Once word of *Nautical Quarterly*'s style and presentation became widespread on the waterfront, however, freelance submissions began to trickle over the transom. In spite of having a small but talented in-house team, in addition to his own remarkable talent, Gribbins was always happy to accept interesting features from the best writers and photographers. As a result, each successive issue proved better than the last.

Early in 1980 Don McGraw brought C. S. Lovelace into the fold. Fresh from a successful two-year turnaround of *Motor Boating & Sailing,* and with 20 years' experience at Time, Inc., Lovelace joined *Nautical Quarterly* as managing director and became *de facto* publisher with the spring issue that year. Lovelace found a less-than-perfect organization. Printing was done at one plant in New York, binding at another. Slipcovers came from a third location on Long Island, and corrugated mailing boxes at another. Then both were shipped to the bindery where the bound softcover magazines were placed in the slipcovers, packed in mailing boxes, and taken to the post office. To add to the confusion, a small Connecticut company, supposedly a computer fulfilment operation, printed subscriber labels. Lovelace commented, "This unique system and movement of all that paper from place to place would have delighted Rube Goldberg . . . ."

In addition to the complicated production process, the New York office arrangement was less than satisfactory. Editors worked out of a small "hole in the wall," while the art department expressed their creativity in Pederson's studio. At that time there was no room in either location for business personnel. In spite of the difficult conditions, Gribbins and his small team continued to produce quarterly masterpieces.

Two weeks after Lovelace took office, the Connecticut fulfilment operation went bankrupt, and as a result their computers and records were removed. This failure, while detrimental to any reasonably accurate determination of circulation figures, proved providential in that the new managing director was able to hire an efficient circulation professional to oversee the subscriber records. By Lovelace's fourth issue (*NQ* No. 13), he had much of the former chaos under control, including the rental of "a small but liveable open-space office on Park Avenue South" to gather all production staff under the same roof.

A potential downside to the move was that co-founder Martin Pederson, the inspiration behind the magazine's design, left the company. Lovelace said, "Joe hired Marilyn Rose to replace Martin beginning with the summer issue of 1982. She filled in seamlessly."

Pederson's unique artistic vision was responsible for *Nautical Quarterly* winning the National Magazine Award for Design that year. Fortunately, even after he left, his genius prevailed and his concept was continued for the magazine's lifetime, a record that C. S. Lovelace attributed to "Joe's wonderful capability to manage the aesthetics of the magazine; Marty's modular design concept that others could adopt fairly easily; and [later] two accomplished young women graphics designers [Marilyn Rose, followed by Clare Cunningham] who readily accepted the challenge to fall in with the genius's mode."

Initially covered with a heavy glossy paper and a slipcase, with issue No. 13 *NQ* finally fulfilled the original dream, becoming a 10x10 hardcover book: an ideal size and style for coffee-table display.

After almost six years, publisher Donald C. McGraw Jr. announced in a letter to all subscribers that with the 25th issue *NQ* would, for the first time, contain advertising. He explained the change of direction to readers by noting the publication had been approached by "potential advertisers almost since our first issue, and we have decided to accommodate them." McGraw went on to stress that the advertising space would be in addition to the existing 120 pages of text, photographs, and other illustrations. In order to maintain the existing clean design, the initial plan was for each advertisement to be either a full page or a two-page spread. Inevitably, financial considerations dictated smaller advertisements, occasionally as small as a quarter-page, which began to appear in later years.

Nautical Quarterly No. 25, in spring 1984, carried seven pages of blue-chip advertisers, none from the nautical world: U.S. Trust, Rolex, BMW, and E.F. Hutton. For the rest of *NQ*'s existence, such top-end advertising, reflecting the overall affluence of the subscriber base, would be placed on selected pages of each issue.

By 1985 the magazine's annual subscription price had risen from an initial $30 to $49.50, but it was not enough, even when backed by valuable advertising revenue. Don McGraw purchased *Soundings* magazine and moved *Nautical Quarterly* "lock, stock, and barrel" out of New York and into *Soundings*' large office in a busy marina on the Connecticut River in Essex, Connecticut. Only designer Marilyn Rose and an assistant editor chose not to make the move. In Essex, Joe tapped Clare Cunningham to re-place Rose, and hired Barbara Lloyd as associate editor. The changes took place without any hiccups or disruptions, as they had with the 1980 move to Park Avenue South. Lloyd eventually expanded her role and contributed a series of beautifully written articles for the magazine.

During the last two weeks before press deadline for each issue, Karen Kratzer worked in the Essex office as a paste-up artist under the direction of Clare Cunningham. She recalled working late on many evenings, then repairing to the Griswold Inn or the Black Whale, in Essex. Most of the staff—Joe Gribbins, publisher's assistant and writer deLancey Funsten, Cun-ningham, sometimes Joe's wife Ethel, and McGraw—went to relax, tell silly jokes, and share a few libations. Karen recalled, "We laughed together a lot, I enjoyed his [Joe's] company, because he was easy to talk to . . . even about stupid things. Joe was so smart, you know. He taught me a lot."

Joe Gribbins had a similar impact on most writers he worked with. John Rousmaniere referred to him as "the best editor I've ever had." Elizabeth Meyer wrote of Joe's ability to take a messy horror of a manuscript and turn it into something special. One adjective, however, crops up repeatedly when writers describe Joe Gribbins: wonderful. It was the same for Joe. "Wonderful" was his own favorite compliment.

Joseph Ditler, whose work on schooners is featured in this book, had high regard for Joe and admitted a certain awe of *Nautical Quarterly*. He recalled a telephone conversation with Gribbins.

"'You know what I need,' said Joe's soothing voice. The editor of *Nautical Quarterly*, the Holy Grail of yachting publications—then, now, and probably forever—was trying to coax me through a flat and windless spot of water, and convince me to write a feature article for his publication.

"'But . . . this is *Nautical Quarterly*,' I squeaked.

"'Forget about that. There is a special magic about schooners that I hear in your voice,' he said. 'I think you're the person to write this story, and all you need to do is sit down and just tell me, not *Nautical Quarterly*, why these sailing vessels are so very special.'"

Gribbins' quiet persuasion had sold another writer and eased him into the broadening *NQ* family. Explaining his feelings about schooners and about working with the best magazine, Ditler said:

Well, there is indeed a special magic about schooners, and yes, as Joe suggested, the story just wrote itself. Of course, it didn't hurt to have the incredible photographs of Bob Grieser at my disposal.

At the time the West Coast had more than its share of great schooners—each boat with a story, each captain with a reputation. Some were legendary, like *Spike Africa* and *Dauntless*. Entire fan clubs would gather on the shore to cheer for them. Bob and I were fortunate to have sailed on most, and to have done what little we could to extend their immortality.

Over my 20 years of covering the waterfront and [working with] dozens of editors big and small, there has never been anyone like Joe

Gribbins. He *was Nautical Quarterly*, as everyone who ever met him will attest. And no other person could have helmed that project.

It is the greatest of honors to be considered part of this tribute to such a fine individual, and such a benevolent professional in our industry. While we may have lost Joe, I look at my wall and see him every day in the many issues of *NQ*, which contain no small amount of his blood, sweat, and tears.

Writer Elizabeth Meyer, who worked with Joe Gribbins on magazine articles as well as on books, was not only impressed by Joe's consid-erable editorial skills and his sense of fun, she was also intrigued by the fact that he knew so many well-known writers. In the summer of 1984, she, Joe, and Michael Levitt wandered into the North Star Pub, opposite the South Street Seaport in New York City. Famed one-legged nautical story-teller Tristan Jones sat at the bar and greeted Gribbins in his customary salty fashion. Jones, of course, had good reason to know Joe Gribbins: Joe had purchased and edited "A Steady Trade," Tristan's first article for *Nauti-cal Quarterly* in 1978 and a feature that Jones would later expand into one of his well-known "autobiographical" books. During his writing years in New York, Jones regularly contacted Gribbins to let him know what he was doing. Two of the four issues in 1984 also featured work by Tristan Jones, as did future issues.

Over the years a steady stream of wonderful writers, many of them previously unknown, were inevitably lured to *Nautical Quarterly*'s pages: names such as John Rousmaniere, Tristan Jones, Elizabeth Meyer, Peter H. Spectre, deLancey Funsten, Reese Palley, Michael Levitt, Stan Grayson, adventurer and sailor Skip Novak, plus works from Jack London and Rockwell Kent. And, it should not be forgotten, Joe Gribbins and Michael Levitt, his right-hand man throughout *NQ*'s existence, contributed dozens of excellent features between them. So, too, fine photographers displayed their artistic skills, including: the legendary Beken of Cowes, Morris and Stanley Rosenfeld, Benjamin Mendlowitz, Allan Weitz, David Doubilet, and the young Thomas Ettenhuber. And great marine artists: Willard Bond, Don Demers, Peter Egeli, Richard Ellis, and Thomas Hoyne, among others.

It is inevitable that the work of Joe Gribbins should be displayed in both volumes of *The Best of Nautical Quarterly*. Joe wasn't just the best editor for the job, he was, without doubt, also way up there as a knowledgeable and extremely talented writer. Some 30 of Joe's own articles appeared in the 50 editions of his magazine. Hubris, however, was never one of Joe's faults. Those who worked with him, either as contributors or staff, remember him as a modest man who was generous in sharing his talents. As an editor he was, without doubt, a writer's best friend. As such, his hand and his expertise touched each and every article published in *Nautical Quarterly*, as they now play an identical role in *The Best of NQ*. Two of Joe's own articles have been selected to decorate *The Lure of Sail*. A similar number will grace the companion volume, *The Lure of Power*.

Nautical Quarterly's illustrated features ran the gamut from the affluent America's Cup racers to individual rowing boats; from fragile sea kayaks to high-performance powerboats; from profiles of important boat designers to the works of great marine artists; from coverage of the top yachtsmen and women to survey reports of vessels great and small. Wildlife, in the form of seals and sea lions, sharks, dolphins, and whales, appeared on the pages, as did travel tales from around the nautical world, describing riverboats from Bangladesh, sailing canoes from Sri Lanka, and schooners of the Java Sea, plus boats from Brazil and the Nile delta. *Nautical Quarterly* took us vicariously from the tropics to the extremes of our polar regions: the Arctic and Antarctica. In addition, we enjoyed features on great maritime art, nautical Christmas cards and postage stamps, all accepted and thoughtfully transformed by Joe's editorial skills into fine literary works, and lovingly laid out and illustrated by a talented and dedicated art department following Martin Pederson's original design concept.

Reese Palley, co-editor of this book, noted with amusement that one of the many things that made *Nautical Quarterly* unique was the publication's rather cavalier attitude toward "Letters to the Editor." Many were made up by the *NQ* staff and one letter, in which the writer complained about a reversed photograph, was itself printed in reverse. That, almost certainly, was Joe Gribbins's subtle sense of humor at work. A further example of his humor can be seen on the magazine's masthead, where—not having any real foreign correspondents—Joe invented a short esoteric list of "Contributing Editors," with names like H. D. "Knots" Nesbitt, The West Coast; T. Fremantle Fong Jr., The Far East; Fortescue Butler-Hall, The U.K.; and Jerome de Chassignac, The Continent. So, too, the eclectic collection of quirky pen-and-ink sketches and occasional black-and-white photographs that enlivened the "Correspondence" and "Credits" pages reflected that impish delight in the ridiculous.

A subscriber study published in 1987 bore its own brand of humor. Right-hand pages were reserved for the serious business of demographics and statistics. Pages on the left carried subscriber comments, most—but not all—complimentary:

"Love it."

"Outstanding!!"

"Excellent material—Quality printing. A real collector's item."

And perhaps with tongue in cheek: "I get a kick from the quality of your photos! I'll bet a poor slob like me has ruined your averages. However you didn't ask if I own a Rolex. I do. Your not so typical reader."

One paid a high compliment. "[I] Find NQ has some of the highest standards for design in a publication. One of [this] country's finest examples of printed material!"

A reader with an income of approximately $400,000 per annum grumbled, "I would have liked to have had the choice of paying a higher subscription rate instead of having advertising."

And from another a sarcastic, "Please—Fractional page advertising is gauche."

The final entry is an enigmatic "Thanks for George . . . I know a cute 5' hairdresser who'd love it!"

Don McGraw Jr. and the editorial staff of *Nautical Quarterly* kept their promise to limit the amount of advertising in each issue. With the advantage of hindsight, however, perhaps they should have increased the number of ads and risked a certain amount of customer displeasure. They could also have increased the number of issues per year to six, but those two additional issues each year would have had a detrimental effect on the magazine as a whole. It took time to prepare each issue, to ensure that the highest standards prevailed. Less time spent on each volume meant a potential slide from perfection, something Joe Gribbins and his staff would never countenance.

Nautical Quarterly's subscriber base was never higher than about 20,000. Even with expensive advertising revenue to boost circulation income, and a few book co-publishing ventures on the side, production costs continued to run too high. In 1990, the 50th edition of *Nautical Quarterly* proved to be the final issue. A short but remarkable era in American publishing had come to an end, but the story continues through the medium of private collectors.

Rarely does one find copies of *Nautical Quarterly* in second-hand book shops; any that do find their way into the marketplace are quickly snapped up by those determined to complete their collections. A full set of *Nautical Quarterly* magazines should include all 50 issues, the first 12 paperback in slipcovers, another 38 in hardcover. Such a collection should also include the two Italian editions; an index of issues 1 through 40, sponsored by Rolex in 1987; a subscriber study, also from 1987; plus a copy of a 2001 tribute to Joe Gribbins entitled *Joseph Gribbins, Recipient of the 2001 W. P. Stephens Award,* in which those who knew him well express their feelings about the man and his works.

Joe Gribbins, who was, himself, the best of *Nautical Quarterly,* spent the two years immediately following *NQ*'s final number freelancing, before going on to achieve even greater acclaim as *the* marine-related editor to work with, and as an author in his own right. He wrote *Wooden Boats: From Sculls to Yachts,* published in 1991; *The Wooden Boat,* 1996; and *Classic Sail,* 1998.

Twelve years after the demise of *Nautical Quarterly,* Joe Gribbins passed away from cancer. His legacy as the finest nautical editor of his time lives on in the books he wrote, in those he edited, and in each and every page of carefully collected editions of *Nautical Quarterly.*

The Best of Nautical Quarterly, both this volume and the forthcoming *The Lure of Power,* is a twin memorial to two unforgettable nautical icons: Joseph Gribbins and his dream creation, *Nautical Quarterly.*

America took shape in an atmosphere of Yankee achievement at sea, and her overwhelming triumph in the summer of 1851 was yet another proof to the New World of its adolescent ascendancy over the Old. A uniquely American vessel of Baltimore Clipper ancestry, built on the quick and weatherly model of the New York pilot boats, *America* was a rakish little ship in character with a U.S. fleet that by the 1850s was acknowledged even in England to be the swiftest and smartest-sailed in the world. In the hundred years of European war which ended in 1815, small American ships had depended upon speed alone for defense against the bat-tlewagons of Europe. The clipper—born as a responsive little schooner much favored by tidewater smugglers and slavers, and destined to become the classic clipper ship with its cloud of canvas—was the 19th-century result of Yankee emphasis on speed and agility rather than cargo-carrying heft in its vessels.

THE UPSTART SCHOONER THAT STARTED IT ALL

BY JOSEPH GRIBBINS

During the first half of the 19th century, fast American ships and skilled American seamen had amazed the complacent Old World with a succession of maritime triumphs. The New York packet ships began to dominate North Atlantic trade in the 1820s with sailings on a regular schedule and passages to Liverpool in as little as 15 days. Trade with the Far East, a thing the British considered impossible for a nation without colonies east of Suez when New York and New England ships first sailed to Canton in the 1780s, grew steadily for 60 years until the American clipper ships of the 1840s surpassed Britain's best efforts in a tea trade that was once her monopoly.

By 1850, the quickest clipper ships in the world were sailing from New York for the gold fields of California and the East River shipyards couldn't build them fast enough. In that year the Collins line steamers of New York began service to Europe on a shorter schedule than the vessels of any foreign flag and the New York clipper *Oriental* astonished the sea-wise citizens of London by finishing first in the year's "tea race" from the East. The first American vessel to deliver tea from China to England following repeal of the Navigation Laws, her 97-day passage from Hong Kong to the Thames was a performance previously considered impossible.

It was a heady time on New York's waterfront. The East River was the shipbuilding center of the U.S. and the port itself was the largest and most lucrative in a nation which ruled the waves in speed and service if not in tonnage. In mid-century, Americans were full of maritime bravado and eager to challenge any nation, especially Britain, in a sailing contest. Two maritime challenges were issued to Britain by the U.S. in 1850-51. The first was for a clipper-ship race between vessels of 1600 tons which would start from a European port and race to the East Indies and return—or around the world—for a purse of $10,000 or £10,000. The second, as it developed, was for the fastest yacht in the world. The result of the first challenge was never in doubt—in fact, no British clipper took up the gauntlet; the result of the second remained in doubt until August 22, 1851.

In commenting on both challenges in the spring of 1851, North American Miscellany noted: "The yacht schooner now building, for competition with the English yachts, is rapidly approaching completion. We have not so much faith in our yacht service, as superior to the British, as in our clipper ships. Still, we hope all success to the new vessel."

America was not built strictly for a racing challenge. She was to be a sailing abassador to the great London Exposition of 1851, an example of American shipbuilding craftsmanship, which even the British conceded to be excellent. In the fall of 1850, a New York merchant received a letter from a correspondent in London suggesting that a New York pilot boat be sent to England during the Exposition. The idea circulated in the city's maritime community and ultimately John Cox Stevens, Commodore of the New York Yacht Club, formed a syndicate to build the finest and fastest New York pilot schooner possible.

Stevens' correspondence with the Earl of Wilton, Commodore of the Royal Yacht Squadron, indicates his own anticipation of a race and the Earl's anticipation of a lesson in shipbuilding. Wilton's February 22, 1851 letter to Commodore Stevens concludes: "For myself I may be permitted to say that I shall have great pleasure in extending to your countrymen any civility that lies in my power and shall be glad to avail myself of any improvements in shipbuilding that the industry and skill of your nation have enabled you to elaborate." Steven's reply concludes: "We propose to avail ourselves of your friendly bidding and take with good grace the sound thrashing we are likely to get by venturing our 'longshore craft on your rough waters." The game had begun.

The New York Yacht Club syndicate chose the best talents on the New York waterfront for the *America* adventure. George Steers, who had pioneered the clipper model of the New York pilot boat as well as fast yachts of similar qualities, got to work on her lines at the Wm. H. Brown Shipyard where he was then subcontracting design and lofting work. Captain Dick Brown, the most renowned of the New York pilots—that fearless fraternity which ranged the coast from Nantucket to Cape Henlopen in every kind of weather to meet incoming ships—was signed on as master. George Schuyler of the syndicate made shipbuilder Brown sign a letter which said: "If it is decided by the umpire that she is not faster than every vessel brought against her, it shall not be binding upon you to accept and pay for her at all."

America was delivered ten weeks late in mid-June of 1851 and she did not prove to be "faster than every vessel brought against her." In a series of trials in the lower harbor, the Steers-designed *Maria*, owned in common by all three of the Stevens brothers, outsailed her. But *Maria*, said to be capable of 17 knots in a decent breeze, was a center-boarder with an enormous spread of sail and a crew that knew her every twitch. *America* was judged to be sufficient for the purpose, and especially sufficient for a transAtlantic passage and for what Commodore Stevens hoped would be "rough waters" and a breeze of wind on the other side. *America* was the first yacht to cross the North Atlantic.

Our upstart schooner dropped Long Island over the horizon on June 21, with 13 men aboard and a set of working sails from Captain Brown's old pilot schooner *Mary Taylor* aloft. Her 20-day passage to Havre was rainy but uneventful, and James R. Steers' log is chiefly a record of the excellent scoff that came out of the galley. He recorded, however, that: "She is the best sea boat that ever went out of the Hook. The way we have passed everything we have seen must be witnessed to be believed." Even the Steers brothers were surprised. They picked up a Channel pilot in the Scilly Isles, a man who shocked Captain Brown by begging food, and James R. noted: "We have every sail set, and the way she slides along 'knocks' the pilot. He wanted to heave the log himself, so we gratified him. He could not believe that she was going 12 knots because she made so little fuss."

left, the New York Yacht Club burgee; at right, the signal of Britain's Royal Yacht Squadron.

James R. Steers wrote in his log: "She is the best sea boat that ever went out of the Hook. The way we have passed everything we have seen must be witnessed to be believed."

The New York schooner was built as an exhibit for the London Exposition of 1851. In the 1851 poster below, she's the centerpiece.

The transAtlantic crew was met at Havre by John Cox Stevens, his brother Edwin Stevens, and Alexander Hamilton's son, Colonel James A. Hamilton. The Commodore and the Colonel also met William C. Rives, the American Minister to Paris, and the great Horace Greeley during their several weeks in France. Rives, who approved *America* as a fit Exposition item for a nation with its sleeves rolled up and disapproved of what he called "objects of mere luxury and artistic elegance," urged that the schooner avoid encounters with British yachts. Greeley was more emphatic: "The eyes of the world are on you," he said. "You will be beaten, and the country will be abused, as it has been in connection with the Exposition." The Yankee exhibits at the Crystal Palace had been looked upon less favorably than the grotesque Victorian furniture and household impedimenta of the civilized world, although a New York lockpicker named Briggs and several threshing machines had been a success.

When *America* crossed the Channel on the night of July 31, the Americans had never seen a British yacht and few among the British had ever seen an American yacht, although some of Britain's more cosmopolitan mariners were familiar with the abilities of the New York schooners. Most members of the Royal yacht Squadron had been surprised, and probably amused, to learn that there was a New York Yacht Club. Although Commodore Stevens intended to race his boat for wagers in England if a promising contest developed, and to get as much from this game as he could, there was no way of knowing what he and the national honor might be sailing into. No man aboard had doubts about her in a breeze of wind, but the dead calm of that first night in England, along with the memory of her poor showing against *Maria*, a 'longshore racing yacht, must have been disquieting. She was also five inches down on her lines with a load of extra gear and with French wines and viands laid on in the expectation of lavish entertaining at Cowes.

Commodore Stevens described the welcome to England: "In the morning early, the tide was against us, and it was a dead calm. At nine o'clock a gentle breeze sprang up, and with it came gliding down the *Laverock*, one of the newest and fastest cutters of her class. The news spread like lightning that the Yankee clipper had arrived, and that the *Laverock* had gone down to show her the way up. The yachts and vessels in the harbor, the wharves, and windows of all the houses bordering on them, were filled with thousands of spectators, watching with eager eyes the eventful trial they saw we could not escape."

The wind had piped up to five or six knots by the time *America*'s sails were raised and the course was to windward, two circumstances to gladden

Captain Brown worked her out to windward and passed the fast
new cutter on the way to the Squadron anchorage. An hour later all of
Cowes knew that the Yankee clipper was a serious adversary.

the heart of Captain Dick. "After waiting until we were ashamed to wait longer, we let her get about two hundred yards ahead and then started in her wake," recalled Stevens. "During the first five minutes not a sound was heard, save, perhaps, the beating of our hearts, or the slight ripple of the water upon her sword-like stem." The drama was soon over. Captain Brown worked her out to windward and passed the fast new cutter on the way to the Squadron anchorage at Cowes. An hour later the Earl of Wilton and a welcoming party were aboard *America*, the champagne was being poured, and all of Cowes knew that the Yankee clipper was a serious adversary.

It was a bad beginning for Commodore Stevens' gambling plans. He issued a low-key challenge to any number of the "schooners of the Old World" for a race offshore in a breeze of not less than six knots. The Stevens brothers and Colonel Hamilton were made honorary members of the Squadron, and there were other civilities, but the Squadron politely ignored the challenge. Finally the Commodore, as George Schuyler put it, "with his usual promptness, and regardless of the pockets of his associates, had posted in the clubhouse at Cowes a challenge to sail the *America* a match against any British vessel whatsoever, for any sum from one to ten thousand guineas, merely stipulating that there should be not less than a six-knot breeze." This was a considerable concession, for the British cutters were inshore racing machines theoretically faster than the schooners in light air, and favored by design and the local experience of their crews to outsail the larger foreigner in a race alongshore. The Ryde Regatta on August 15 was such a race, and Stevens declined to enter because the morning's breeze was barely perceptible.

While all this was going on, interest in the peculiar American yacht became a mania. The Illustrated London News dismissed her as "a rakish, piratical-looking craft" and commented that she "seemed rather a violation of the old established ideas of naval architecture." The old established ideas consisted of a full-bowed, weight-carrying hull combined with a complex and towering rig of many spars setting baggy sails that were designed that way. When he first saw her, the Marquis of Anglesey remarked: "If she is right, then we are all wrong." She was very different from anything ever seen at Cowes, although the British Admiralty, in its role as the sea's policeman, knew her type well after several decades of chasing American slavers.

The London Times' "Own Correspondent at Cowes" was delighted with her clean, straightforward hull and the way she seemed rigged "without an extra rope." She was, he reported, "The *beau ideal* of what one is

accustomed to read about in Cooper's novels." He was also delighted with the stir she had created: "Day after day, gentlemen in most wonderful costumes, ranging in style from Dirck Hatterick to Wright in an Adelphi farce, sit at the windows or in the porch of the clubhouse with telescope to eye, staring at the phenomenon, or they row around her in grotesque little punts, or go on board and have a chat with the Commodore, his brother, and Colonel Hamilton, three very cautious and gentlemanly persons—as downright 'cute and keen as the smartest in the States, but who can hardly disguise, nevertheless, their pleasure at John Bull's astonishment and evident perturbation, owning, as he does, a fleet of about 800 yachts of all sizes—from nearly 400 tons down to three tons."

Aboard *America*, Captain Dick and the crew enjoyed themselves equally. According to Colonel Hamilton: "There was at one time a very general impression among the lower classes of the people about the docks at Cowes that the *America* had a propeller which was artfully concealed; and our crew amused themselves by saying to the boatmen who came

The Currier & Ives interpretation of the great event shows an out-of-scale

America, with typical tars on deck, sailing past a rough approximation of The

Needles under the whipped-cream skies of the 19th-century imagination.

James E. Butterswoth, whose small dynamic portraits of yachts were the standard of aesthetic excellence in the last half of the 19th century, represented the upstart schooner meeting an East Indiaman in the Straits of Dover. She was never near the Straits of Dover under Commodore Stevens' ownership, but when she was sold to Lord Jon de Blacquiere of England in the fall of 1852, she led an adventurous life in Europe, which included a victory—interestingly enough—over a Swedish schooner named *Sverige*, and cruises to the Mediterranean, during one of which she rode out a storm that sank many ships. The cruising/racing Lord |was very impressed with her.

America was unbeatable going to windward, and when she came
around the corner she left them all behind. "Her canvas," wrote the
admiring Special Correspondent, "was as flat as a sheet of paper."

alongside with visitors (there were thousands, as people of all classes were permitted to examine the vessel) 'In the stern sheets, under the gangway, there is a grating which the Commodore does not allow any person to open.'"

Propeller or no, the ordinary boatmen of Cowes were disgusted that the gentry had ignored the challenge. One of them offered to man a crack cutter with the best of his mates if some gentleman would put up the wager, to race *America* out to Cape Clear and back in the worst weather that turned up, and "to crack on till the masts went to Hell."

America took an occasional afternoon sail if the wind piped up. Although Stevens had remained at anchor when the Ryde Regatta ghosted off that morning, he took an unofficial turn on the course the afternoon of August 15. As the London Times reported: "She went along very steadily and well up to Ryde but did not show any great superiority till she was off the pier, about 3:20, when she seemed as if she had put a screw into her stern, hoisted her fore and aft foresail, and began 'to fly' through the water. She passed schooners and cutters one after the other just as a Derby winner passes the 'ruck,' and as the breeze freshened slid with the speed of an arrow out towards the Nab, standing upright as a ramrod under her canvas, while the schooners were staggering under every stitch they could set, and the cutters were heeling over under gaff topsails and balloon jibs. She went about in splendid style, a little short of the Nab, spinning round like a top, and came bowling away toward Cowes as fast if not faster than ever. As if to let our best craft see she did not care about them, the *America* went up to each in succession, ran to leeward of every one of them as close as she could, and shot before them in succession, coming to anchor at Ryde at least two miles, as it seemed to me, ahead of any of the craft she had been running against."

This was a performance to make the Commodore wish he had challenged the Squadron that morning, and it may have influenced his decision to sail for the Hundred Guineas Cup a week later in a race with no time allowances but with tricky tides and currents that would favor those who knew them well. For their part, the Squadron considered the August 22 free-for-all around the Isle of Wight their best bet for redeeming their sullied reputation with the press and public. It was not to be a money race, for one thing, and a light breeze would favor their fleet of heavily-canvased cutters.

"The anxiety attending this race is deep and earnest" wrote the Special Correspondent on August 20. The old salts of Cowes were predicting disaster and the town was crowded from the beaches to the rooftops on the morning of the contest. Anxiety was equally deep and earnest aboard *America*.

Several British crewmen had been taken on and a pilot had been hired to advise Captain Dick on local conditions. The Americans had been warned not to trust any English pilot and even this one, guaranteed honest by the Admiral of the Portsmouth Dockyard, had been damned as a liar in an anonymous letter. The Commodore was still wishing for a six-knot breeze, if not a full gale.

"But no one not present can realize the anxieties of that contest," Colonel Hamilton recalled years later, "for we knew the ground was most unfavorable for us. When the yachts got off, while the wind was fresh, we got away easily, but twice the wind failed us, and, with a strong head tide, we were actually drifting back, while lighter vessels with a greater and loftier spread of canvas, taking advantage of small draught of water and eddies known to them, were gradually overhauling us."

America had her sails up before her anchor, and she slewed around her warp in some disorder before starting the course in last place. "We got off before the wind," recalled Commodore Stevens, "and in the midst of a crowd that we could not get rid of for the first eight or nine miles." The Squadron fleet, their sails boomed out before a freshening breeze, bunched up to keep the schooner at bay on the run to the Nab, and Captain Dick was forced to maneuver in ways that risked an all-standing jibe. "Shall I put her bowsprit through that fellow's sail?" he asked Stevens at one point.

He worked her patiently through the first dozen of the fleet, and when she passed the Noman's Land buoy she was only two minutes behind *Volante*, the leader, with *Freak*, *Aurora* and *Gipsy Queen* between. *Volante* and *Aurora* had stood out to round the Nab Light while most of the rest of the fleet, including *America*, turned the corner inshore. In the two circulars issued for the race, one had put the course inside the Nab, the other outside. As a result, *Bacchante*, *Arrow*, *Volante*, *Constance* and *Aurora* rounded the light and returned on a course nearly dead to windward. There were protests from all five.

America was unbeatable going to windward, and when she came around the corner she left them all behind. "Her canvas," wrote the admiring Special Correspondent, "was as flat as a sheet of paper." He continued: "While the cutters were thrashing through the water, sending the spray over their bows, and the schooners were wet up to the foot of the foremast, the *America* was as dry as a bone." *America* broke her jib-boom at 12:58 powering against the wind and current, but her lead was already substantial and the delay was of no consequence. Tightened up and heeling, she beat down the back of the island and increased her lead by miles. "At 5:40 the *Aurora*,

The royal party took a complete tour, during which Captain Dick reminded Prince Albert to wipe his feet before going below. "I know who you are," said Captain Dick, "but you'll have to wipe your feet."

the nearest yacht, was fully 7 1/2 miles astern, the *Freak* being about a mile more distant, and the rest being 'nowhere'," said the Times.

The steamers anchored at Alum Bay gave three cheers as *America*, now under the lee of the land, ghosted past on a run. As they passed the royal yacht *Victoria and Albert*, reported the Special Correspondent, "the Commodore took off his hat, and all of the crew, following his order and example, remained with uncovered heads for some minutes till they had passed the yacht—a mark of respect to the Queen not the less becoming because it was bestowed by republicans."

America ghosted to the finish at 8:37; *Aurora*, a cutter with an excess of sail, had gained in the faint winds of evening and finished at 8:45. It was all over, as the man says, but the shouting.

The shouting started with the five protests. *America*'s crew stayed awake all night to await the results and were told before morning that they had won the ornate urn which still sits in its glass vitrine at the New York Yacht Club. All the protests had been disallowed.

The next day, Queen Victoria asked that *America* sail down to Osborne House to receive a royal visit. The Queen, Prince Albert and a retinue of ladies and gentlemen in waiting came aboard. It was an unprecedented gesture and it became the subject of a week's gossip. The royal party took a complete tour, during which Captain Dick reminded Prince Albert to wipe his feet before going below. The Prince, a trifle astonished, stood still at the top of the companionway. "I know who you are," said Captain Dick, "but you'll have to wipe your feet." Victoria asked to see the bilges and the way the ballast was stowed, and she ran a royal handkerchief over the shelves of the galley and found no dust. Back on deck, she presented each member of the crew with a gold sovereign. The next day Captain Brown received from a representative of the Crown a package which contained a gold pocket compass and a note which said that Her Majesty hoped he might keep it as bright as he kept his ship.

America's victory was literally staggering to the British yachting establishment, and its implications of American prowess at sea and elsewhere were unacceptable to much of the British public in that summer when the Crystal Palace stood in Hyde Park as a symbol of the Empire's greatness. The weeks of correspondence and comment which followed show both a tough realism and a blind arrogance in British response, with hardly anything in between.

"It is a remarkable incident, and not satisfactory to the national pride," wrote the London Spectator, which ascribed the schooner's superiority to the "accident" of George Steers' discovery of the sharp, clipper type of vessel in the midst of the wilderness. The more realistic—indeed, pessimistic—London Merchant wrote: "We write to record our opinion that the empire of the seas must before long be ceded to America; its persevering enterprise, its great commerce, are certain to secure this prize; nor will England be in a condition to dispute it with her. America, as mistress of the ocean, must overstride the civilized world."

A writer signing himself An Old Cruiser expressed to the London Times the cruising side of that ancient debate between sailors who like to race and sailors who value their comfort: "The order shipbuilders in general receive is to build a roomy comfortable vessel and a good seaboat of a certain tonnage, and, as the owner pays by the ton, he expects as much accommodation as possible for the size." Confessing that he was "at first astonished and confounded" by *America*, he goes on to condemn her as a racing machine unfit for comfortable cruising. Another writer, evidently a racingman, cited three cases of "piratical vessels" built on the Baltimore Clipper model and seized by Her Majesty's Navy, which were "improved" by British rigging technology and badly compromised. "Now, it is not an unfair inference," he wrote, "that if American schooners, altered in their rig according to English notions, are injured, that British schooners altered by Americans would probably be improved." He suggested sending the best of the Squadron's yachts to Baltimore or New York to be fitted with "two beautiful sticks with immense rake."

As the letters pro and con appeared in the press, Colonel Hamilton received a note of congratulation from the cautious Mr. Rives in Paris. "And what a victory!" crowed the American Minister. "To beat Brittania, 'whose flag has braved a thousand years the battle and the breeze,' to beat her in her own native seas, in the presence of her Queen, and contending against a fleet of seventeen sail of her picked models of naval architecture, owned and personally directed by the proudest names of her nobility—her Marlboroughs and her Angleseys—is something that may well encourage us in the race of maritime competition which is set before us."

It was a great victory, yet another proof of the New World's adolescent ascendancy over the Old.

LORD JIM LIVES!

BY BRIAN DOWLEY

Off our stern a Walker log spins through mile after mile of the 2600 between San Francisco and Acapulco. Slicing into moderate Pacific swells with a westerly breeze on the starboard quarter, the 72´ schooner *Lord Jim* is five days out on her maiden voyage after four years of rebuilding. At the helm bundled in heavy sweaters and wet gear, we see in *Jim*'s cockpit a little world of warmth and security as the day drops and we reach southward 200 miles out in the Pacific. A muted sunset glows on brasswork already turning salty green. A heavy rain poured down though fog thickening over the Golden Gate when a big crowd of well-wishers—craftsmen, engineers, friends—many of whom had put years of their lives into reviving this grand old campaigner—waved and hollered as the crew of six cast off. Many of them even then couldn't believe that there wasn't some last detail to be seen to as *Lord Jim* began a round-the-world odyssey. The black hull with her glassy brightwork and powerful North Atlantic spread of sail slid under the big bridge with owner/skipper Holger Kreuzhage at the helm and with the shouts of her supporters ringing in the ears of the crew. *Lord Jim* was alive again!

THE ALDEN SCHOONERS

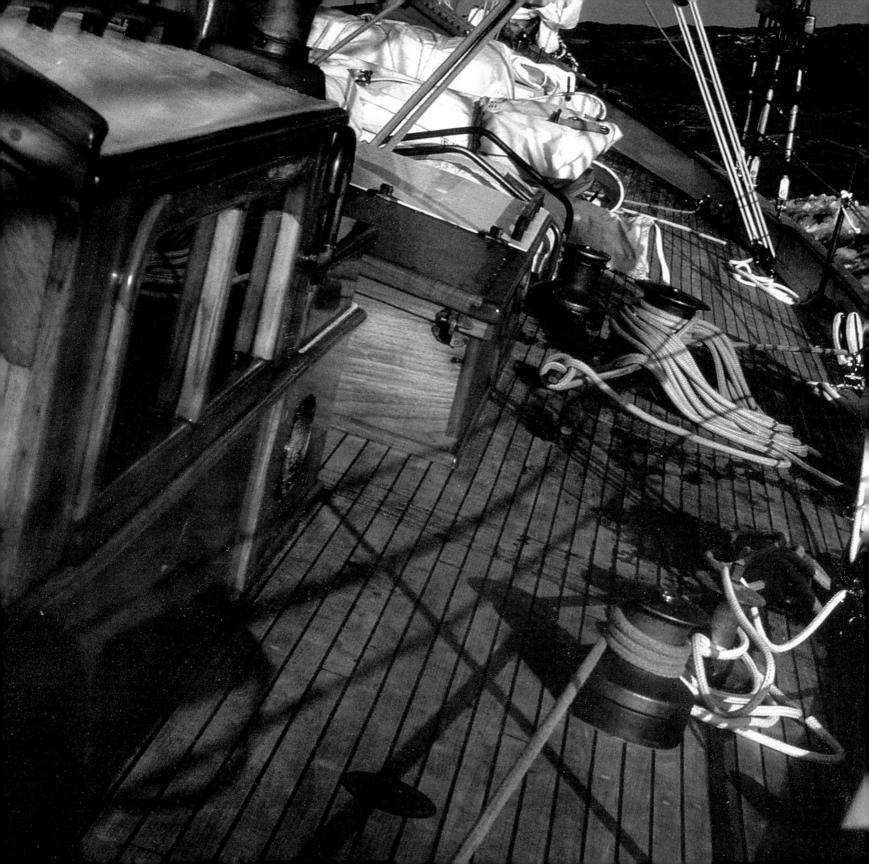

Schooners twice *Jim's* size were the goldplaters of racing and cruising at the turn of the century. The great schooners each had a personality, an identity that linked a name with feats on blue water and some of the best of yachting seamanship. But only a few of them would ever live beyond the few years they fulfilled an owner's needs.

While Joseph Conrad was writing his novel *Lord Jim* about youth, ambition and courage in the Far East, the schooner age was coming to an end for both yachtsmen and fishermen. Yet the schooner *Lord Jim* eighty years later sails into seas familiar to readers of Conrad's stories. She will, in a different age, star in a tale for television. She is a fortunate survivor of many hard times, and her story has something of the mystique of her namesake.

While she now sails the Pacific, her roots are in New England, and her survival is due in part to an inherent Yankee toughness. Now, after restoration, her owner estimates that she is stiffer and 80% stronger in her rigging than she was when she was built in the mid-1930's.

John Alden, her designer, knew his boats could endure and live for years if they were given proper care. A careful man, he would have applauded the efforts of Jim's new owner to ready her for big seas and winds, for Alden learned early what strength in a boat meant.

In the winter of 1908, Alden and his brother, along with four others, sailed a fishing schooner out of Halifax, Nova Scotia, on a clandestine mission for their employer. Canadian authorities and Alden's boss were involved in litigation over some long-forgotten infraction of Admiralty law. To make matters worse, the regular crew was quarantined ashore with smallpox. With no time to consult the crew or worry about weather (The Canadians were about to seize the vessel.) Alden and his five friends set sail in the dead of night on a big schooner that normally shipped a fishing crew of 23 men. They sailed into a blizzard, and for three weeks the violent seas and bitter cold of a winter storm in the North Atlantic was the little ship's world. They headed roughly south, keeping sea room, and struck for land several hundred miles off course. The Coast Guard towed the schooner and six half-starved men into New York Harbor. There was surprisingly little damage. Glad to be ashore, John Alden began to consider the inherent seaworthiness of that North Atlantic fishing vessel, and his thoughts were to give the world of

Shortly before the start, Prior announced that his wife
would be aboard for the run to Halifax. At that point, two-thirds of the crew jumped ship,
and those who stayed did so because of friendship or good wages.

THE NEW SCHOONER *MERIDIAN*

yachting a series of superb "Alden schooners." The "fisherman" style—deep draft, full keel, spoon bow, broad transom, all with a tall topsail rig—became an Alden hallmark.

Lord Jim was hull #614 at the George Lawley & Sons Shipyard in Neponset, Massachusetts. Two M.I.T. professors, Milton Knight and his brother, had come to Alden for a bluewater cruiser. As the design section of Yachting noted in 1936: "Her construction is quite heavy with double-sawn frames. The decks are of teak as is the rail and deck joinerwork. A comfortable deck shelter is built at the forward end of the cockpit, similar to that used on other Alden boats . . . The gaff-head rig with fiddled topmast was adopted at the owners' request as the boat is designed for extended offshore cruising, speed being a secondary consideration."

That last phrase has an odd ring for me. On a blustery night in the Pacific, I was at *Lord Jim's* helm with main, foresail and #1 Genoa up on a beam reach. A sudden surge of wind and a big queer wave sent the schooner on a sleighride I'll never forget. We seemed to be surging along already at 11+ knots, although with no instrument lights on (sailing more by feel than electronic gadgetry) I can't say for sure. With that wave, though, I know we must have approached *Lord Jim's* hull speed of 15 knots. I was alone on deck, and thus the only witness to this exhilarating burst of speed. They wouldn't believe me when I went below. And later on, drinks in hand, the story grew to 17 knots in fearful seas. Whatever really happened, the fact remains that a 72´ "fisherman" schooner is fast!

In the spring of 1936, the Knights launched their new Alden/Lawley yacht and named her *Meridian*. There was speculation that she would sail the Newport-Bermuda Race that year, but it didn't work out. The brothers cruised the Atlantic coast for the next five years until war interrupted their recreation. In 1941 *Meridian* was signed over to military duty as a submarine patrol boat off the East coast. One can imagine a German U-Boat surfacing to find that a graceful schooner painted dull grey had discovered them. This, of course, was the idea. Her name was changed to *Blue Water* during her wartime duty.

In 1946 Roscoe Prior, a sailor from Boston, bought *Blue Water* from the U.S. Coast Guard. Prior was the owner of the Lenox Hotel in Boston, headed a shipping firm, and had an interest in the marine railways of Rockport, Mass. The new owner gave her an extensive cleanup after her rough-and-ready military experience, had her completely rerigged, installed a new diesel, and ordered a new suit of sails cut. *Blue Water* became *Shoal Water*, and she looked as fresh as she did a decade before on the ways.

Prior's propriety of command, befitting a Hub hotelier, expressed itself when he hired a prim and proper steward complete with white jacket and matching shoes. Then he went to the other extreme and hired an old Down-East schooner captain complete with arm garters for his working shirt. The two didn't get on too well. Prior had bought the boat for cruising, but in the spring of 1948 he entered the Marblehead-Halifax Race.

Walter McInnis (former chief engineer at the Lawley yard) and his son Alan were among the full complement of crew gathered for the race. Shortly before the start Prior announced that his wife was to be aboard for the run to Halifax. At that point, two-thirds of the crew jumped ship, and those who stayed did so because of friendship or good wages. Prior started the race anyway, with two youthful hands forward and four elderly yachtsmen in the afterguard. And Mrs. Prior, of course. Fortunately for all, the race was a one-tack affair for its 350 miles. It was not quite a milk run, nevertheless, for the few able hands who pulled the strings for what was then heavy canvas sail. The skipper held steady on the rhumb line, and *Shoal Water* finished second only to the remarkable L. Francis Herreshoff ketch *Ticonderoga*. It was *Shoal Water's* first race, and the last one she would know for another 13 years.

In the fall of 1949 Roscoe Prior, then in his early sixties, was ready to put his schooner up for sale for $16,000. He died before she could be sold, and ownership passed to his wife. *Shoal Water* lay idle until Mrs. Prior donated her to the New York State Maritime Academy in 1953.

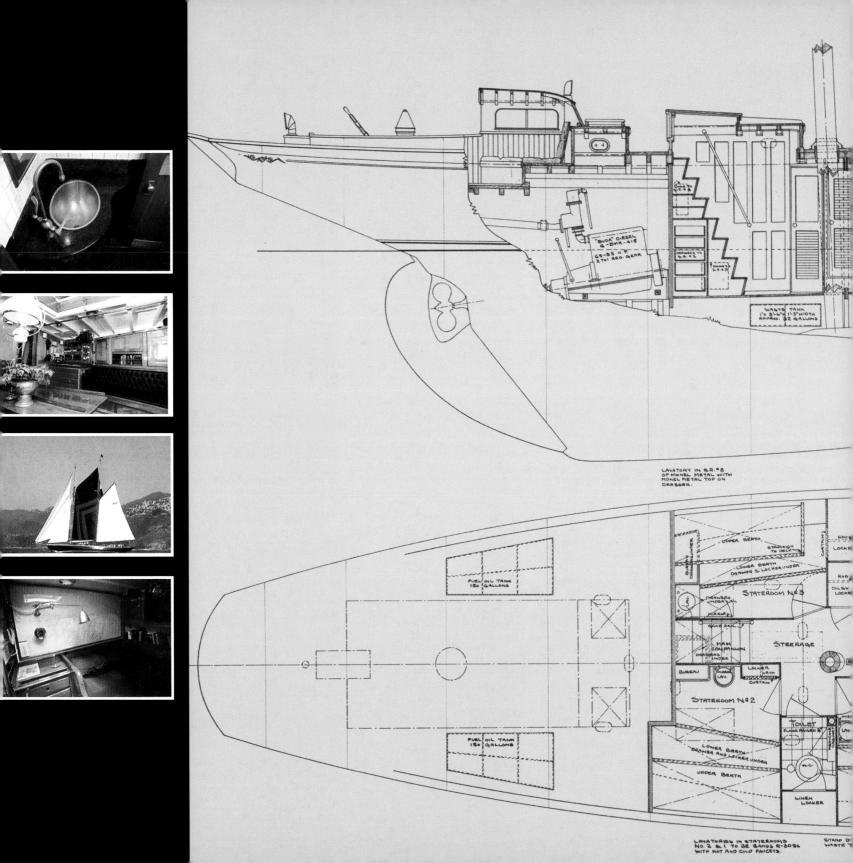

"BUDA" DIESEL
6-DHR-415
65-55 H.P.
2 to I RED. GEAR

WASTE TANK
1'x 2'6"x 1'3" WIDTH
APPROX. 52 GALLONS

LAVATORY IN S.R. #3
OF MONEL METAL WITH
MONEL METAL TOP ON
DRESSER.

FUEL OIL TANK
150 GALLONS

FUEL OIL TANK
150 GALLONS

UPPER BERTH

STANCHION
TO DECK

LOWER BERTH
DRAWER & LOCKER UNDER

CURTAIN

STATEROOM No3

STEERAGE

MAIN
COMPANION
DRAWERS
UNDER

STATEROOM No 2

TOILET
FLOOR RAISED 3"

BUREAU

W.C.

LOWER BERTH
DRAWER AND LOCKER UNDER

UPPER BERTH

LINEN
LOCKER

LAVATORIES IN STATEROOMS
NO. 2 & 1 TO BE SANDS R-3056
WITH HOT AND COLD FAUCETS.

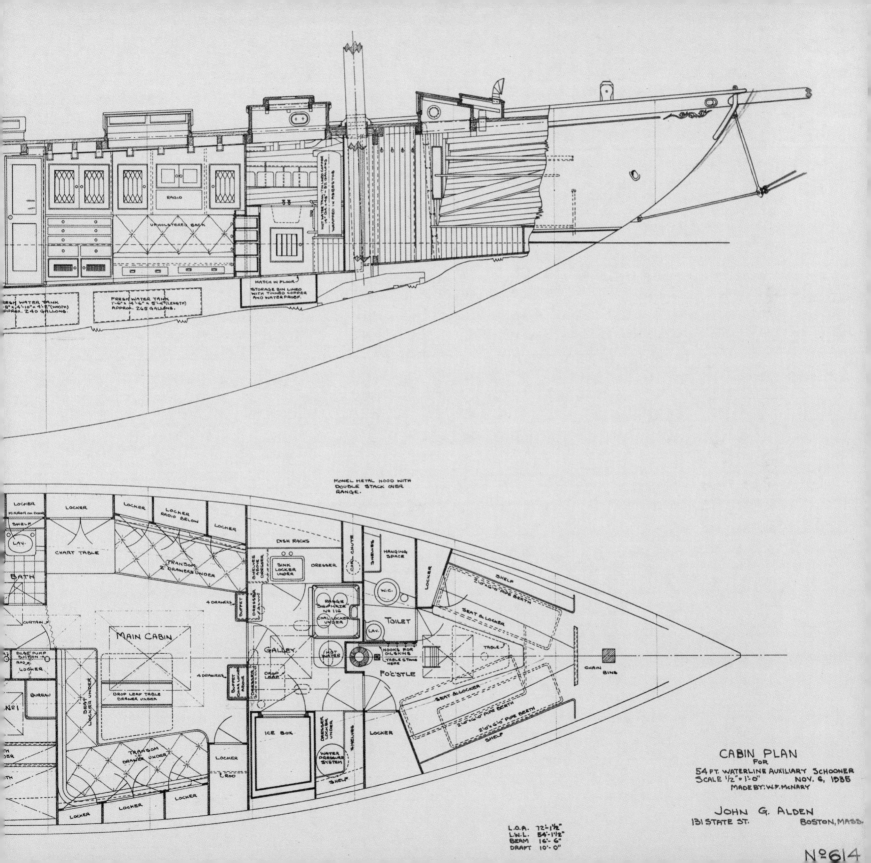

CABIN PLAN
FOR
54 FT. WATERLINE AUXILIARY SCHOONER
SCALE 1/2" = 1'-0"   NOV. 6, 1935
MADE BY: W.F. McNARY

JOHN G. ALDEN
131 STATE ST.   BOSTON, MASS.

L.O.A. 72'-1½"
L.W.L. 54'-1½"
BEAM   16'-6"
DRAFT 10'-0"

Nº 614

Victory over the formidable *Niña* was the high point of a
racing career for *Lord Jim*, the schooner that had been built as a cruiser.
It was one of the last great contests between schooners.

THE RACE WITH *NIÑA*

Sailing enthusiasm was abundant at the Academy, but the money for maintenance was not, and the big schooner lay neglected for another four years.

In 1957, when she was put up for auction, the old girl was bought by a professional magician from New York. Not much magic was performed on her, except to change her name to *Genie*. She was sold again in 1959 to radio producer Phillip H. Lord. Lord apparently bought the schooner as an investment, and he had hopes of reselling her immediately. Along about this time, Alan McInnis, through the brokerage office of Eldredge-McInnis, sold a 68´ schooner to Ross Anderson, prominent Boston sailor and Commodore of the Boston Yacht Club from 1960 to 1962. Anderson named his new boat *Lord Jim*, but he enjoyed her only briefly. She went down on a reef off Fishers Island that summer. Anderson went looking for a replacement. He wanted a yacht that would rival that of his counterpart at the New York Yacht Club, Commodore De Coursey Fales, owner of *Niña*.

Phillip Lord meanwhile had moored *Genie* in the lee of his island off the Maine coast. When word came to Commodore Anderson that she was for sale he didn't hesitate. Anderson brought her down to Falmouth Marine Railways in Buzzards Bay where he had her completely rebuilt. There had been a fire in her galley, and most of her interior had been badly damaged. With meticulous attention to her original plans and details, she was brought back to life in only six months. She became Ross Anderson's new *Lord Jim*. In July of 1960, her topsides gleaming and her brass and brightwork polished, *Lord Jim* glided into Marblehead Harbor on a perfect midsummer day. She was a sight to be long remembered, and with cannons booming from the Boston Yacht Club seawall, Commodore Anderson neatly steered the new flagship in for a landing at the clubhouse pier. It was a flag-flying day long overdue for the graceful creation of John Alden and the Lawley yard of Boston.

Down in New York, De Coursey Fales and the Burgess-designed *Niña* were pursuing ocean racing in an ageless way; no schooner, let alone a mere ketch or yawl, was able to beat the 35-year-old N.Y.Y.C. flagship. Commodore Anderson was eager to do battle, and he chose to challenge the mighty *Niña* in the Marblehead-to-Halifax Race. As Don McNamara recounted the adventure in his book *White Sails, Black Clouds*, the boat was old, and no one seriously thought she could be outfitted well enough and pushed hard enough in an offshore race. Anderson and McNamara inspected every inch of *Lord Jim* late in the fall of 1960, and they found her sound and potentially able to meet the challenge. It wasn't long before Ted Hood, a friend contracted to cut new sails, came up with a way around the old vessel's CCA handicap rating. In the spring of 1961, *Lord Jim* was sporting a new 82´ aluminum mast, a thing that was to prove useful on the race course although it left a lot to be desired in aesthetics. *Lord Jim* was about to make ocean-racing history.

In her first race of the 1961 season, she walked away from all contenders flying a tremendous #1 Genoa and a "monster" drifter that stretched from the bowsprit all the way aft to a block abeam of the wheel. It was a race for reaching, a condition in which a schooner will fly. The initial victory brought Anderson and *Lord Jim* the Lambert Cup, and there was optimism in the air at Marblehead. But the real battle was still to be fought. Bring on *Niña*! *Niña* did come forward, soundly trouncing Anderson's reborn vessel in three consecutive races. Off the wind, *Lord Jim* could hold her own; going to windward it was embarrassing. The Halifax Race, however, was still ahead.

Light northerly winds at the start made the rhumb line to Nova Scotia a dead beat, an uphill struggle that promised disaster for Anderson and crew. With little choice, *Lord Jim* crossed the line, laying off on a beam reach for Provincetown while the rest of the fleet inched up the coast to windward.

For four days Lord Jim sailed her own course, playing the wind for her reaching strength. The rest of the fleet, with Fales' *Niña* in the van, was never to be seen, and news reports of the race's progress identified *Niña* as the obvious leader, *Lord Jim* not in sight and way behind. The

She arrived in Antigua unscathed and on time. It was just
another challenge taken in stride by this excellent little ship. And it
was the dramatic beginning of a ten-year charter career.

THE CHARTER TRADE

gamble to go East paid off, and to the astonishment of the race committee, the little world of ocean racing, and especially De Coursey Fales, *Lord Jim* charged out of the haze at Halifax going like a freight train and crossed the finish line first overall. *Niña* had been beaten, and the celebration that followed was not soon forgotten in Halifax.

Anderson continued to race the old schooner for the next five years, sailing the Newport-Bermuda Race and various coastal contests. But victory over the formidable *Niña* was the high point of a racing career for *Lord Jim*, the schooner that had been built as a cruiser. It was one of the last great contests between schooners.

In 1966, Commodore Anderson, older now and weary of the classic burden of a wooden yacht's full-time upkeep, was ready to sell. Jolyon Byerley came north from Antigua representing the Nicholson Yacht Sales and Charter Company to look over New England's collection of grand old schooners and yawls. Byerley's eyes soon fell on *Lord Jim*, and very soon she was his. He powered her into Stamford, CT, on a cold, still November evening. She was to be put into charter service in less than a fortnight, so Byerley and crew geared up and set sail direct for Antigua. November is a bad, late time to sail for the south.

Reminiscent of John Alden's encounter with a winter storm in the Atlantic, *Lord Jim* slid down towering seas before 60-knot winds under bare poles, with every extra warp on the vessel strung out astern in a bight nearly a mile long. In one 24-hour stretch she made better than 250 miles without a stitch of sail.

She arrived unscathed and on time. It was just another challenge taken in stride by this excellent little ship. And it was the dramatic beginning of a ten-year charter career.

The schooner's pride was diligently preserved by Jolyon Byerley and his wife Jenny. An enthusiastic crew sailed her as the queen of all the charter vessels of the West Indies. The Byerleys raced her in the annual Antigua Sailing Week, and *Lord Jim* was the toast of the event twice running. While on charter they rarely used the engine; they always sailed in and out of harbor.

After seven years the all-too-familiar need of a major refit came due, and the dilemma of the expense forced the Byerleys to sell. Her new owner, Denny Warner, quickly sailed into disaster in the most unlikely of conditions. On a clear, blue day in the Caribbean, a fleet of lovely vintage yachts was racing off Antigua. The ageless *Clover* (now

She lay over on the coral, her death certificate all
but signed. The tragic loss of Irving Johnson's *Yankee* was being compared with
her end. But miraculously she came off the reef in one piece.

DIFFICULT DAYS IN THE ISLANDS

based in San Francisco) was matching *Lord Jim* tack for tack. In the heat of the competition, *Clover's* crew confirmed with a chart that a reef lay dead ahead and got busy tacking away. They watched unbelieving as the crew on *Lord Jim* failed to dodge the reef. With a sickening crunch, *Lord Jim's* stem and forefoot were splintered and torn apart. She lay over on the coral, her death certificate all but signed. The tragic loss of Irving Johnson's *Yankee* was being compared with her end. But miraculously she came off the reef in one piece. Warner had her fitted with a new stem and some fresh frames, and he held her together for another three years in the charter trade. But not enough was done, and in 1975 she lay in the Caribbean all but forgotten when another sailor came to her rescue.

Holger Kreuzhage grew up in postwar Germany. He spent summers sailing off the small Baltic islands of Northern Germany. When he was a teenager he went to a summer sailing school run by a pair of hardnosed ex-German naval officers, one of them a former sub commander. They tended to treat their pupils like their former subordinates. Ability to endure difficulty, and a plain toughness at sea, were to be with Holger Kreuzhage forever as a result of his training in the little Baltic sailing school. He progressed to the Hamburg Yacht Club. There, as a skipper with a reputation for winning, he raced intensely, sailing the 80′ yawl *Hamburg V*. The earlier *Hamburgs* were well-known, most notably *Hamburg I & II* of the early 1900's, both of which were 150′ three-masted schooners.

Business and a career in commercial photography brought him to the United States. Keeping up with racing, let alone any sailing at all, proved difficult. Every season, however, Holger would return to the Hamburg Yacht Club, of which he is still a member, and race in the old races. TransAtlantic races became part of his annual international schedule.

Working out of a home and studio in San Francisco for the past ten years, Kreuzhage has kept in touch with the sea by occasionally skippering big Class A boats in Bay-area racing. As a successful photographer

in this country and in Europe, he was soon able to make certain dreams become realities. The big dream was a schooner of his own. "Schooning!" is what Holger likes to shout. Doing what a schooner does best (reaching) has always had a grip on him.

The first two decades of this century were the last of the true "schooning" era. Opening a book on the mighty yachts of 50 to 100 years ago, you can't help but wonder what it must have been like to stand at the wheel of the 150′ *Atlantic*, or the powerful *Westward*, or Germany's original *Hamburgs*. To be aboard such machines, to feel the power of a gaff-rigged cloud of canvas driving through the sea, was Holger's big dream.

To find and afford any vessel of such size today is not likely unless you've struck oil (or, in Baron Marcel Bich's case, ballpoint pens). But something half the size and equally majestic would certainly do. Holger hired a broker in Miami to track down something appropriate. He got a call that a boat had been found, and that she was just what he was looking for. He wired a down payment, arriving within a week in the Bahamas to find that the boat had been sold out from under him and that the agent had decamped with his $20,000. Holger pursued his money and his boat until both had been recovered, then he headed for Antigua where he found *Lord Jim* in a quiet cove.

He assembled an ample crew of 15 to 20 hands, then sailed in stages over a period of three months through the Panama Canal and north to San Francisco. Crew members came and went throughout these passages. One is still with the boat today. He was picked up and offered passage after his own boat was wrecked in the Bahamas. They sailed the old hooker only in fair weather. A hurricane was narrowly dodged off the west coast of Mexico. The old sails blew out continuously, and several of the crew became expert at sewing in strong patches. The mainsail looked like a map of Kansas when *Jim* finally sailed under the Golden Gate Bridge.

Holger sailed straight for the Anderson and Cristofani Shipyard, where the old schooner was hauled. For the first time, the new owner could see what he was dealing with. He picked up a large screwdriver and

Testing the wood in the stem, the tool pushed straight
through the rot. The amount of restoration was awesome. Holger didn't hesitate
for a second. This was his dream, after all . . .

LORD JIM REBORN

climbed the ladder to the forepeak. Testing the tool in the stem, the tool pushed straight through the rot. The amount of restoration was awesome. Holger didn't hesitate for a second. This was his dream, after all. Nothing is impossible. Or is it?

That was the fall of 1975. And it did seem impossible. In the spring of 1979, the miracle of devoted care and craftsmanship has prevailed, preserving—indeed, creating—something extraordinary. *Lord Jim* was entirely replanked below the waterline when she sailed for Acapulco. A new stem was in place. Frames were replaced or sistered, and many of her deck beams were new. The deck was more than four inches thick. Over the old 1-3/4˝ teak deck a 5/8˝ marine plywood subdeck was laid, then covered with a fresh layer of 1-1/2˝ teak. The rigging was all new, and it was personally wrapped and payed by Holger and his crew. Only the spars were original. Below decks, gangs of as many as seven carpenters completely rebuilt the interior spaces, changing the original plan only in the master cabin and galley.

The Lawley yard was crawling with talented shipwrights 43 years ago when this little ship was built. In the mid-1970's in San Francisco two old-timers at the Anderson and Cristofani yard, men who knew the last of a lost age of wooden boatbuilding, directed young volunteers in the art of a gone time. Proper wood was hard to find, and so was hard labor; but the will and sweat of an inspired restoration crew prevailed. The revived *Lord Jim* is a tribute to the ageless knowledge passed on, and to the young men and women who executed the work.

It was a clear, crisp day, and a typical brisk wind was sweeping San Francisco Bay. It was Master Mariner Race Day, 1978. Most of Pelican Harbor, Sausalito's exclusive haven for wooden boats, emptied into the Bay to watch the traditional yachts. *Lord Jim* was there, and Holger was at the helm with a gleam in his eye. It was the look of a man overdue for some competitive pleasure, for hard wind on a spread of gaff-rigged canvas—for schooning! *Jim's* structural and rigging work was complete and recently tested. With a green crew (It's tough to find a brawny bunch of deckhands who know the difference between a peak and a throat, let alone what a gollywobbler is.) he powered *Lord Jim* over the line, startling the competition with a magnificent sight. A genoa clew blew out on the second leg and caused Holger to ease off. But *Lord Jim* was racing again; her strength was back. She looked and felt colossal, racing be damned.

We are at sea off the Mexican coast. Hauling down on a foremast halyard, Phil, Pam and Fred send up the gollywobbler. The moderate westerlies have held into the tropical air south of Cabo San Lucas. Laying off on a starboard reach, the giant sail fills with an awesome bend, arcing back to the tip of the main boom. We smash along at a steady 11 knots.

Straddling the seat behind the wheel, Holger cranes forward to watch the foredeck work, his weight on the wheel to hold the inevitable lee helm the mass of sail creates. The gollywobbler is his own design, and it is a crowning touch to the exhilaration of sailing this vessel—of schooning! Now on a southeast heading, Acapulco is three days ahead, the end of the first leg of an open-ended adventure.

Lord Jim's latest adventure represents a level of
serious activity that no previous owner ever attempted, and it eclipses
even the World War II service she saw as *Blue Water*.

HER NEW ADVENTURE

An impressive sight wherever she goes, *Lord Jim* will soon become the star of a European television series, a show-biz connection that enables a big, expensive sailing yacht to pay her way in these expensive times. *Lord Jim* and Holger seem uniquely suited to make it work. Holger is the producer, with some of the money spent on the vessel's refitting provided by investors in the television production company. Holger remains very much in control of both the schooner and the company. The business and the sailing adventure nicely complement each other.

The television series will center on young sailors traveling and living aboard the schooner, encountering the contemporary ports of the Orient and any number of adventures. Scripts have been drafted with promising plots for locations in Samoa, the Phillipines, Malaysia, and other places in Conrad's Far East. There is no pressure of production schedules for the moment, and Holger figures that it will take as much as two years to shoot and edit. Photographing *Lord Jim* on the high seas is the first big project. The plan is to outfit the boat and its film crew to sail intentionally into the best and worst weather conditions imaginable. Spectacular drama at sea—almost unfilmed before—will be cut together with near-documentary footage in port. Actors and actresses will be engaged with the real people of Far East locations.

There will be times when *Lord Jim* and crew will sail into such lawless areas as Southeast Asia, and the need to be armed, and to keep a constant watch for pirates, will be a very real part of their lives. The adventure of filming promises to be as dramatic as the TV-series film itself. There is something incongruous about a sailing vessel from a bygone age of New England yachting sailing into the contemporary strife of Southeast Asian waters. *Lord Jim's* latest adventure represents a level of serious activity that no precious owner ever attempted, and it eclipses even the World War II service she saw as *Blue Water*.

We glided into Acapulco Bay under a full moon. When I left her she seemed straining on her mooring lines, impatient to race the high seas yet again, impatient like Holger to be off over the horizon, to have the sheets tight and thrumming, to be—schooning!

THE HOOLIGAN NAVY

BY JOSEPH COOPER

The grey yawl nosed into a clear patch of pewter sea as the morning's fog burned off, and a man in the cock pit and another on the bow stood and looked aloft to where the growl of an engine grew louder. It was a familiar Lakehurst blimp, for sure; but a grey blimp in grey clouds that started just over the masthead couldn't be seen. In the companionway, the cook took orders for more coffee and the men sat again by the forestay and by the lashed wheel, the yawl making just over a knot with a scrap of storm jib, a storm trysail and her mizzen. It was the spring of '43 and these men were not yachting – they were patrolling.

It was a tense time, when the beaches of New Jersey
were tarred by oil from torpedoed tankers and when attacks not only from submarines
but from carrier-based aircraft were considered a possibility.

TWO PICKET PATROL KETCHES AND A SCHOONER, ALL FORMER YACHTS, RETURN FROM A 96-HOUR PATROL IN EASY WEATHER DURING WORLD WAR II.

In making a case for their proposed anti-submarine
activities, the Cruising Club of America cited eight "primary tactical
advantages of using sailboats" . . .

Between June of 1942 and November of 1943, yachts like this yawl played an active role in guarding most of the Eastern Seaboard of the U.S., and until war's end a fleet of them patrolled the approaches to New York Harbor. The Navy's name for this volunteer effort was the Coastal Picket Patrol, and the Coast Guard called it for a time the Corsair Fleet, a romantic monicker for a ragtag aggregation of small fishing vessels, coastal freighters, motorboats and sailing auxiliaries. The crews of ocean-racing yachts in this service, many of them grey-painted goldplaters, called themselves the Hooligan Navy; and although the term would imply otherwise, they carried out their missions with skill and discipline.

The Coastal Picket Patrol offered offshore eyes and ears at a time when Allied shipping of all kinds was under submarine attack and the security of the U.S. East Coast was uncertain. Along with yacht clubs, U.S. Power Squadrons, fishing fleets, marine supply houses, and other establishments with shore facilities or activities which took them to sea, their missions were to report evidence of submarines and suspicious activities of small craft—particularly anything equipped with peculiar signaling or communications gear, or ferrying extraordinary quantities of supplies. They were to be a deterrent against efforts to sabotage navigational aids and port facilities; they were to watch for the dropping of mines and other floating objects by aircraft and surface vessels; they were to discover the placement of any obstruction that might impede convoy traffic. It was a tense time, when the beaches of New Jersey were tarred by oil from torpedoed tankers and when attacks not only from submarines but from carrier-based aircraft were considered a possibility. Even floating garbage—an egg crate with German lettering—could be a clue to an enemy presence that was clandestine but real until war's end. During a ten-day period in January of 1942, only weeks after Pearl Harbor, three German submarines destroyed 200,000 tons of shipping off the U.S. East Coast, and U-boats were a threat until the very last day of the war, when U-853 was sunk off Block Island.

The Coastal Pickets were also to serve as a vital link in search and rescue work. Shipping losses in the spring of 1942 off the U.S. East Coast had been for a few periods greater than the combines losses in all other sectors of the Atlantic. This collection of Corsair vessels and crews was inspired by the resourcefulness and courage of the small-boat seamen who made history in 1940 with the evacuation of Dunkirk. Fittingly, the Corsair Fleet came about not at the instigation of the U.S. Navy or the Coast Guard, but through the suggestion of British authorities and the influence of a determined band of web-footed citizens.

Early in 1942, the British representative of the Ministry of War Transport wrote to the Office of the British Merchant Shipping Commission to discuss "a rather alarming sense of disquiet among many merchant seamen in vessels arriving at Canadian ports," caused in part by the way the British had been handling announcement of ship losses. The British representative suggested that "morale would be enormously improved if the U.S.A. could organize and publicize a voluntary fleet of small craft which would undertake certain patrols." He continued: "Of course, I do not know what sort of arrangements have been made, but there must be any number of Americans who, if the government could supply them with some sort of craft, would be only too willing to have a crack at it. After all, we have the example of Dunkirk where every available craft that could float was pressed into service."

While this letter was making its way through the British Admiralty and the British Embassy in Washington, and on to the Chief of U.S. Naval Operations, the Commander of the Eastern Sea Frontier was considering a proposal from the Cruising Club of America that offshore sailing vessels, owned and manned by CCA members and other volunteers, be commissioned for anti-submarine patrol duty. It was an idea whose time had come. And while the effectiveness of such a fleet in deterring submarine attacks may be debated, the Corsair patrols promised to be very helpful in reconnaissance and rescue missions. In making a case for their proposed anti-submarine activities, the Cruising Club cited eight "primary tactical advantages of using sailboats," which, as it turned out, made them perhaps as valuable in other offshore roles:

"1. A vessel under sail gives no warning of her presence or approach to a submarine. (This advantage is shared by no other type of craft, either water or air. Even a blimp can be heard or, in the day, be seen, in time for the surfaced submarine to submerge into deep water. The minor water noises of a sailing vessel allow her to come very close to a submarine before detection on listening apparatus.)

"2. A vessel 'hove to' (headsails backed, helm up) is a steadier type of observation platform than a destroyer or other type of patrol craft. (This is due to the keel in the water and the counterbalancing keel action of the sail in the air. An observation post aloft at the hounds, 40´ to 60´ from the deck, gives approximately the same or better height of eye as the bridge of a large patrol vessel.)

"3. There is less leeway or drift with a sailing vessel properly 'hove to' due to the counterbalancing action of the rudder forcing the ship up into the wind and the backed headsail or reefed foresail tending to drive the bow off. (Under gale conditions this leeway will not amount to more than 1 1/2K or at the most 2K. Thus a small vessel can comfortably, safely,

The Navy envisioned Cruising Club boats and crews assuming aggressive roles, and it was thought that sailing yachts of 50´ and more could be armed for combat against enemy submarines.

and effectively hold her station at sea, as has been demonstrated many times in our members' experience.)

"**4.** There is less noise on a sailing vessel—there is no engine noise to compete with the audible submarine Diesel proceeding on the surface at night or charging her batteries. It is surmised that this submarine Diesel exhaust can be heard 2-5 miles depending on conditions.

"**5.** A sailing vessel is cheap and quick to build. While in war, economy is not a governing consideration, speed of production is. We estimate the rough-finish production cost of a 50´ sailing vessel as being about $20,000–$25,000, and on a production basis, maybe lower. There are probably in excess of 100 small yards on the Atlantic Coast not now engaged in naval contracts that could be geared up to handle this type of production. (A fleet of only 80 such vessels—40 operating, 40 relief—could constitute an observation and patrol screen at 10-mile intervals from Cape Cod across the Gulf of Maine to Cape Sable and up the coast to Halifax; or from Ambrose Light Vessel down the Jersey Coast, across the Delaware Bay area to Cape Hatteras.)

"**6.** Construction of a fleet of such wooden sailing vessels—should the experiment prove successful—would not compete for steel plate, specialized welding and riveting shipyard labor.

"**7.** Having only auxiliary power, these vessels would not require engineer personnel. (A regular crew member could be quickly trained to give the relatively simple power installation such attention as it might require afloat.)

"**8.** Cruising range, due to tankage being available for water rather than fuel and space for provisions rather than machinery, would extend far beyond normal for patrol craft of considerably greater size. (Such vessels as are being proposed could keep the sea for a two-week tour of duty easily, 30 days in emergencies.)"

This scheme made sense to the CCA, but it was apparently an annoyance to the hard-pressed U.S. Navy. It took the persistence and persuasiveness of Alfred Stanford, Commodore of the Cruising Club, to win orders to set sail. Stanford took his case to Washington, where he had what he describes as "a hard time" getting to see Admiral Adolphus Andrews, Commander of the Eastern Sea Frontier. "I had to use a lot of pull," Stanford recalls, "and he wasn't favorably disposed to our proposal. He seemed unduly concerned about the status and safety of the patrols rather than the ships we hoped to protect. There were at least 16 CCA members who were ready to donate their boats, and they weren't unaware of the risks. But Andrews. . . Well, he just couldn't find a place for us. He didn't have time for us, so he pushed us off on the Coast Guard."

Stanford, a former newspaperman who left the New York Herald-Tribune to devote himself to the publishing of a Connecticut newspaper and a boating magazine (the fondly-remembered BOATS), was working in an advertising

agency when he visited Admiral Andrews. He describes the advertising game as "good fun if it weren't for the clients." One can't help but imagine this man's balanced and economical presentation having the desired effect, which it finally did. With the CCA as a client, and the offshore patrol as the service to be sold, Stanford was perfect for the job. He claims to have made a tactical error, however: "I should have gone to F.D.R. with the idea—he would have been delighted with it. According to one of the White House boys, Roosevelt had his CCA mail brought to his bed with his breakfast and the night dispatches and cables. We had decided by this time to honor the yachtsmen of Dunkirk for their role in the evacuation. It was our way of celebrating the solidarity of the cause; but we hadn't been able to present or even deliver the Blue Water Medal, our highest award. I had called the White House in the hope of getting someone interested in this little symbolic effort. I told our story to a Naval aide, and the next thing I know F.D.R. is on the phone telling me 'You get me that medal and I'll see that it's presented' . . . I should have gone to F.D.R. with our patrol idea."

Even before the Navy Department approved the use of yachts for war duty, the Cruising Club was lining up vessels for such patrols. On 5 March, 1942, the CCA offered the Eastern Sea Frontier 30 auxiliaries between 50´ and 90´ with experienced skippers and skeleton crews, even though there was no commitment from Washington that the yachts would be given public status (putting them under charter to the Navy or enlisting them in the Coast Guard Auxiliary Reserve) to keep them repaired, provisioned and fueled at government expense.

There were ample precedents for such pleasure-boat service. Even before December 7, 1941, the Coast Guard Auxiliary had accepted the services of civilians and civilian-owned-and-operated powerboats for anti-sabotage vigilance on rivers, harbors and back bays. While the Command of the Eastern Sea Frontier was to godfather the Coastal Picket Patrol, the first offshore patrols under sail were organized and controlled by the Coast Guard.

Curiously, it was an admission by the Army Air Force that influenced Naval authorization of what became the Hooligan Navy. The Army had admitted that its Warning Net of civilian lookouts along the Atlantic coast "could not furnish information about enemy aircraft approaching from the sea in sufficient time to permit adequate organization of defenses." The Army Air Force suggested that reports from small boats equipped with radio transmitters stationed at strategic points 50 to 100 miles offshore would "permit interception of enemy aircraft before they reach their objectives." Official assignments began in June of 1942, and were supervised by Commander Vincent Astor, U.S.N.R., a yachtsman in his own right. It should be noted, however that the Coast Guard in New England had seen

Life aboard a Coastal Picket Patrol boat was like
yachting, but it was a lot more intense. It was like ocean racing in its
disciplines of observation, navigation and keeping the little ship.

the value of anti-submarine patrols early in the game. Doug Turner, now a yacht broker at Falmouth Marine Railways, volunteered himself at the age of 39 to the Boston Coast Guard the day after Pearl Harbor. By nightfall, he was on the deck of the 62′ schooner *Ellida* in Boothbay Harbor, charged with guarding the freighters then loading munitions at Searsport.

While the program proposed by Alfred Stanford was in its planning stages, the Navy envisioned Cruising Club boats and crews assuming aggressive roles, and it was thought that sailing yachts of 50′ and more could be armed for combat against enemy submarines. The Navy discovered, however, after "a few unhappy experiments," that even the swiftest sailing vessels were not fast enough to dodge their own explosives nor constructed to withstand the shocks that follow the explosion of depth charges. So instead of being fitted with a row or two of 300-pound depth charges, machine-gun stanchions were stepped on the decks of larger sailboats and machine guns were issued to the crews of smaller yachts. When Doug Turner took charge of the schooner *Ellida* at Boothbay Harbor, her arsenal consisted of a .38 and a .45. "But after things became a bit more organized," he recalls, "they took our sidearms and gave us a World War I Browning machine gun. We never fired the damned thing because we knew it would blow the face plate right off."

Ed du Moulin, yachtsman, chairman of the *Freedom* syndicate in the latest America's Cup campaign, and in 1942 the master of a 47′ Alden-designed motor yacht in the Corsair Fleet, remembers dropping a few of the 25-pound depth charges that were finally issued, and that "the fact that the hull bounced readily kept it from damage." Joe Choate, later to be president of the National Association of Engine and Boat Manufacturers for many years, recalled in an article he wrote for Yachting that the depth charges aboard his command, the 58′ yawl *Zaida*, "would do little more than blow off our stern if we were ever foolish enough to use them." The Eastern Sea Frontier War Diary for July of 1942 described this weaponry as "tragically inadequate for combat against 720-ton submarines." It soon became obvious that the duties for which the Coastal Pickets were best suited were those recommended by the British Merchant Marine and the U.S. Army Air Force—observation and rescue.

The Cruising Club had contended—and the Army Air Force had suggested—that sailboats would be particularly useful in sighting enemy, and otherwise suspicious, vessels. An example of just how effective the Coastal Pickets were in this role can be found in the War Diary of the Eastern Sea Frontier for September of 1942. It was known that a U-boat had been lurking south of Long Island for a week or more before moving to a position about a hundred miles south of Nantucket. A Naval report quoted in the Diary is quoted here:

"It is significant to note that the U-boat was reported five times by drifting Coast Guard Reserve picket boats. These contacts were made at night, and in every case the submarine was under way on the surface. The sound of diesel engines was in most cases heard fifteen to twenty-five miles before the sub was sighted. Navy patrol craft operating in the same area, but under way—and in some cases making sound sweeps—never obtained a contact on this U-boat during the period it was patrolling off Long Island. The value of drifting patrols by numerous small craft off a strategic area such as New York Harbor is thus indicated. Coordination of such a patrol with craft capable of taking rapid offensive action once contact has been established has promising possibilities."

This vigilance was not confined to sub-spotting. On 13 August, 1942, the Army Air Base at Westover, MA, sent out without notice a flight of ten planes to test the Army's own aircraft warning system. The squadron came across Cape Cod, flew south of Nantucket, then turned west and south for Philadelphia. No shore station or Naval vessel spotted them, but four vessels of the Coastal Picket Patrol did.

The value of small boats in submarine "warfare" was elaborated on by the Eastern Sea Frontier War Diary for October, 1942. Submarines operating on the surface at night, noted the Diary, had great difficulty in seeing a small vessel riding low in the water and, therefore, approached close enough for the silent sailboat to get a good fix on the sub's position, speed and likely course. Even when U-boats were able to discover Coastal Picket vessels, they were not inclined to pick on them. In the calculus of war, a sailboat—even a large one obviously on observer duty—was apparently not sufficiently important prey. Sinking a small boat was not worth the risk of bringing on larger foe, and perhaps a U-boat skipper three thousand miles from his source of torpedoes would take care not to squander his offense on a small bit of defense. Whatever their motives, Nazi submarine commanders left the yachts alone throughout the war, although sometimes they acknowledged their presence. Alfred Stanford remembers his son's most exciting experience in the service his father helped create: "John commanded *Nordlys*, Chester Bowles' yacht. They sailed to within a few hundred feet of a German sub that had surfaced to recharge her batteries. John got close enough to get a good fix on their position before sending his signal to shore. With the sub's six-inch gun in mind and sight, John got ready to high-tail it out of range. He was hailed by someone on the sub—in perfect English, with only a slight accent. The voice said 'Don't you fellows know this is no time for yachting?'"

Life aboard a Coastal Picket Patrol boat was like yachting, but it was a lot more intense. It was like ocean racing in its disciplines of observation, navigation, and keeping the little ship. Lawrance Thompson wrote about

"The fellows on watch often shouted 'submarine'
too quickly, and got a razzing from the others when they came on deck
to see where the sub was."

THE FOREDECK LOOKOUT SCANS THE HORIZON, A PLACID BUT EXHAUSTING DUTY THAT WAS THE PRINCIPAL OCCUPATION OF A PATROL'S "ON" WATCH.

"They took our sidearms and gave us a World War I
Browning machine gun. We never fired the damned thing because we knew
it would blow the face plate right off."

PATROL VESSELS, SOME WITH BOXY WINTERTIME PILOTHOUSES, AWAIT ORDERS AT ONE OF THE HOOLIGAN NAVY'S PRINCIPAL BASES IN GREENPORT, L.I.

Normal patrols were 96 hours, although the larger sailing vessels might keep the sea for weeks, and normal patrol areas in the northeast were along the 50-fathom curve.

the experience in a book and in articles for Harpers, and his remarks on sub-searching give some flavor of it: "When there was nothing in sight on the horizon, there was always the business of trying to keep a bright eye peeled for periscopes or telltale feathers of wake where periscopes might be. We would keep imagining that we were seeing things. Let the wind change enough to kick rollers into a chop, and there would be all kinds of lights and shadows on the water, so that you would be sure that you saw at least a dozen periscopes before the end of each watch. Every time you saw a whale or a porpoise it gave your stomach a sudden turn; the fellows on watch often shouted 'submarine' too quickly, and got a razzing from the others when they came on deck to see where the sub was."

Sometimes the sightings were all too real. In Yachting, Joe Choate described *Zaida*'s encounter with a convoy on a grey day with 300-yard visibility: Then both lookouts yelled simultaneously—a freighter bow was looming at us from each quarter. Good! We were in between the columns, and all we had to do was stay between them until they got past us. Those first two rushed by at a good 15 knots, about 100 yards on either side of us, and were closely followed by six more pairs, while we veered a little one way, a little the other, to keep out of their paths."

The Picket Patrol plan, announced 14 July, 1942, organized five task groups: Northern, Narragansett, New York, Delaware, Chesapeake and Southern. Six weeks later the Northern group had 51 sailing yachts from 50' to 75' on patrol, including the schooner *Blue Goose*, the ketch *Tioga* (better know by her second name, *Ticonderoga*) and the schooner *Grenadier*. Only the 7th Naval District in New Orleans fielded more vessels, mostly fishboats. Between the Virginia Capes and Pensacola, most of the patrol boats were power cruisers, one of them Ernest Hemingway's Wheeler sportfisherman *Pilar*. Each vessel carried a radiotelephone, sonic listening gear, the poor arsenal already noted, and Army Interceptor Command grid charts for 200 to 300 miles offshore, each grid defining a patrol area 15 nautical miles square. Normal patrols were 96 hours, although the larger sailing vessels might keep the sea for weeks, and normal patrol areas in the northeast were along the 50-fathom curve.

Dead-reckoning navigation was a constant discipline. "We didn't do celestial at that time; but even if we did, many a patrol didn't have the required visibility," remembers Ed du Moulin, whose Alden motor yacht was nicknamed *The Rolling Bettine* despite the best efforts of her steadying sails. "An accurately timed run and a steady helm from the Fire Island entrance buoy to our grid would be good for starters. On the grid we would head for the upwind end, always keeping an accurate running plot, logging each change of wind direction. With any kind of a breeze, we would set the jib and trim it flat. The trysail was usually for steadying going out and returning, and whenever we were under power. The trysail could be

trimmed well to windward to keep it full when going upwind. Over the stern we rigged a bridle with heavy line and a big, strong canvas sea anchor with a trip line. Plenty of chafing gear helped—and a handy axe. Then we would lock the wheel, take a compass reading, drop a block of wood from the bow and time its drift to the stern. We kept oil ready to empty through the head if seas got too bad. The duties of the on-watch included sound detection by one man, and another acting as lookout who also had to log all compass changes. Interestingly, the course would always remain steady—yawing back and forth—unless the wind changed. With wind changes, they would usually wake me to adjust the plot. After dead reckoning down to the other side of our grid this way, we would secure the sea anchor and very slowly work our way back upwind using only one engine to conserve fuel."

Aboard *Rolling Bettine*, recreation for the off-watch included "planning how to become heroes," according to du Moulin. One daring plan, devised by Tom O'Sullivan, who later became a combat artist, involved a drawing of the latest type of U.S. Navy destroyer which du Moulin and crew hoped to hold up in front of an enemy periscope to encourage a panic dive. Another *Bettine* crewman brought fishing gear aboard and spent off-watch hours trolling for fresh fish. What du Moulin recalls as "the main event" of their battle against boredom was "an eating contest to the death" between Seaman First Class Charles Purcell and Coxswain O'Sullivan. The contest began with an appetizer of three inches of peanut butter between two saltines, proceeded to the rinds of breakfast's grapefruit and other barely-edible courses, and ended when Charlie asked for a Gillette Blue Blade and proceeded to chew it up and wash it down with a glass of water. He won the contest—and lived.

Weather was the principle hazard of these year-'round patrols. No vessels were lost on picket duty, a tribute to the seamanship and navigational skills of their crews, but there were some close calls. The closest call of all was the 27-day odyssey of the 58′ yawl *Zaida*, damaged by a winter storm and blown over more than 3000 miles of wild sea. *Zaida*, an ocean racer donated to the cause by George Ratsey of the sailmaking clan, was fighting through a gale on the last day of a tough week's patrol on December 3, 1942, when the shackle at the peak of her storm trysail carried away. The sail burst from its bolt ropes and *Zaida* fell off the wind and swung broadside into the trough of a big sea. She was knocked on her beam ends twice while green water filled her mizzen and snapped the spar. Water cascaded below, soaking much of the food supply and putting her engine and generator out of commission. When things were squared away, her nine crew members, one with a battered head and another with broken ribs, found themselves in a building storm aboard a boat that could barely be controlled. They got busy surviving. *Zaida* was sighted a few times despite snow squalls and freezing rain, but several rescue attempts had to be aborted in seas that made any duet between the yacht and a destroyer too

> Nearly 400 "frontier vessels" were officially in the several coastal
> patrol programs during World War II, and there is no doubt that they saved
> lives, perhaps many more than can ever be reckoned.

WINTER TARGET PRACTICE WITH A WARM GUN

A PATROL SCHOONER, RIGGED FOR COLD WEATHER, BROAD REACHES THROUGH WINTER SEAS IN THE ATLANTIC

perilous. At one point she made an out-of-control run through a convoy bound for North Africa, passing so close to one freighter that water from the ship's bilge pumps poured on her deck. On December 23, she was spotted by a blimp only 15 miles off Ocracoke Inlet. Her adventure had started near Nantucket Shoals and ended in even more treacherous territory near Cape Hatteras. *Zaida* was towed into Ocracoke; her men were flown home for Christmas; and she was repaired and back on patrol in a few weeks.

Was it all worthwhile? "I can't honestly say that the patrol made a significant contribution," says Alfred Stanford, the man who had so much to do with its creation. "In theory, it made a lot of sense. It was probably worthwhile in preparing the younger men for other duties at sea." In the first volume of his History of the United States Naval Operations in World War II, titled *The Battle of the Atlantic*, Samuel Eliot Morison observed that "the Coastal Picket as well as the Ship Lane Patrol became an excellent training school in fundamental seamanship, both for the Navy and the Coast Guard. Hundreds of Coastal Picket 'graduates' were detached for duty on regular cutters, transports and landing craft, to the great profit of the service. This undesigned byproduct of the two patrols justified the effort and expense, whatever one may think of their main performance."

Morison also commented on their performance, writing that "with few exceptions, the yachtsmen personnel proved keen, competent and rugged." He credited Picket Patrol vessels with keeping their stations while taking "everything that old man Neptune uncorked." By way of example, he cited the "tough assignment" of the schooner *Primrose IV*, which patrolled from Quoddy Roads out around Grand Manan and across the Bay of Fundy. "It was typical of the 'Hooligan Navy' that she was commanded by a sixty-year-old Harvard professor who had been a Naval Reserve officer in the last war, but accepted the rating of Chief Boatswain's Mate in this."

But did they deter submarines? The War Log of the German Navy's High Command noted on July 22, 1941: "1. The main problem of the submarine war is still that of locating the foe when traveling in convoy. 2. The attempt to control a concentration of sea routes farther to the west has not been successful. Fog and adverse weather conditions have been mainly responsible." The Picket Patrol began to operate a year later in the "fog and adverse weather conditions" of the U.S. East Coast, and a case can be made that their presence harassed the U-boats if it did not directly threaten them. Under similar conditions off the Japanese coast later in the war, U.S. submarine commanders were wary of Japanese patrols in motorized sampans which could detect them unawares and quickly radio their locations to aircraft and subchasers. Submarines, ours and those of the Germans, were sitting ducks for aircraft while surfaced, and in equal peril dodging depth charges while submerged. It was vital for their survival that they operate unobserved.

Nearly 400 "frontier vessels" were officially in the several coastal patrol programs during World War II, and there is no doubt that they saved lives, perhaps many more than can ever be reckoned. Lt. Ben W. Morris of the Miami Coast Guard wrote of a just-grey-painted motor yacht's exploit in the January, 1943, issue of Motor Boating: "Before the paint was really dry, it will interest you to know, a ship was torpedoed some 50 miles away and our boat, together with others available at the base, was ordered under way to the scene of action—*muy pronto*, boys! East and North into the Gulf Stream, a matter of several hours' run though a particularly black and blowy night, went the 46-footer; and with a crew which had been aboard only a few hours she finally reached the scene of the disaster, saved the lives of eight men, and returned to port . . ."

It all seems to have been worthwhile.

Spare no money," I said to Roscoe. "Let everything on the *Snark* be of the best. And never mind decoration. Plain pine boards is good enough finishing for me. But put the money into the construction. Let the *Snark* be as stanch and strong as any boat afloat. Never mind what it costs to make her stanch and strong; you see that she is made stanch and strong and I'll go on writing and earning the money to pay for it." And I did . . . as well as I could; for the *Snark* ate up money faster than I could earn it. In fact, every little while I had to borrow money with which to supplement my earnings. Now I borrowed one thousand dollars, now I borrowed two thousand dollars, and now I borrowed five thousand dollars. And all the time I went on working every day and sinking the earnings in the venture. I worked Sundays, as well, and I took no holidays. But it was worth it. Every time I thought of the *Snark* I knew she was worth it.

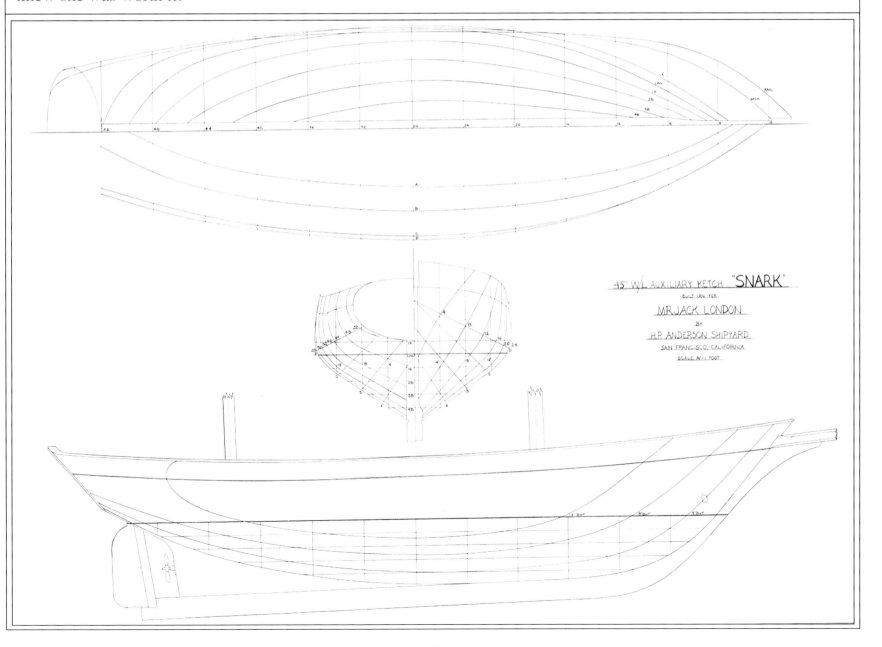

45' W/L AUXILIARY KETCH "SNARK"

BUILT 1906 FOR

MR. JACK LONDON

BY

H.P. ANDERSON SHIPYARD

SAN FRANCISCO, CALIFORNIA

SCALE ¾"=1 FOOT

There is no explaining it; if there were, I'd do it. I, who am an artisan
of speech, confess my inability to explain why the *Snark* was not ready. As I have said, and
as I must repeat, it was inconceivable and monstrous.

For know, gentle reader, the stanchness of the *Snark*. She is forty-five feet long on the water-line. Her garboard strake is three inches thick; her planking two and one-half inches thick; her deck-planking two inches thick; and in all her planking there are no butts. I know, for I ordered the planking especially from Puget Sound. Then the *Snark* has four water-tight compartments, which is to say that her length is broken by three water-tight bulkheads. Thus, no matter how large a leak the *Snark* may spring, only one compartment can fill with water. The other three compartments will keep her afloat anyway, and, besides, will enable us to mend the leak. There is another virtue in these bulkheads. The last compartment of all, in the very stern, contains six tanks that carry over one thousand gallons of gasolene. Now gasolene is a very dangerous article to carry in bulk on a small craft far out on the wide ocean. But when the six tanks that do not leak are themselves contained in a compartment hermetically sealed off from the rest of the boat, the danger will be very small indeed.

The *Snark* is a sail-boat. She was built primarily to sail. But, incidentally, as an auxiliary, a seventy-horse-power engine was installed. This is a good, strong engine. I ought to know. I paid for it to come out all the way from New York City. Then, on deck, above the engine, is a windlass. It is a magnificent affair. It weighs several hundred pounds and takes up no end of deck room. You see, it is ridiculous to hoist up anchor by hand-power when there is a seventy-horse-power engine on board. So we installed the windlass, transmitting power to it from the engine by means of a gear and castings specially made in a San Francisco foundry.

The *Snark* was made for comfort, and no expense was spared in this regard. There is the bathroom, for instance, small and compact, it is true, but containing all the conveniences of any bathroom upon land. The bathroom is a beautiful dream of schemes and devices, pumps, and levers, and sea-valves. Why, in the course of its building, I used to lie awake nights thinking about that bathroom. And next to the bathroom come the lifeboat and the launch. They are carried on deck, and they take up what little space might have been left us for exercise. But then, they beat life insurance; and the prudent man, even if he has built as stanch and strong a craft as the *Snark*, will see to it that he has a good lifeboat as well. And ours is a good one. It is a dandy. It was stipulated to cost one hundred and fifty dollars, and when I came to pay the bill, it turned out to be three hundred and ninety-five dollars. That shows how good a lifeboat it is.

I could go on at great length relating the various virtues and excellences of the *Snark*, but I refrain. I have bragged enough as it is, and I have bragged to a purpose, as will be seen before my tale is ended. And please remember its title, "The Inconceivable and Monstrous." It was planned that the *Snark* should sail on October 1, 1906. That she did not so sail was inconceivable and monstrous. There was no valid reason for not sailing except that she was not ready to sail, and there was no conceivable reason why she was not ready. She was promised on November first, on November fifteenth, on December first; and yet she was never ready. On December first Charmian and I left the sweet, clean Sonoma country and came down to live in the stifling city—but not for long, oh, no, only for two weeks, for we would sail on December fifteenth. And I guess we ought to know, for Roscoe said so, and it was on his advice that we came to the city to stop two weeks. Alas, the two weeks went by, four weeks went by, six weeks went by, eight weeks went by, and we were farther away from sailing than ever. Explain it? Who?—me? I can't. It is the one thing in all my life that I have backed down on. There is no explaining it; if there were, I'd do it. I, who am an artisan of speech, confess my inability to explain why the *Snark* was not ready. As I have said, and as I must repeat, it was inconceivable and monstrous.

The eight weeks became sixteen weeks, and then, one day, Roscoe cheered us up by saying:

"If we don't sail before April first, you can use my head for a football."

Two weeks later he said, "I'm getting my head in training for that match."

"Never mind," Charmian and I said to each other; "think of the wonderful boat it is going to be when it is completed."

Whereat we would rehearse for out mutual encouragement the manifold virtues and excellences of the *Snark*. Also, I would borrow more money, and I would get down closer to my desk and write harder, and I refused heroically to take a Sunday off and go out into the hills with my friends. I was building a boat, and by the eternal it was going to be a boat, and a boat spelled out all in capitals—B-O-A-T; and no matter what it cost I didn't care, so long as it was a BOAT.

And, oh, there is one other excellence of the *Snark*, upon which I must brag, namely, her bow. No sea could ever come over it. It laughs at the sea, that bow does; it challenges the sea; it snorts defiance at the sea. And withal it is a beautiful bow; the lines of it are dreamlike; I doubt if ever a boat was blessed with a more beautiful and at the same time a more capable bow. It was made to punch storms. To touch that bow is to rest one's hand on the cosmic nose of things. To look at it is to realize that expense cut no figure where it was concerned. And every time our sailing was delayed, or a new expense was tacked on, we thought of that wonderful bow and were content.

The *Snark* is a small boat. When I figured seven thousand dollars as her generous cost, I was both generous and correct. I have built barns and houses, and I know the peculiar trait such things have of running past their estimated cost. This knowledge was mine, was already mine, when I estimated the probable cost of the building of the *Snark* at seven thousand dollars. Well, she cost thirty thousand. Now don't ask me, please. It is the truth. I signed checks and I raised the

And not one union man and not one firm of all the union men and all the firms ever delivered anything agreed upon, nor ever was on time for anything except pay-day and bill-collection.

money. Of course there is no explaining it. Inconceivable and monstrous is what it is, as you will agree, I know, ere my tale is done.

Then there was the matter of delay. I dealt with forty-seven different kinds of union men and with one hundred and fifteen different firms. And not one union man and not one firm of all the union men and all the firms ever delivered anything at the time agreed upon, nor ever was on time for anything except pay-day and bill-collection. Men pledged me their immortal souls that they would deliver a certain thing on a certain date; as a rule, after such pledging, they rarely exceeded being three months late in delivery. And so it went, and Charmian and I consoled each other by saying what a splendid boat the *Snark* was, so stanch and strong; also, we would get into the small boat and row around the *Snark*, and gloat over her unbelievably wonderful bow.

"Think," I would say to Charmian, "of a gale off the China coast, and of the *Snark* hove to, that splendid bow of hers driving into the storm. Not a drop will come over that bow. She'll be as dry as a feather, and we'll be all below playing whist while the gale howls."

And Charmian would press my hand enthusiastically and exclaim:

"It's worth every bit of it—the delay—and expense, and worry, and all the rest. Oh, what a truly wonderful boat!"

Whenever I looked at the bow of the *Snark* or thought of her water-tight compartments, I was encouraged. Nobody else, however, was encouraged. My friends began to make bets against the various sailing dates of the *Snark*. Mr. Wiget, who was left behind in charge of our Sonoma ranch, was the first to cash his bet. He collected on New Year's Day, 1907. After that the bets came fast and furious. My friends surrounded me like a gang of harpies, making bets against every sailing date I set. I was rash, and I was stubborn. I bet, and I bet, and I continued to bet; and I paid them all. Why, the womenkind of my friends grew so brave that those among them who never bet before began to bet with me. And I paid them too.

"Never mind," said Charmian to me; "just think of that bow and of being hove to on the China Seas."

"You see," I said to my friends, when I paid the latest bunch of wagers, "neither trouble nor cash is being spared in making the *Snark* the most seaworthy craft that ever sailed out through the Golden Gate—that is what causes all the delay."

In the meantime editors and publishers with whom I had contracts pestered me with demands for explanations. But how could I explain to them, when I was unable to explain to myself, or when there was nobody, not even Roscoe, to explain to me? The newspapers began to laugh at me, and to publish rhymes anent the *Snark's* departure with refrains like, "Not yet but soon." And Charmian cheered me up by reminding me of the bow, and I went to a banker and borrowed five thousand more. There was one recompense for the delay, however. A friend of mine, who happens to be a critic, wrote a roast of me, of all I had done, and of all I ever was going to do; and he planned to have it published after I was out on the ocean. I was still on shore when it came out, and he has been busy explaining ever since.

And the time continued to go by. One thing was becoming apparent, namely, that it was impossible to finish the *Snark* in San Francisco. She had been so long in the building that she was beginning to break down and wear out. In fact, she had reached the stage where she was breaking down faster than she could be repaired. She had become a joke. Nobody took her seriously; least of all the men who worked on her. I said we would sail just as she was and finish building her in Honolulu. Promptly she sprang a leak that had to be attended to before we could sail. I started her for the boat-ways. Before she got to them she was caught between two huge barges and received a vigorous crushing. We got her on the ways, and, part way along, the ways spread and dropped her through, stern-first, into the mud.

It was a pretty tangle, a job for wreckers, not boat-builders. There are two high tides each twenty-four hours, and at every high tide, night and day, for a week, there were two steam tugs pulling and hauling on the *Snark*. There she was, stuck, fallen between the ways and standing on her stern. Next, and while still in that predicament, we started to use the gears and castings made in the local foundry whereby power was conveyed from the engine to the windlass. It was the first time we ever tried to use that windlass. The castings had flaws; they shattered asunder, the gears ground together, and the windlass was out of commission. Following upon that, the seventy-horse-power engine went out of commission. This engine came from New York; so did its bedplate; there was a flaw in the bed-plate; there were a lot of flaws in the bedplate; and the seventy-horse-power engine broke away from its shattered foundations, reared up in the air, smashed all connections and fastenings, and fell over on its side. And the *Snark* continued to stick between the spread ways, and the two tugs continued to haul vainly upon her.

"Never mind," said Charmian, "think of what a stanch, strong boat she is."

"Yes," said I, "and of that beautiful bow."

So we took heart and went at it again. The ruined engine was lashed down on its rotten foundation; the smashed castings and cogs of the power transmission were taken down and stored away—all for the purpose of taking them to Honolulu where repairs and new castings could be made. Somewhere in the dim past the *Snark* had received on the outside one coat of white paint. The intention of the color was still evident, however, when one got it in the right light. The *Snark* had never received any paint on the inside. On the contrary, she was coated inches thick with the grease and tobacco-juice of the multitudinous mechanics who had toiled upon her. Never mind, we said; the grease and filth could be planed off, and later, when we fetched Honolulu, the *Snark* could be painted at the same time she was being rebuilt.

The controversial *Snark* is shown here on Oakland's 1907 waterfront. Her lines are shown in first-draft form on page 49, drawn this past August by Bill Elliott of Bay Ship and Yacht Company in Novato, CA. Bill Elliott drew her lines, with what he admits is one small error in numbering, from a body plan he was given by Dean Anderson, grandson of her builder, supplemented by information from photographs. Al Cristofani, partner and patriarch of what is now San Francisco's celebrated Anderson & Cristofani yard, helped out with his memories of *Snark*. Bill Elliott has found similarities between *Snark*'s lines and the lines of San Francisco pilot schooners of her time, as well as resemblances to ketch-rigged and schooner-rigged yachts whose lines were

By main strength and sweat we dragged the *Snark* off the wrecked ways and laid her alongside the Oakland City Wharf. The drays brought all the outfit from home, the books and blankets and personal luggage. Along with this, everything else came on board in a torrent of confusion—wood and coal, water and water-tanks, vegetables, provisions, oil, the life-boat and the launch, all our friends, all the friends of our friends and those who claimed to be their friends. to say nothing of some of the friends of the friends of the friends of our crew. Also there were reporters, and photographers, and strangers and cranks, and finally, and over all, clouds of coal-dust from the wharf.

We were to sail Sunday at eleven, and Saturday afternoon had arrived. The crowd on the wharf and the coal-dust were thicker than ever. In one pocket I carried a check-book, a fountain pen, a dater, and a blotter; in another pocket I carried between one and two thousand dollars in paper money and gold. I was ready for the creditors, cash for the small ones and checks for the large ones, and was waiting only for Roscoe to arrive with the balances of the accounts of the hundred and fifteen firms who had delayed me so many months. And then—

And then the inconceivable and monstrous happened once more. Before Roscoe could arrive there arrived another man. He was a United States marshal. He tacked a notice on the *Snark's* brave mast so that all on the wharf could read

that the *Snark* had been libelled for debt. The marshal left a little old man in charge of the *Snark*, and himself went away. I had no longer any control of the *Snark*, nor of her wonderful bow. The little old man was now her lord and master, and I learned that I was paying him three dollars a day for being lord and master. Also, I learned the name of the man who had libelled the *Snark*. It was Sellers; the debt was two hundred and thirty-two dollars; and the deed was no more than was to be expected from the possessor of such a name. Sellers! Ye gods! Sellers!

But who under the sun was Sellers? I looked in my check-book and saw that two weeks before I had made him out a check for five hundred dollars. Other check-books showed me that during the many months of the building of the *Snark* I had paid him several thousand dollars. Then why in the name of common decency hadn't he tried to collect his miserable litte balance instead of libelling the S*nark*? I thrust my hands into my pockets, and in one pocket encountered my check-book and the dater and the pen, and in the other pocket the gold money and the paper money. There was the wherewithal to settle his pitiful account a few score times and over—why hadn't he given me a chance? There was no explanation; it was merely the inconceivable and monstrous.

To make the matter worse, the *Snark* had been libelled late Saturday afternoon; and though I sent lawyers and agents all over Oakland and San Francisco,

published in Rudder in 1905 and 1906. There is much more inquiry to be done, he says, but he makes these notes from his own research and his experience as a yachtbuilder: "One very distinctive feature in the *Snark*'s design is the lack of hollow in the garboards, and particularly the futtock heels running up the aft deadwood. The *Snark* was built with the scantlings of a sawn-frame vessel, but her frames were all steam-bent, these of 4″ or 5″ molded dimensions. Her body plan is obviously designed to make this type of construction practical, a method which was common in the Anderson yard for many years. My feeling is that while the design was no doubt inspired by other, distant yachts of the time, the *Snark* was modeled to suit local construction methods by Anderson, Lester Stone or someone associated with these yards."

neither United States judge, nor United States marshal, nor Mr. Sellers, nor Mr. Sellers' attorney, nor anybody could be found. They were all out of town for the week end. And so the *Snark* did not sail Sunday morning at eleven. The little old man was still in charge, and he said no. And Charmian and I walked out on an opposite wharf and took consolation in the *Snark*'s wonderful bow and thought of all the gales and typhoons it would proudly punch.

"A bourgeois trick," I said to Charmian, speaking of Mr. Sellers and his libel; "a petty trader's panic. But never mind; our troubles will cease when once we are away from this and out on the wide ocean."

And in the end we sailed away, on Tuesday morning, April 23, 1907. We started rather lame, I confess. We had to hoist anchor by hand, because the power transmission was a wreck. Also, what remained of our seventy-horse-power engine was lashed down for ballast on the bottom of the *Snark*. But what of such things? They could be fixed in Honolulu, and in the meantime think of the magnificent rest of the boat! It is true, the engine in the launch wouldn't run, and the life-boat leaked like a sieve; but then they weren't the *Snark*; they were mere appurtenances. The things that counted were the water-tight bulkheads, the solid planking without butts, the bath-room devices—they were the *Snark*. And then there was, greatest of all, that noble, wind-punching bow.

We sailed out through the Golden Gate and set our course south toward that part of the Pacific where we could hope to pick up with the northeast trades. And right away things began to happen. I had calculated that youth was the stuff for a voyage like that of the *Snark*, and I had taken three youths—the engineer, the cook, and the cabin-boy. My calculation was only two-thirds off; I had forgotten to calculate on seasick youth, and I had two of them, the cook and the cabin-boy. They immediately took to their bunks, and that was the end of their usefulness for a week to come. It will be understood, from the foregoing, that we did not have the hot meals we might have had, nor were things kept clean and orderly down below. But it did not matter very much anyway, for we quickly discovered that our box of oranges had at some time been frozen; that our box of apples was mushy and spoiling; that the crate of cabbages, spoiled before it was ever delivered to us, had to go overboard instanter; that kerosene had been spilled on the carrots, and that the turnips were woody and the beets rotten, while the kindling was deadwood that wouldn't burn, and the coal, delivered in rotten potato-sacks, had spilled all over the deck and was washing through the scuppers.

But what did it matter? Such things were mere accessories. There was the boat—she was all right, wasn't she? I strolled along the deck and in one minute

We started rather lame, I confess. We had to hoist anchor by hand,
because the power transmission was a wreck. Also, what remained of our seventy-horse-power
engine was lashed down for ballast on the bottom of the *Snark*.

counted fourteen butts in the beautiful planking ordered specially from Puget Sound in order that there should be no butts in it. Also, that deck leaked, and it leaked badly. It drowned Roscoe out of his bunk and ruined the tools in the engine-room, to say nothing of the provisions it ruined in the galley. Also, the sides of the *Snark* leaked, and the bottom leaked, and we had to pump her every day to keep her afloat. The floor of the galley is a couple of feet above the inside bottom of the *Snark*; and yet I have stood on the floor of the galley, trying to snatch a cold bite, and been wet to the knees by the water churning around inside four hours after the last pumping.

Then those magnificent water-tight compartments that cost so much time and money—well, they weren't water-tight after all. The water moved free as the air from one compartment to another; furthermore, a strong smell of gasolene from the after compartment leads me to suspect that some one or more of the half-dozen tanks there stored have sprung a leak. The tanks leak, and they are not hermetically sealed in their compartment. Then there was the bathroom with its pumps and levers and sea-valves—it went out of commission inside the first twenty hours. Powerful iron levers broke off short in one's hand when one tried to pump with them. The bathroom was the swiftest wreck of any portion of the *Snark*.

And the iron-work on the *Snark*, no matter what its source, proved to be mush. For instance, the bed-plate of the engine came from New York, and it was mush; so were the casting and gears for the windlass that came from San Francisco. And finally, there was the wrought iron used in the rigging, that carried away in all directions when the first strains were put upon it. Wrought iron, mind you, and it snapped like macaroni.

A gooseneck on the gaff of the mainsail broke short off. We replaced it with the gooseneck from the gaff of the storm trysail, and the second gooseneck broke short off inside fifteen minutes of use, and, mind you, it had been taken from the gaff of the storm trysail, upon which we would have depended in time of storm. At the present moment the *Snark* trails her mainsail like a broken wing, the gooseneck being replaced by a rough lashing. We'll see if we can get honest iron in Honolulu.

Man had betrayed us and sent us to sea in a sieve, but the Lord must have loved us, for we had calm weather in which to learn that we must pump every day in order to keep afloat, and that more trust could be placed in a wooden toothpick than in the most massive piece of iron to be found aboard. As the stanchness and the strength of the *Snark* went glimmering, Charmian and I pinned our faith more and more to the *Snark's* wonderful bow. There was nothing else left to pin to. It was all inconceivable and monstrous, we knew, but that bow, at least, was rational. And then, one evening we started to heave to.

How shall I describe it? First of all, for the benefit of the tyro, let me explain that heaving to is that sea manoeuvre which, by means of short and

balanced canvas, compels a vessel to ride bow-on to wind and sea. When the wind is too strong, or the sea is too high, a vessel of the size of the *Snark* can heave to with ease, whereupon there is no more work to do on deck. Nobody needs to steer, The lookout is superfluous. All hands can go below and sleep or play whist.

Well, it was blowing half of a small summer gale, when I told Roscoe we'd heave to. Night was coming on. I had been steering nearly all day, and all hands on deck (Roscoe and Bert and Charmian) were tired, while all hands below were seasick. It happened that we had already put two reefs in the big mainsail. The flying-jib and the jib were taken in, and a reef put in the forestaysail. The mizzen was also taken in. About this time the flying jib-boom buried itself in a sea and broke short off. I started to put the wheel down in order to heave to. The *Snark* at the moment was rolling in the trough. She continued rolling in the trough. I put the spokes down harder and harder. She never budged from the trough. (The trough, gentle reader, is the most dangerous position of all in which to lay a vessel.) I put the wheel hard down, and still the *Snark* rolled in the trough. Eight points was the nearest I could get her to the wind. I had Roscoe and Bert come in on the main-sheet. The *Snark* rolled on in the trough, now putting her rail under on one side and now under on the other side.

Again the inconceivable and monstrous was showing its grizzly head. It was grotesque, impossible. I refused to believe it. Under double-reefed mainsail and single-reefed staysail the *Snark* refused to heave to. We flattened the mainsail down. It did not alter the *Snark's* course a tenth of a degree. We slacked the mainsail off with no more result. We set a storm trysail on the mizzen, and took in the mainsail. No change. The *Snark* rolled on in the trough. That beautiful bow of hers refused to come up and face the wind.

Next we took in the reefed staysail. Thus, the only bit of canvas left on her was the storm trysail on the mizzen. If anything would bring her bow up to the wind that would. Maybe you won't believe me when I say it failed, but I do say it failed. And I say if failed because I saw it fail, and not because I believe it failed. I don't believe it did fail. It is unbelievable, and I am not telling you what I believe; I am telling you what I saw.

Now, gentle reader, what would you do if you were on a small boat, rolling in the trough of the sea, a trysail on that small boat's stern that was unable to swing the bow up into the wind? Get out the sea anchor. It's just what we did. We had a patent one, made to order and warranted not to dive. Imagine a hoop of steel that serves to keep open the mouth of a large, conical, canvas bag, and you have a sea-anchor. Well, we made a line fast to the sea-anchor and to the bow of the *Snark*, and then dropped the sea-anchor overboard. It promptly dived. We had a tripping line on it, so we tripped the sea-anchor and hauled it in. We attached a big timber as a float, and dropped

On my return to California after the voyage, I learned that the Snark was forty-three feet on the water line instead of forty-five. This was due to the fact that the builder was not on speaking terms with the tape-line or two-foot rule.

the sea-anchor over again. This time it floated. The line to the bow grew taut. The trysail on the mizzen tended to swing the bow into the wind, but, in spite of this tendency, the *Snark* calmly took that sea-anchor in her teeth, and went on ahead, dragging it after her, still in the trough of the sea. And there you are. We even took in the trysail, hoisted the full mizzen in its place, and hauled the full mizzen down flat, and the *Snark* wallowed in the trough and dragged the sea-anchor behind her. Don't believe me. I don't believe it myself. I'm merely telling you what I saw.

Now I leave it to you. Who ever heard of a sailing-boat that wouldn't heave to?—that wouldn't heave to with a sea-anchor to help it? Out of my brief experience with boats I know I never did. And I stood on deck and looked on the naked face of the inconceivable and monstrous—the *Snark* that wouldn't heave to. A stormy night with broken moonlight had come on. There was a splash of wet in the air, and up to windward there was a promise of rain-squalls; and then there was the trough of the sea, cold and cruel in the moonlight, in which the *Snark* complacently rolled. And then we took in the sea-anchor and the mizzen, hoisted the reefed staysail, ran the *Snark* off before it, and went below—not to the hot meal that should have awaited us, but to skate across the slush and slime on the cabin floor, where cook and cabin-boy lay like dead men in the bunks, and to lie down in our own bunks, with our clothes on ready for a call, and to listen to the bilge-water spouting knee-high on the galley floor.

In the Bohemian Club of San Francisco there are some crack sailors. I know, because I heard them pass judgment on the *Snark* during the process of her building. They found only one vital thing the matter with her, and on this they were all agreed, namely, that she could not run. She was all right in every particular, they said, except that I'd never be able to run her before it in a stiff wind and sea. "Her lines," they explained enigmatically, "it is the fault of her lines. She simply cannot be made to run, that is all." Well, I wish I'd only had those crack sailors of the Bohemian Club on board the *Snark* the other night for them to see for themselves their one, vital, unanimous judgment absolutely reversed. Run? It is the one thing the *Snark* does to perfection. Run? She ran with a sea-anchor fast for'ard and a full mizzen flattened down aft. Run? At the present moment, as I write this, we are bowling along before it, at a six-knot clip, in the northeast trades. Quite a tidy bit of sea is running. There is nobody at the wheel, the wheel is not even lashed and is set over a half-spoke weather helm. To be precise, the wind is northeast; the *Snark's* mizzen is furled, her mainsail is over to starboard, her head-sheets are hauled flat; and the *Snark's* course is south-southwest. And yet there are men who have sailed the seas for forty years and who hold that no boat can run before it without being steered. They'll call me a liar when they read this; it's what they called Captain Slocum when he said the same of his *Spray*.

As regards the future of the *Snark* I'm all at sea. I don't know. If I had the money or the credit, I'd build another *Snark* that *would* heave to. But I am at the end of my resources. I've got to put up with the present *Snark* or quit—and I can't quit. So I guess I'll have to try to get along with heaving the *Snark* to stern-first. I am waiting for the next gale to see how it will work. I think it can be done. It all depends on how her stern takes the seas. And who knows but that some wild morning on the China Sea, some gray-beard skipper will stare, rub his incredulous eyes and stare again, at the spectacle of a weird, small craft, very much like the *Snark*, hove to stern-first and riding out the gale?

P.S. On my return to California after the voyage, I learned that the *Snark* was forty-three feet on the water line instead of forty-five. This was due to the fact that the builder was not on speaking terms with the tape-line or two-foot rule.

From *The Cruise of the Snark*, copyright 1911 by The Macmillan Company.

SKÛTSJ

Poised on the weather rail, sailors aboard two skûtsjes crossing tacks look like crewmen aboard IOR boats in a round-the-buoys contest. These brawny barges do race around the buoys every summer on the waters of Holland's northern province of Friesland, but the boats and the racing are a far cry from the IOR. Both the skûtsjes and their racing traditions are hundreds of years old, and the furious action on the windy lakes and bays of Friesland is largely unencumbered by rules. The 14 restored and wonderfully maintained former working vessels meet every July in 11 races over a period of two weeks, drawing huge crowds ashore, in spectator boats, and aboard the motor barges which have replaced the great old skûtsjes as vehicles in which Frisian watermen make their livings.

From end to end of Holland, watermen and yachtsmen have kept alive the vessels and traditions of the past, and among the botters, jachts and tjalks, the most dramatic vessels are the skûtsjes, those majestic sloop-rigged barges that still sail the steel-gray waters of Holland's northern province of Friesland. Although no longer used for their original purpose as freight vessels for loads of brick, peat, manure and fertile soil to supply the farms and towns of a once-remote place, the skûtsjes remain radiant visions on the water. It is impossible not to fall in love with them at the first sight of their sturdy, snub-nosed and flat-bottomed hulls and the amazing quantities of heavy cotton in their mainsails and jibs. Seeing them in a good breeze under full billowing sail, all 50 tons of them heeling sharply and pushing a hill of flashing water under their bows, is more than just visual pleasure. One is moved by their simplicity and straightforwardness; they are tough and purposeful and essentially Dutch.

BY FLORINE BOUCHER
PHOTOGRAPHS BY FARRELL GREHAN

ESILEN

And every summer they race. Skûtsjesilen— a yearly contest among a dozen or more of these barges on the inland waters of Friesland—keeps alive both the vessels and the tradition of competition among Frisian sailing families, which challenge each other now in 11 races for the championship of skûtsjesilen. The informal beginnings of this racing can undoubtedly be traced to the cosy country inns, where in the old days skûtsje skippers

Classic Dutch vessels, the skûtsjes are on record as freight carriers back as far as 1450. On the shallow bays and "lakes" of Friesland's sandy coast, and in the tide-swept passages between them, this broad, flat vessel with draft of as little as 16″ did its work efficiently for more than 500 years. Leeboards make these big barges surprisingly

would dispute one another's sailing skills over small but numerous glasses of Genever (Dutch gin). The proof of the pudding being always in the eating, the earliest races were organized by local innkeepers and held on the nearby shallow lakes. Cash prizes could be won; but the real prize was honor for the skipper, his family and his boat. These were spontaneous trials of strength, endurance and skill, without any rules or organization, but with a bag full of tricks. For these events, a skûtsjesilen family would strip their vessel—which was also

weatherly; huge sloop rigs with loose-footed mains give them their power; barndoor rudders make them maneuverable even in the close-quarters racing seen here; and masts are strikeable to enable the skûtsjes to pass under bridges. The last skûtsje in commercial service retired in 1962, joining her 13 sisters in a new life as a restored piece of Frisian history owned and maintained by a Frisian town or, in a few cases, an individual or family.

their home—of all superfluous weight. Wife and children would be stationed ashore for the day, together with the furniture and cooking equipment. Even the iron pot-bellied stove was removed.

It was not until 1945—when the skûtsje's role as a freight vessel had almost ended—that a handful of skûtsje lovers formed a "Central Commission for Skût-sjesilen" (SKS) to structure the races and ensure their continuity. In doing this, they ensured the survival of the vessels as well. What started out as a survival

project turned over the years into a complete revival. The year 1956 changed for good and for all the nature of skûtsjesilen when the village of Eernewoude—backed by a foundation—brought the skûtsje *De Nijverheid* from owner/skipper Berend Mink and began a trend that was soon followed by others. It happened just in time. By the 1950s, maintaining a barge of this size just for pleasure wasn't within a skipper's means any more. And keeping a vessel in the old trade was just as difficult. In 1962, skipper Jan Brouwer marked the end of a 500-year-old commercial-sailing tradition when he entered the race for the very last time with a skûtsje that was still the means to his living. Today, all but two of the skûtsjes that race each summer are backed by a town or village in Friesland.

Skippering, however, remains as in former days. Commercial captains from the same renowned families—Zwaga, Brouwer, Meeter, Van der Meulen and Van Akker—now masters of modern diesel barges—proudly take the helms of the skûtsjes that are entrusted to them. The sailing that was once the means to a hard-won living for Frisian skippers has now become a sailing spectacle that lasts for two weeks and brings every hog, dog and poor devil in the whole of Friesland to an utter pitch of excitement. And the vast and green stretches of flat polderland—seemingly reaching for the world's end—where thick white clouds sweep the sky and reflect on the water—is the stage set. It is a glorious symphony of the elements for the thousands of sailing-barge lovers who flock every July to the windswept lakes of Friesland to watch 14 skûtsjes compete in a way that defines the Frisian character: never budge a fraction of an inch.

Throughout the three-hour races, hot rivalries among skippers frequently bring spectacular duels and challenges, great displays of daring and professional skill. Old hands watching the races with Frisian taciturnity will only approvingly nod their weather-beaten heads when a skipper pulls off an especially clever maneuver. Although regulations have come to these contests over the years, the determination to win at all costs obsessively overrules a skipper's

Skûtsje racing frequently involves collisions between these 50-ton boats, definitely part of the excitement of skûtsjesilen for spectators and participants alike. As one may imagine, the damage can be enough to take a boat out of the race. Although the skûtsjes are kept with typically Dutch (or Frisian) spit and polish, all is sacrificed in the fervor of racing, just as in the earliest days of these contests, when a skipper would move his live-aboard family and most of their furniture ashore to prepare his boat for a challenge. The revival of the racing tradition on an organized basis after World War II insured the survival of the remaining boats.

decorum, not to mention his prudence. Skûtsje sailors often snatch right-of-way from rivals, and they don't shun encounters between these heavy and cumbersome barges. In 1983 on De Veenhoop—a particularly difficult lake—all 14 skûtsjes running off the wind were fairly well matched; it was a question of inches when they came to the mark. Rounding the first buoy in a narrow space turned the race into a battlefield. The crowd got a good run for its money, and it is said that the thundering clashes and crashes of that afternoon still echo over the lake. While crewmembers ducked and dashed for their lives, mainsails clattered down or were ripped open by the yard, fittings snapped like matchwood, bollards were torn away, and one of the skûtsjes even lost her rudder. Though the race continued with ten boats, it was not to end before two more had bashed each other out of the lists.

Skûtsjesilen, for the Frisians, is something like an Indian pow-wow or a traveling circus, for it contains ingredients of both. An important and charming aspect is the tradition that the 11 races for the championship are sailed on no fewer than seven lakes and at ten different places, carrying on from the days when these contests were locally organized. So strong is the Frisian love for tradition that the SKS still refuses to exclude the lake at Veenhoop from the series, although many voices have suggested that this narrow stretch of water is no place to race 50-ton sailing barges. Two-time champion Rienk Zwaga, son of the illustrious Ulbe Zwaga who won 11 championships between 1946 and 1972, discounts the fancied drawbacks of Veenhoop with the remark that "If you can't steer clear in narrow waterways, you can't become champion either."

With that, Zwaga touched upon the quintessence of Frisian sailors and their barges. As early as 1450 the skûtsje is on record as a type of freight vessel. With its wide beam, strikeable mast and draft of as little as 16 inches, it proved to be the perfect design for load-carrying combined with maneuverability in the tidal estuaries and shallow landlocked waterways that lace the Frisian countryside. Zwaga's hard-nosed attitude is typically Frisian,

too. Throughout history, the Frisians have been famous for their independence, typified by their stubborn refusal to accept the feudal system in the time of Charles the Great. "We only curtsy for God" was their boast and their attitude. Living record of their long-standing and many-splendored individualism is the Frisian language, which is practically incomprehensible to the Dutch. Woe betide the wretch who even thinks Frisian to be a Dutch dialect or jokingly calls it Double Dutch. "Fries" is an ancient language, the direct ancestor of English among all the old Germanic tongues. In Frisian, skûtsje means little

Above, five skûtsjes reach around the course, watched by a crowd of spectators in the background. As Florine Boucher notes, the racing "brings every hog, dog and poor devil in the whole of Friesland to an utter pitch of excitement." The racing is also a yearly gathering for Frisian families who spend most of the rest of the year on their motor barges, carrying cargo all over northern Europe.

tub, or even better, cockleshell. It indicates a former littleness as a freight vessel.

In the old days, skippering a skûtsje was a guarantee of poverty. Stuggling for some sort of a living, the skipper and his family had to be continuously under sail, day and night, carrying loads back and forth. It was a hard but self-supporting life that suited the freebooting character of the skippers. The names of some skûtsjes still bear witness to those days—*The Industry, The Simplicity, The Good Hope*. Nowadays, being appointed master of a skûtsje is, by Frisian standards, about the greatest honor that can be bestowed. To these "chosen men," the honor to defend the town or village their skûtsje represents is of such importance that they take as much as a two-week vacation from their barging businesses to compete for the championship. When skûtsjesilen time comes, a staggering number of motor barges descend upon the lake near Grouw, the first in the row of seven to be honored by the racing. Aboard are all those that belong with the 14 competing skippers in one way or another—friends and family, all of their offspring, and last but not least a menagerie of dogs, cats, kittens and puppies, always largely represented in Dutch households.

Skûtsjesilen is a spectacle of traditional boats and passionate sailing; but it is also a lively, warm and crowded reunion of Frisian barging families—a yearly highlight in their gypsy-like existence of traveling the commercial waterways of Holland and the neighboring countries on their giant motor barges. As 18-year-old Jikke Zwaga—who started as a crewmember on his father's skûtsje in 1981—defined it last summer, while celebrating a victory that day on the "Fluessen" near Woudsend: "This is the best time of the whole year. I just love it, and I can't think of a better way to spend my vacation."

Like a cluster of migrating birds, the families on their barges move from lake to lake, from race to race, towing the old skûtsjes, the ancestors of their motor vessels. Settling for the day, they shift into smaller groups. Every skûtsje has her own "clan" of barges solidly behind her stern. Floating islands of black motor barges scatter around the lakes in dancing attendance for the next race. But however strong their family ties may be, when the skippers maneuver their big sloops across the starting lines at full tear, they are forgotten. Blood may be thicker than water, but here it is thinner than adrenaline. Brothers compete with one another in virtual Cain and Abel style if they are sailing separate vessels. Good examples are the notorious Meeter brothers, Lodewijk and Siete, often nicknamed the gypsies of Friesland, who have three championships between them. Pleasure-seeking Siete likes the taste of first

Aboard a diesel barge, which is also home, a skûtsjesilen family eats, drinks and makes merry after a race, using the vessel's empty cargo space to set up tables and host friends, distant family members on hand for the races, even rivals in the contests. The man at right, with his daughter bringing him a cigar, is toasting the victory of his family's sailing barge in the day's racing.

blood so much that he puts up a barrel of the best Dutch beer for his crew for every race they win.

When the races have been run, the glorious moment of holding the fiercely desired "Silver Skûtsje" belongs only to the champion. But what has happened has been more than just a series of races. The skûtsje skippers, their crews and their families have had the delight of sailing once more on the waters and in the old vessels of their homeland, greeting old friends, settling old scores, telling stories, touching times remembered.

During *Outward Leg*'s crossing of the European continent by way of the Rhine and Danube rivers, being trapped in thick ice for three months, and the subsequent need for repairs, meant that we missed the 1985 season of the southwest monsoon in the Indian Ocean. It couldn't be helped, and it gave us a prolonged stay in Turkey, Greece, Cyprus and Israel. Sailing around the world eastabout, north of the Equator, and via Central Europe, is like a combination Commando obstacle course, a ballet to "The Flight of the Bumble Bee," running the gauntlet, and a slow, cunning game of chess. Without doubt, it is the Everest of world voyaging. It has to be; it had never before been successfully completed by a small sailing craft—so softly, softly catchee monkee. And we did. To do it with a total of $300 at the start (from San Diego) and $22.50 on arrival in Istanbul made us proceed even more softly, even more slowly. On *Outward Leg*'s way south from Istanbul, through the Sea of Marmara and the Dardanelles (with $300 onboard—the proceeds of a lecture at the U.S. Consulate in Istanbul, where the Golden Eagle shat with even greater profligacy than customary), the thing was to live as do the locals ($5 a day *maximum* expenditure) and seek out a place to repair the ravages of the Rhine and Danube.

THE LEVANT

BY TRISTAN JONES
PHOTOGRAPHS BY THOMAS ETTENHUBER

asier said than done, for with the rip tide of rampant yachting/tourism flooding north at a rate of knots along the coast of Turkey these days, where we found a slipway wide enough for our 26′ beam we found no machinery for hauling. All the old donkey/horse/man winches have rusted away, their human attendants now serving as table waiters at vast, ugly concrete hotels. Where there was machinery, in the shape of French-made travel hoists, the slipways were nowhere near wide enough, having been installed to accommodate ever-slimmer fleet-charter vessels to lug around ever-fatter office workers on their summer holidays in an ever-more-expensive "cruising Paradise."

Being broke in a voyaging boat has two compensations: it keeps your waistline down and it forces you to discover out-of-the-way places and remote anchorages. That's the way it should be—with poverty anyway, which is a private matter. Only when it's shared in crowded places does it become unbearable.

The fabled Levant can be said to start at Rhodes. It does, that is, if you're going east. If you are heading west, like the sane sailor I'm sure you are, then the Levant ends at Rhodes. It always has done, ever since the first packaged tours from Northern Europe arrived nearly a thousand years ago in the form of Crusaders. The harbor at Rhodes is just as packed now, six deep all around, as it was when carracks and caravels crowded in and landed kings, earls, fancy-Dans, remittance-men, family-black-sheep, released criminals and a rainbow of the odds and sods of medieval times. Then they came in iron armor, with feathers on their helmets. Now they come—in droves and squadrons, *gruppen* and legions—in shorts and funny hats to be herded around the castles and feasting halls of the Knights of St. John, paying their deutschmarks, pounds, francs or lire at the massive, iron-bolted gates, and wondering all the while when they will reach the beach, the bratwurst stand, the bathroom. It was so badly crowded in Rhodes in August that I wrote a letter to the Times of London suggesting that the Greek government should *pay* people to go there. Anyone who went there twice should receive a medal for heroism.

For the yatties, though, apart from being moored six-deep, and the noise all night of what young people have become convinced is *music*, Rhodes is a suitable place for a short stop before tackling the Eastern Mediterranean. But not for repairs. Anything more technical than a candle in a jam-jar, if it goes wrong before or in Rhodes, is likely to end up worse if local "technicians" are brought in. Don't let a pair of overalls or rimless spectacles fool you. Rhodes may be the start of the Levant, but it is still the Levant.

For me, though, Rhodes had one good thing going for it: there was a spare berth in a shallower part of the harbor hard by the old Italian church, only yards away from the post office. When you have one leg and no money, and leave the typewriter at odd times to send stuff to a dozen lands, a few yards to the post office makes all the difference between purgatory and hell.

By the end of August someone was making threatening noises about collecting harbor-dues from *Outward Leg*. Nothing was said to me personally; but various official-looking chaps, some in uniform, some without, were seen on the jetty weighing up the length and breadth of *Outward Leg* a little too observantly. So, to the concerted whistles and horns of a hundred and more sailing craft from foreign parts, *Outward Leg* slid gracefully and gratefully out of Rhodes Harbor, between the stag-decorated columns at the entrance. We were off east, to find a free mooring for a month, so that I might write my twelfth book, the one about the trans-Europe adventure, *The Improbable Voyage*. If I could finish that there would be a further advance from the British publisher, and then I could refit *Outward Leg* and make her ready for the lonely, demanding waters beyond Suez.

The berth I found was in one of the last completely unspoiled islands or ports I had found in the Eastern Mediterranean. It was in the easternmost Greek territory, and therefore the easternmost patch of Europe, the island of Kastellórizon, about 120 miles east of Rhodes. In the days of Levantine glory, in the days of commercial sail, Kastellórizon was a thriving island-city of 20,000 people, with a sailing fleet of barkentines and feluccas by the hundreds. Kastellórizon was strategically placed, windwise, to trade between the Turkish south coast, Cyprus, Syria, Egypt and the Greek mainland. From the Italo-Turkish War of 1912 on, it was Italian territory; but the decline of sail, together with Mussolini's grand ambitions in the Levant (which established a seaplane base in Kastellórizon, and nothing else), started a long agony of rot for the island. On the collapse of Mussolini's influence in 1943, the Nazis occupied the island, which the British promptly bombed. The Nazis withdrew, and the British evacuated everybody from the island. Most of the inhabitants were sent to Egypt. Their diaspora then took the vast majority to Australia. A tiny number of survivors, no more than a couple of hundred, returned to find the island after World War II not only ruined by foreigners but despoiled by their own countrymen, who operated as "freedom fighters" (pirates) during the British occupation. Word has it that many treasures from Kastellórizon found their liberated way to Britain. The islanders are still fighting the British for compensation 41 years later. Some of the Australian-Greeks have returned home now, and it is curious to be greeted by a little old man, dressed in black, with a collarless shirt and three days' growth, perhaps carrying a fiddle, who will ask, in round, rich Australian-English: "How's it gowin', cobber?"

Back in Romania, on our emergence from the Danube, the local mast-raising gang, supplied courtesy of the Constanta Communist Party, had wrecked the mast tabernacle. This had been cast in aluminum. There was no possibility of getting it replaced in aluminum east of Athens and west of Haifa, so I decided to go for stainless steel, which could be made up in Rhodes. This meant lowering the mast. There were no cranes in Kastellórizon, but there were some ruined houses around the harborfront with bedroom windows ideal for lowering a mast by block and tackle. Getting the mast up again was another thing; but in the back-of-beyond only present priorities matter. You must have faith that the Lord, or whatever you believe in, will provide for future needs. If you don't—or if you can't believe that—then for God's sake stick to suburbia.

There was another thing to consider. I wear two hats: the sailor's and the writer's. I knew, deep down, that I would never be able to concentrate for a month or more singly and solely on one thing—The Book—if my mast remained in place and the boat sailable. On the first ideal day for sailing that came along, half my mind would be on what I was missing. With the mast down I could deaden that half of my mind and give myself wholly to my ethereal lover—The Reader. So down came the mast. It took as long to get the tabernacle made in Rhodes—made properly, including two returns of the item to the workshop by local ferry—as it did for me to write the 150,000 words of *The Improbable Voyage* and draw the 15 maps to go with it—a matter of 28 days.

Kastellórizon was ideal to my purpose. We berthed *Outward Leg* only a foot from Jack's Restaurant on the waterfront, and Jack supplied me with coffee in the morning, a light lunch served onboard, and a good hearty supper in the evening. And that's the way it was done. There were no telephones—if there were they must have been installed before Alexander Graham Bell was

THERE WERE NO CRANES
IN KASTELLÓRIZON, BUT THERE WERE
SOME RUINED HOUSES AROUND THE HARBORFRONT WITH
BEDROOM WINDOWS IDEAL FOR LOWERING
A MAST BY BLOCK AND TACKLE.

born—and there was only one mail delivery a week, if the Rhodes post office remembered to put out mail on the ferry.

Getting the mast up again was simple. By God's grace the Greek government had decided to re-wire the island's electricity system, and to this end they had sent over, by steamer, one of those man-raising booms. It had a ten-ton capacity and a reach of 20´. It visited the island for three days, and the driver earned himself another twenty bucks putting my mast back, while I made yet a few more friends. That's what the back-of-beyond faith of the true cruising sailor brings, and it is part of the serendipitous pleasure of the sport. Still, we had to redrill the mast step holes through a quarter inch of stainless steel—and by hand at that.

With my book written, and dispatched to England by way of a very kind, intelligent returning English tourist (they have to be intelligent merely to *find* Kastellórizon), it was time, at the end of September, to get underway again, to find a place to work on the hulls. For a month, after 14-hour days pounding away at the typewriter in my cabin, I had stared across the four-mile gap between Greek territory and the Turkish coast, at the twinkling lights of a small town set between the feet of mighty mountains, and so we fetched Kas to us.

The first night in Kas found us hanging on by our toenails, it seemed, while great gusty williwaws roared down the mountainside in godlike contest with our anchors and rodes, trying to blow us onto the already wrecked seawall. The following morning saw peace and beauty all around us, and meals at $2 apiece, instead of the $8 apiece in Kastellórizon. Better food, too, fresh from the fields.

We stayed four days in Kas, while Thomas Ettenhuber completed, with my help here and there, his drafting of a complete Small Craft Pilot for the Danube River, from Kelheim, in West Germany, the head of navigation, to the Black Sea. We had been working on it ever since Istanbul—drawing out, in every factual detail that we could, all 2453 kilometers of the River Danube, from our pile of notes, all made behind the Iron Curtain, under the noses of otherwise unsuspecting Communist officials. Purely in the interest of small-craft safety, you understand. Every island, every buoy, every possible haven, every berthing pontoon, every blockhouse, every sentry-post, every riverside shop.

In Kas, strolling around, I found that there was an old mooring buoy on display at the town crossroads as an ornament. I was curiously touched by this memorial, intentional or not, to local fishermen and sailors. That old buoy told me more of a tale than any heroic statue or modern abstract sculpture. It was right outside the town mosque, so it would be the first thing worshipers would see when they emerged from their devotions, a definitive reminder of our own mortality. I was so struck by this symbol that I stopped hobbling for a good ten minutes, staring at it, until Thomas tugged at my sleeve and brought me back to the world of the land and the people of the land and their strange ways. Then we wended our way back over the cobblestones to *Outward Leg* and sailed away for Cyprus.

Once clear of the effects of the high Taurus mountains—say, 30 miles out—the wind and sea settled down to the usual Mediterranean nervousness in place of local frenzy. It seems to me that people in more steady climes than that of the Mediterranean and informed by romance think of this sea in terms of graceful mermaids and boys riding dolphins, all sheening in the sun, playing in the calm, wine-dark sea. Not me. I've messed around in boats in the Mediterranean too many times for that. For me, the Mediterranean is a bitter old spinster, ancient and frustrated, with nowhere to go, who gets agitated every time a man shows his face or makes a move anywhere near her. She's either sitting on a fence glowering or flying around like a provoked poltergeist. Outside of the high summer, when she's sleeping, that's what this sea is like most of the time. The Med has every bad female trait without much sign of the best—largeness of heart and fondness for life, as have the other seas. Yes, the sea of Homer seems to love self-indulgence; but that's not what I mean by fondness for life. Very little compassion she has, and on our way to Paphos, at the western end of Cyprus, I found myself, as we jerked and bounced our way over this old, bitter sea, thinking more and more of the generous rolls of the Atlantic and Pacific, and missing them and wanting them, and half tempted to turn right and head for Gibraltar and the Western Ocean, which is my home.

Paphos in Cyprus turned out to be tiny and dust-blown, a half-wrecked haven wide open to the west and south. As the southwest wind is the hardest in a hard sea, I decided to curtail our stay; and after we had entered Cyprus, we beat our way the 160 miles eastward to Larnaka, where I knew there was a change of refitting the battered hulls of *Outward Leg*. Beating 160 miles, hard against the wind, means covering about 350 miles over the ground, which, in the steep, short Levant seas, means tiring work. We headed into Limassol to find, perhaps, a night's rest. There was none of that; the harbor authorities demanded $80 for a night's stay at anchor! No sooner did they demand this than we were headed out again into the churlish chop, and beat all day and night until we fetched Larnaka Marina, which is no more than the old British harbor jetty, covered by a seawall and fitted with pontoons and mooring buoys. But

THE MAN-RAISING BOOM
HAD A TEN-TON CAPACITY AND A REACH OF 20´.
IT VISITED THE ISLAND FOR THREE DAYS, AND THE DRIVER
EARNED HIMSELF ANOTHER TWENTY BUCKS
PUTTING MY MAST BACK.

On previous pages, *Outward Leg* is shown moored along the waterfront of Kastellórizon in Greece where her mast was sent down and the mast-step replaced. After Greece, she sailed to Cyprus for hull repairs, then to Israel to spend the winter before transiting the Suez Canal and the Red Sea to catch the southwest monsoon in the Indian Ocean. All spruced up, she is shown here on the Israeli coast making a passage from Haifa to Akko.

the rates there, we had been told, were reasonable and the harbor was quite safe in winter. It was Saturday afternoon when we arrived. That, anywhere else, might mean little; but in the Levant *everything* means *something*, and the *something* usually means a disadvantage for you and advantage for someone else. In the case of Cyprus it meant that if a boat enters on a Saturday or Sunday the Customs and Immigration Officers will charge overtime fees for attendance over a weekend. The overtime charge seems to vary, but usually it is about $8 extra. So we anchored inside the breakwater until exactly 8:05 a.m. on Monday morning, and then requested entry. One advantage to poverty is that it teaches patience.

I won't bore my readers with details of our haul—it took four days to drag *Outward Leg* bodily out of the Mediterranean, and with the aid of a British Army truck and some stout chaps—nor

will I go far into the nitty-gritty of our refit, except to say that we ground the hulls down to the marrows, repaired all the bumps and bruises, and completely rebuilt the battered cool-tubes on the bottom of the keel. Anyone who has had anything to do with major repairs on a fiberglass hull knows already what's involved—all the searching for tools and materials, all the dusty grinding, the messy patching, the groping around in semidarkness late at night, the fending-off of curious idlers seeking gossip to liven their winter days and nights. I'll just say that the consensus among the marina denizens was that the repairs would take us at least a month, if not two. We finished the whole caboodle in ten days flat. Shipshape and Bristol (no, *San Diego*) fashion.

It was the end of November when we relaunched the boat. The commanding officer of the Cyprus United Nations Peacekeeping Force,

Brigadier Duchesne, British Army, himself an ocean sailor when he's not keeping squabbling factions from getting at each others' throats, honored us by attending the launch with two Irish Army officers from his staff, along with a piper from the Royal Irish Rifles, a braw lad from Ulster. They brought two bottles of Irish whiskey with them, too, which, along with a crane supplied at cost by the marina, saw *Outward Leg* all pristine and glistening under her hulls and back afloat.

The next passage was to Haifa, Israel. There were various reasons for wanting to winter in Israel, and the best one was that in a storm the quietest place to be is at its center. There had already been a murderous attack on a yacht by thugs in Larnaka Marina in September. I was planning to leave the boat and, with Thomas, fly to the U.S. in January to attend the Houston and New York boat shows, to raise the wherewithal for the voyage east of Suez. That meant that the boat would have to be left in a clean, well-lighted place. Through the cruising grapevine I knew where that place was—at Akko, ten miles north of Haifa.

The voyage from Larnaka to Haifa was lively enough, with a 40-knot wind from the northeast to start with, dropping to a zero wind from nowhere, ending with a southwester of 35 knots as we zoomed inshore hard by Ras En Naqura, where the frontier between Lebanon and Israel shows clearly in the sun as a wide livid scar across the face of the hills of the Holy Land. Of course we were buzzed by fighter planes first, then a helicopter, then two gunboats, then two harborpolice launches outside Haifa port. In Haifa, everyone was welcoming and official formalities were quickly over.

It was soon obvious how much the sailing scene in Israel had changed since I was last in

THE NEXT PASSAGE WAS TO
HAIFA, ISRAEL. THERE WERE VARIOUS REASONS
FOR WANTING TO WINTER IN ISRAEL, AND THE BEST ONE
WAS THAT IN A STORM THE QUIETEST PLACE
TO BE IS AT ITS CENTER.

Haifa in *Barbara* back in 1969. Now there was a full-fledged yacht club and marina on the south side of the port in the mouth of the River Kishon. In it were about a hundred sailing yachts of cruising size (22′ and over), and all around were healthy looking youngsters practicing rowing and sailing in 17′ daysailers. I promptly invited their instructors to bring the kids over "five at a time" to look around *Outward Leg*. Like the Jesuits, I'm a great believer in "catching 'em young." Get them interested in sailing as soon as they are able to walk and you've got them for life. Think how different the world would be now if someone had done that with Adolf Hitler at the age of six . . . To cut a long story sideways, before you could drop a marlinspike we had Israeli youngsters all over the boat, not five at a time but fifty or sixty. It was an *invasion*. In two hours 350 of them went through the boat, asking a million questions about everything in sight. Two things impressed me: their questions were intelligent and to the point, and each and every one of the kids shook my hand and Thomas's and thanked us for letting them look around. As for us, we both collapsed as soon as the boat was clear.

Next day we sailed north ten miles to the new marina-like harbor at Akko. This is built off the ancient town that was known as Acre to the Crusaders. There, under the walls of old fortifications, half-destroyed by Napoleon, in the shadow of a fisherman's mosque, we moored *Outward Leg* securely to the piles and settled down to await the early spring, when it would be time to head down the Red Sea, so as to arrive there for the change of the monsoon wind.

Akko turned out to be a gem. The inhabitants of the old town are mostly "Arabs" (which, in fact, is a misnomer; "Levantines" would be better), mainly of Moslem but some of Christian persuasion. These people treated us like honored visitors. At first we had to watch the small change, it's true, when we went shopping in the lively, Kashbah-like market place, all cobblestones, colors, and rich smells; but after we had—as any good sailor should—become part of the furniture, there was not enough the Arabs could do for us. We found they had impeccable manners and apparently no politics. They know that various plans are afoot to "modernize" their town and turn it into some sort of tourist Disneyland, and they knew that we knew this, too, and that we were for them and against any degradation of what is one of the jewels of the Levant. Anything that changes the character of Akko, as it is now, apart from perhaps some small improvement in the harbor protection, will be yet another social crime. The best thing for Akko will be completion of the harbor work to prevent the present surge that enters in heavy winds, and the provision of berths for cruising yachts based there for the winter. In the main the yatties will not want to change the place, and the craft themselves will provide income and work for the local youths, many of whom are at present merely battening on visiting tourists for pittances as "guides," and going to the bad, one way or another.

The figures for such a project are simple and understandable even by planners and promoters: 200 yacht berths a day at $4 equals $800 a day. A hundred boats with average crew of three living on board equals daily expenditure, all included, of $20 per day per boat. This is *$2000 a day* going into the town, where it matters among the small traders and craftsmen. With a better port, Akko can grow from the inside instead of having outside "developers" come in and destroy the nature of the place, as has happened so frequently and disastrously in Turkey and Greece.

By mid-February we had re-supplied the boat (having recuperated our fortunes in a flying three-week visit to the U.S.) and made ready for the long voyage to Singapore. Food, canned and dried, in Israel, is not cheap; but we could not depend on being allowed ashore in Egypt, nor of the quality of stores available there. A nearby port in Lebanon had a duty-free area for visiting craft; but the risks involved in visiting Lebanon in a U.S.-flag vessel were far more than the saving of a few hundred dollars warranted. So we concluded that the next necessity for the port of Akko is a duty-free area for departing yachts. Given that, I foresee Akko becoming a major yachting center in the future, and I foresee that future being far sooner than most people seem to think it will be. Larnaka and Tel Aviv are crowded already.

Akko is well-served by restaurants and little tea shops. Just opposite the post office in the old town is "Dick's Shamrock Inn," a bar/restaurant run by New York Irishman Dick Lambert, who originally came to Israel with the Grumman Aircraft Corporation, married an Israeli wife and settled in Akko. This is the official yatties meeting place on the Levant coast. At the western end of the Med there is the Rock Hotel, Gibraltar; at the eastern end there is Dick's Shamrock Inn, Akko, and I thoroughly recommend it to any salt worth his salt.

Then next port of call for *Outward Leg* was Tel Aviv Marina, right in front of the Hilton Hotel. There are several hundred sailing vessels berthed there, and hardly room for any more during the winter months. The marina has a very difficult entrance, and should not be approached at night. The best time is the afternoon when the sun is in the west, shining on every feature of the narrow fairway between the high combers and the hard rock walls. Tel Aviv Marina, being only yards from a major highway and a youngsters' roller-skating rink, is noisy by day and night from traffic, and by night from what is, I am told, "music" blaring from the rink. But there are plenty of restaurants and bars close by, for those who miss civilization in its more concrete forms.

The weather on the Israeli coast in winter is variable, from full southwest gales (the only safe entrances are Haifa and Ashdod) to long spells of weak winds and sloppy seas. Mornings usually feature thick low mists, which clear up around noon. The rule is to stand off well at night, and don't approach the coast until forenoon. At all times expect to be challenged very suddenly by patrol craft; and when this happens, have everyone onboard stand on deck so that the Israeli Navy or Police can see all hands. At two a.m. this is a nuisance, but in the present circumstances understandable enough.

Formalities for clearing Tel Aviv were minimal. The Police checked that we'd paid the marina's dues, returned our passports, and off we set, for the offing and Port Said. About five miles off Tel Aviv we were hailed by the requisite gunboat, in a most friendly fashion, with the hooting of her siren in farewell. Shortly after, we encountered the quasi-legal shipboard radio station *Peace*, which, Israeli-owned, hovers off the coast broadcasting pop music and messages of peace on Earth and goodwill to all mankind. I was told she has been there for some years; at first the Israeli Government would not allow *Peace* into territorial waters; but persistence in a good cause will always win through sooner or later, and eventually the vessel was allowed to put into Ashdod in very bad winter weather and for repairs. Long before "Band Aid" was mooted with such show-biz palaver, the *Peace* people were collecting funds for the relief of the starving millions in East Africa.

I sent the lads over to the ship-side of *Peace* with a bottle of Johnny Walker as a respect offering. My thought was that if the Ethiopian government could take the pains to import shiploads of the stuff from Scotland for political gatherings in their otherwise benighted land, surely the folk who were working so hard to relieve Ethiopia's starving millions ought to have at least a bottle. But alongside the heaving *Peace* ship my lads were gently waved off. All onboard were, it seems, teetotallers. Now that's

AT ALL TIMES EXPECT TO BE
CHALLENGED VERY SUDDENLY BY PATROL
CRAFT; AND WHEN THIS HAPPENS, HAVE EVERYONE ONBOARD
STAND ON DECK SO THAT THE ISRAELI NAVY
OR POLICE CAN SEE ALL HANDS.

At Akko —Acre to the Crusaders— *Outward Leg* shared a marina-like harbor with yachts and working boats in the shadow of the minaret of a fisherman's mosque. This ancient port, with its Kasbah-like market place and hospitable mostly-Arab population, is now becoming a port of call for cruising yachtsmen in the eastern Med. Tristan Jones feels that it will become a major yachting center with some harbor improvements and, he hopes, no further attention from "developers."

what I call dedication, sitting out off the coast of Tel Aviv, month in and month out, with a noisy generator churning out the amps for the transmitter day and night, and not one wee drappie onboard. So I dipped our ensign in salute, and off we flew, on a beam reach with a northerly wind . . .

"Take me somewhere east of Suez,
Where the best is like the worst,
And there ain't no ten commandments,
And a man can raise a thirst . . ." I sang as we whizzed along in a confused sea. Soon both Thomas Ettenhuber and Sven Wagenius, German and Swede, were joining in . . .

"For the wind is in the palm trees,
And the temple bells they say,
Come you back . . ." But here I had to change Kipling's words to something more appropriate, so it was . . .

"Come you back you bloody sailor,
Come you back to Mandalay!"

The 160 miles to Port Said took only 24 hours. Just outside the entrance to the great canal, dodging an inquisitive cargo-steamer—let's be kind and say she was Ruritanian—*Outward Leg* managed to get a fishing net tangled up with her screw. We were not running the engine at the time, but we knew we had caught the net because the boat came almost to a halt from six knots. I headed to windward and backed all sail, making a stern-board out of the net; but we still had bits and pieces tangled in the propeller, so it was sail all the way, under twin headsails, right up to the Port Said Yacht Centre, where we dropped the hook and let her swing stern to the wooden jetty. (A notice board proclaimed: *"Welcome to Centre, Hull, Machinry and Reeging Repairs can be executed and enginners and technicians at very reasonable rates . . . trimarans pay Double the rates. Monthely rate 120 dollars."*)

On the way to the Yacht Centre basin we were overhauled by at least ten different launches, all with several ship's agents and chandlers' "runners" on board. Each launch was doing its best to outmaneuver all other competitors for our business. Some went to the extreme of claiming to be the Port Doctor, demanding to clear us for health regulations. Challenged for identification, they could only scrabble in their incredibly grotty briefcases and wave tattered business cards at us. They were waved away. The Port Said "chandlers" are that in the true sense of the word—they supply the ships with everything, not just ship's equipment, but food and drink and duty-free supplies, too.

Eventually we contacted an honest agent through the immigration officer, a cultured and civil gentleman. The "honest agent," Ibrahim, even though he is based in Suez, at the south end of the canal, 80 miles away, was with us the next morning. After filling out fourteen forms for separate functions in different offices, together with six copies of the crew list, we were officially cleared to pass through the Suez Canal, as long as we had onboard a pilot to make sure that we successfully navigated what must be the easiest, most straightforward, well-marked passage on Earth. I could have done it . . . Well, on one leg, for Chrissake.

When it comes to a ship's agent in the Suez Canal, the amount of bureaucratic nonsense is so extensive and pervasive that not to have one would be tantamount to consigning yourself, after a week's untangling of the intangible, to a madhouse. If you must have one—and you must—the only way to get true value for your money (about $200) is to get some entertainment out of the deal. Ibrahim and his "pilots" are truly better actors and much funnier than Charlie Chaplin and the Keystone Cops combined—and just about as efficient, too. There is no need to be concerned about the ship's ensign, whatever nationality it represents. Ibrahim & Co. recognize one flag and one only, and it is green and white. On top of the flag is the legend "Federal Reserve Note" and below that are pictures of various gentlemen no longer, unfortunately, with us. Ibrahim's phone number is Suez 20982. His telex number (despite his protestations of poverty) is 66041.

Before clinching the deal with Ibrahim it will be wise (unless you are inclined to the contrary, in which case Egypt will suit you to the ground) to be firm with him about not being kissed on both cheeks and the lips. The camels of Gizeh are not the most pungent creatures in Egypt, believe me.

IF YOU MUST HAVE A SHIP'S AGENT
FOR THE SUEZ CANAL—AND YOU MUST—THE ONLY
WAY TO GET TRUE VALUE FOR YOUR MONEY (ABOUT $200)
IS TO GET SOME ENTERTAINMENT
OUT OF THE DEAL.

WHITBREAD

THE TOUGHEST PROJECT GOING

BY SKIP NOVAK

This is Skip Novak's third attempt at getting the 27,000-mile Whitbread Round the World Race "all right." The 33-year-old American sailed on *King's Legend* in 1977-78—the boat finished second—then he skippered *Alaska Eagle* in the 1981-82 race. This time Novak skippered the Maxi *Drum* for British rocker Simon le Bon. In the photo to the right, the crew reefs the main on Leg II, from Cape Town to Auckland. In the adjoining photo, crewmembers pack a headsail as the boat rocks and rolls through the South Atlantic. *Drum* is a 77´ Ron Holland design, originally called *Colt Cars*, and designed for the late Rob James. While sailing a multihull, also called *Colt Cars*, James was lost at sea, and the Whitbread boat was never completed until Simon le Bon and his business associates, brothers Paul and Mike Berrow, bought the hull and deck in January 1985. No doubt the lack of continuity contributed greatly to her troubles.

Sometimes it seems like nothing more than an exercise in setting yourself up for failure. Big boats with big crews have big problems, and it's safe to say that 27,000 sea miles over seven months will expose the most subtle of weaknesses in a project—if the project makes it at all. But to get it all right is what the Whitbread Round the World Race is all about. Unlike short-course races, the results tell little of the real story of untallied victories and defeats that make it a human drama indeed. Join *Drum* for her adventure around the world.

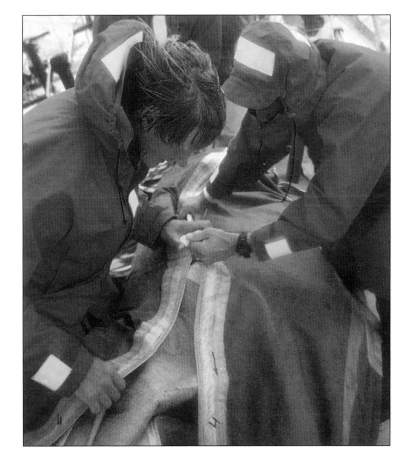

Overhead the massive carbon-fiber deck would creak
and groan in a visible deflection (by an "acceptable" amount, the
builder had vaguely assured me last summer).

Last night in the early morning hours of the genoa-tack fitting, a hefty piece of 16mm stainless steel bar, gave way on the No. 3 genoa. One of our bowmen spent most of the morning watch in an immersion suit pressing eyes into a jury-rigged wire strop passed down through the stemhead. A good repair with no ground lost. This afternoon a 20mm rope genoa sheet parted only seconds after a man had clipped in the Kevlar change sheet as a backup. Any earlier and the clew might have taken his head off. Well, I thought to myself, if that's all that happens we'll be lucky.

That was October 27th, 1985. *Drum* was less than a 1000 miles from Cape Town and the finish of Leg I, which began in Plymouth, England. Off Cape Agulhas it was blowing 50 to 60 knots from the southeast and what was until then a cakewalk down the Atlantic for the Whitbread fleet had turned into an endurance test in a dead beat. For the six Maxis up front, the tactics were obvious, and any breakdowns would determine the results. After 6000 miles of racing they were all only 100 miles apart, and with this new weather the leg was up for grabs.

Lifting up into an unusually steep seaway, the simple pleasure of lounging around back aft in the nav area was more like being trapped in a chamber of horrors. Behind me, the disturbing crackling noise from the rudder shaft was getting worse, and overhead the massive carbon-fiber deck beam supporting the traveller would creak and groan in a visible deflection (by an "acceptable" amount, the builder had vaguely assured me last summer) with every surge. But when the helmsman inevitably missed a wave, and this 78´ misguided missile belly-flopped in the trough—if only for an instant—it made you feel your little world was just flying apart.

For the next two days in worsening conditions, it was as if one's senses were pushed to the limit. On deck bloodshot eyes would gaze aloft at a mast that gyrated wildly and below, wedged into our bunks, sleep all but impossible, ears would prick up to the slightest variation against the familiar background of yacht-and-emotional torture. It was no secret to the crew or to myself that I was feeling the strain. Frankly, I was a nervous wreck.

With only 560 miles to go on the 29th under a misconception that these Maxis could actually live up to this sustained punishment, the message was loud and clear on the 1100 radio sched: "*Côte d'Or* running off with delaminated bow sections." "*New Zealand Enterprise* running off with a broken main halyard and unable to reeve a new one." I thought to myself, Well, there's two in the bag.

As if for my satisfaction in the misfortune of others, retribution was exacted almost immediately. I was summoned to the forepeak to witness our portside bowsection across three panels panting like a slack bass drum.

This was accompanied by the undoubted sound of the Nomex honeycomb core crushing between the two skins of Kevlar.

We immediately reduced sail while teams of guys shored up the inside with bedding, floorboards and the jockey poles. After a look at the outside of the hull, where only filler cracks were visible, it was obvious the hull was not likely to breach, but we certainly couldn't push the boat. We were now out of it.

It was here that a suspected problem with the keel attachment revealed itself as we wallowed our way towards shore in the direction of the Namibian port of Lüderitz. Under a press of sail a slight movement in the mast step and keelson areas had been an area of slight concern; but now, without directional stability, it was apparent the keel was flagging dramatically and flexing the bottom structure of the boat. Not only was the crew's confidence in the boat completely shaken (and don't forget we had little else to do then but to worry about it), but thoughts about getting to shore at all were starting to run high.

Before the seas eased and we were able to continue the race to Cape Town, life on board became a protracted exercise in trying to convince everyone that we were doing the right thing. Not a simple matter with 17 individuals on board; understandably, plans varied from calling for a rescue to going for it, seeing what would happen on the southern board. Heavy-handed tactics would have certainly polarized the crew in a negative way, and I knew that if this thing was repairable, and we were to continue the race, we would have to stand together. How we got to Cape Town was a group decision.

We were not alone in our tribulations. The South African favorite, *Portatan*, only 220 miles from her home, dropped the whole rig overboard when the D1 shroud parted, and after a series of misfortunes with a jury rig erected in Lüderitz retired from the leg. *Enterprise* would finish well behind the leaders with a topmast of her fractional rig bent 30 degrees to the vertical. *Côte d'Or* also made it, but with serious hull damage. Only *UBS Switzerland*, the leg winner, and *Lion New Zealand* came through unscathed, and they both made no bones about the fact that they had been the best-prepared before the start. *Drum* finished fifth out of six Maxis, almost three days behind the leader.

The four-week stopover in Cape Town was really the turning point for the *Drum* project, but not before the boat was dismembered and the crew subjected to a siege of emotional hardship. The pitiful look on the faces of the few there to meet us in the gray South African dawn was enough to convince me that we had better do something positive, and it was without mercy or clemency that I summoned the crew back on board in five hours time to offload the sails and gear and pull the mast. This was a lot to ask after 36 days at sea and I wasn't too popular at the time.

The "Great Test" had had its desired effect; I was emotionally shattered and took to the bottle. I doubted whether we could make it, and more importantly whether I could continue to cope.

The seemingly star-crossed *Drum* is hoisted out of the water in Cape Town. *Drum* dropped her keel in the '85 Fastnet. On the first leg of the Whitbread, the new keel began to flex the hull. Then, after a long repair, when the hull was being mated to the keel, a hoist sling broke, crushing the rudder and nearly the spirit of her skipper. *Drum* started Leg II with 10 miles of sailing under her repaired hull.

After hauling and surveying the damage, a team of local builders and fitters assisted by Rob Lipsett (Vision Yachts in Cowes, the builder), Adrian Thompson (designer of the structural layout of *Drum*) and Butch Dalrymple-Smith (from yacht designer Ron Holland's office)—all flown in for the occasion—got together and formulated a plan. These men, with their names on the boat in varying degrees obviously felt responsible for the failure (no doubt in varying degrees), and after little persuasion from me dropped all former disagreements that went back to a construction and design concept noted for its lack of continuity—a fascinating story too lengthy to delve into in these pages. In short, they all pulled together and did the right thing.

The right thing for *Drum*'s illness was to gut the middle of the boat and drop the keel. This involved removing all the water tanks, the V-drive for the engine, the generator and all the attendant plumbing and wiring. A broken carbon-fiber ring frame and other stress cracks were discovered after the epoxy paint was shot-blasted off, so a simple solution here was to overlay the entire bilge area with 15mm of glass fiber. To arrest any further movement, a steel "space frame" was erected in situ below that would spread the keel loads out into the hull as well as absorbing mast compression—the two forces at work that quickly exposed the poorly designed keel-to-hull interphase in the pounding conditions off South Africa.

Of course the bow section had to be repaired, a relatively simple case of replacing the Nomex core with end-grain balsa as well as adding two additional stringers in the forward panels. Simple; but, as any boat builder will tell you, time-consuming. The endless list of minor but significant tasks in addition to all the normal servicing of the mast, deck gear and machinery put a tremendous strain on the crew.

Being all experienced boat hands working under pressure was not new; but we all had to endure a constant stream of advice. Parents and friends offered sincere caution—fair enough. But on the other side, with the word "keel" being bandied about like a red flag, the press was having a field day, and on site a casual remark like "I wouldn't put to sea in this thing, mate!" didn't exactly serve to brighten one's day. It was common knowledge that we would be hard-pressed to make the restart; and, if we did, how could we justify taking a suspect repair out into the Southern Ocean without the benefit of a proper sea trial (something we had promised ourselves in a crew meeting, fully realizing there would be no time)? For all their pessimism these were some reasonable questions indeed.

Because of the gravity of the situation, I had decided from the beginning that we must approach the repair as objectively as possible and with the facts and plans laid bare. Each man would have to decide for himself whether to do the second leg. If this solution to *Drum*'s problem was wrong, there was the overriding possibility that more would be at stake than just a few reputations. Whether ethically right or wrong I became comfortable in leading the team by hard work and unflagging optimism—only hoping there were no sheep that could come back and haunt the shepherd if things went wrong offshore.

It's as if the gods had declared the night of November 27th, only eight days before the start, to be the last great test of our wills. We were working late refitting the keel, and that's when we "bottomed out." Two mobile cranes had the hull suspended in two slings over the keel, and after a successful "dry fit" we raised her four inches up to lay in the bedding. It was then that the aft sling, the one we had used earlier in the day, the one *Côte d'Or* had used, parted abruptly and the unfortunate *Drum* settled on her safety slings and keel with a bang, but not before pitching aft and crushing the bottom third of her rudder. Holding back the tears, we righted the hull (no damage) and finished bolting on the keel with almost an air of resignation. The rudder was dropped out and hidden under a tarpaulin in anticipation of the presence next day of the press who ghoulishly awaited our every move.

One by one on the upturned hull, we cheered the heads
popping up from below until our numbers totaled. All were accounted for
in what must be the happiest of endings . . .

The crew should have seen its skipper later that evening. The "Great Test" had had its desired effect; I was emotionally shattered and took to the bottle. For the first time I doubted whether we could make it, and more importantly whether I could continue to cope.

The popular story going around at the time—that *Drum* was somehow star-crossed—was certainly fueled by this latest incident and even prompted the three owners in London to carry out an investigation into the joss of the now familiar Aztec Eagle, which is the *Drum* logo. There was no denying the fact that *Drum* had had an unfortunate history, beginning with the tragic death of British yachtsman Rob James, who drowned off the Devon coast after falling overboard from his trimaran *Colt Cars*.

With continuing sponsorship from Colt, Rob had conceived and had designed the Maxi hull for this Whitbread while finishing his commitments on the trimaran, but his death and later a change in management at Colt Cars Ltd. UK, stopped the project in its tracks with the hull and deck already completed. That was in the spring of 1984, and it wasn't until nine months later that the story would continue.

Enter rock star and teen idol Simon le Bon, figurehead of the three-man partnership including Mike and Paul Berrow, the brothers who masterminded the success of Simon's group Duran Duran. For reasons personal as well as commercial, these sometime sailors intended to enter the Whitbread Race as the penultimate challenge in ocean racing, a concept not uncommon to people who have little time to come up through the ranks of yacht racing in the normal way.

It has always been axiomatic that you need three things to be successful in the Whitbread; a Maxi boat (to reap Maxi publicity), enough money well-managed, and time. With only eight months before the start, the committee of the owners, designers, builders and myself as designated skipper went into the project with our eyes wide open, knowing full well it would be an accomplishment in itself just to make the start, let alone be prepared enough to win the race. Most of our competitors were already on the water when the *Colt Cars* hull was purchased in January of 1985, and it was a case of being on the bus or off. However, owner Paul Berrow made his intentions quite clear when he said to me then, "There is one thing we cannot afford and that is to come in sixth out of the six Maxis in the Whitbread." I confidently assured him we would not.

"Don't worry, Simon," said the boatbuilder, Rob Lipsett, as he banged his fist against the cavernous Kevlar/carbon-fiber hull one day late in February, "She's tighter than a drum!" And so *Drum* she became.

A well-managed construction schedule launched her only three days late of her projected target date of June 15th. Much to our satisfaction, and to the delight of *Drum* supporters, we maintained a disciplined schedule of local racing and sea trials that was an amazement to some segments of the British public, and especially to the Fleet Street press who take an unseemly pleasure in seeing people fail.

On the blustery summer's day of August the 11th, they were more than satiated. "Pop Star Simon in Sea Terror," "Pop Star in Sea Rescue Drama" and "Simon le Bon Yacht Sinks—Pop Star is Trapped in 'Tomb' Terror" were some of the headlines that announced *Drum*'s capsize in the Fastnet Race in the summer of 1985.

Certainly not the most tragic, the capsize quickly became the most publicized in yachting's history for two reasons: "keels just don't fall off," and the fact that our rock star le Bon had been one of the six crew who had been trapped below inside the upturned hull.

Everything had been going fine that Sunday afternoon. We were wearing a No. 5 jib and three reefs in the main, short-tacking up the Cornish Coast after a hard night in the Channel. There was almost a holiday atmosphere on board, now that we were in the flat water in the lee behind the Lizard Lighthouse.

John Irving and I were back aft at the chart table after I had just asked helmsman Phil Holland to drive her off a little more for more speed. Two loud bangs up forward, and I thought the rig had gone, but an increasing list to port turned the odd 20 seconds it took *Drum* to turn turtle into a simple case of "every man for himself." In addition to those on deck and the ones that made it through the hatch before and after she went over, six had been caught completely unaware and it was this lapse in time, when they could gather their senses and realize the boat wasn't going to sink, that saved Pascal Pellet-Finet's life. He had been back aft and trapped under half a ton of sails, and by the time the others had freed him, the water was rising above his chin pinned to the overhead.

In what must also be the most fortuitous rescue circumstance, we had capsized in full view of the cliff walkers who had called out the Culdrose Air-Sea rescue helicopter that within 20 minutes had a diver down who brought out the six from inside. One by one on the upturned hull, we cheered the heads popping up from below until out numbers totaled. All were accounted for in what must be the happiest of endings in the most dramatic of circumstances.

In a simple world the keel had failed due to poor welding of the alloy spacer between the hull and lead. In a complicated world of long-term litigation to determine ultimate responsibility, I can only offer the more curious of readers an explanation the *Drum* crew had learned only too well: "NO COMMENT!"

Stuffed with Cornish cream teas and sporting borrowed boiler suits and old clothes lent to us by a guest house, we were on our way by chartered bus

After the capsize the Daily Telegraph printed an observation
by one of the men in the helicopter: "It seemed that not many of them knew
very much about the sea." This was devastating . . .

to Falmouth that same afternoon. In an air of bravado we all proclaimed that "somehow" we had to refit *Drum* in the six weeks left before the start. Not only was the main capital spent, but reputations were in jeopardy; Simon's head was on the chopping block and the Berrow brothers' credibility as organizers was now in question.

The day after the capsize the Daily Telegraph printed an observation by one of the men in the helicopter that read—and I quote: "It seemed to me that not many of them knew very much about the sea." This was devastating for a crew who had spent most of their lives working offshore, and it only made us more determined to make it.

The reality of the situation would have made the most optimistic of men think otherwise. John Irving was already in Falmouth beginning a telephone marathon to organize the subsequent salvage and towage into Falmouth. In five days, we had rolled the boat over, pumped her out, offloaded a tangle of abraded sails, rigging, clothing, bedding and food and ballasted the boat with five tons of sand before she was smartly towed back to the Hamble for an extensive survey of what was left, which wasn't much. The survey luckily proved positive.

Knuckling under, the owners forked out the £300,000 necessary to replace damaged sails, electronics, the electrical system and, of course, a new keel and mast (the original was lost in the salvage), as well as extensive servicing and cleaning of everything else. I'm sorry to say that we lost three of the original crew because of the capsize. In what can be described as an inordinately severe test of moral fiber I can hardly blame them. The rest of us got down to work.

The morning of the start on September 28th was a triumph for the *Drum* crew because the five weeks of labor had paid off; we had made the venue on time. In spite of a mere 172 miles of sea trials after the repair, the guys on board attempted to portray an air of confidence—of being fully prepared—while thousands of spectators looked on. These were people not especially interested in the shape of our new keel, but very interested in catching a glimpse of Simon who was seeing us off. He had music commitments during the fall and would only join the boat for the last two legs.

Just then New Zealander Chris Barker calmly pointed out that there were no hacksaws on board, probably misplaced ashore in the fray. With half an hour to departure I sent him against the tide of humanity, already dangerously submerging the dock's pontoon, to the hardware store to purchase two. Now alert to the problem and always thinking of these things, I casually asked Richard Freeman, the cook, if he remembered the matches. (I had already seen the toilet paper come on board.) He had forgotten. Up to the marina shop he

went while I thought to myself, My God, what else has he missed? Of course, this black comedy was picked up by a few astute observers who must have wondered, Do these guys really have their act together?

For a light-hearted farewell, and knowing only too well the value of "the circus aspect" that has become such a part of sponsorship in yachting, I had Simon, in full view of the crowd, plant his lips on a piece of discarded ceiling batten. We had learned that for Duran Duran fans, any bit of rubbish from *Drum* was worth something and instead of used, balled-up masking tape or bits of epoxy resin, this was a quality piece of garbage indeed. I flung the length of wood to the throng, whereupon the little girls savagely ripped it to splinters while the gang of journalists and photographers, more mature but no less predatory, looked on in gales of laughter. We backed out of the marina at Camper & Nicholsons in Gosport and made our way to the Solent.

After one postponement due to an unruly spectator fleet numbering in the thousands, we broke free in the hazy afternoon and led the 15-strong Whitbread fleet down the Solent and out through the Needles Channel; for us, that was a major publicity coup.

Our support craft was the last to leave us abeam of St. Alban's Head, our last piece of land for a while, and as John Irving, girlfriends and well-wishers waved us goodbye, we suddenly blew out the old .75 ounce spinnaker, a survivor of the capsize, in the light easterly. In spite of our early lead and the fact we had made it at all, the incident was perhaps a grim reminder to owners Simon and Paul Berrow of what they had to face back on shore: the threads of a project that in the end would cost them over £2 million.

Leg I is highly tactical as the fleet encounters several major weather systems with vast options to consider. A light easterly run was kind to *Drum*, and we maintained our lead out the English Channel until we passed Ile d'Ouessant at the northwest corner of the Brittany coast. Here the wind swung through the south putting the fleet on the wind with the lead almost an arbitrary claim depending upon how much searoom you planned to give Cape Finisterre across the Biscay. As if for a last look at his homeland, the legendary Frenchman Eric Tabarly skippered his Joubert-Nivelt Maxi, *Côte d'Or*, in between Ushant and the mainland to cut the corner, but fell foul of tide and wind and had to kedge off of a buoy in some little bay, as the other Maxis left them behind. A soon-to-be disillusioned crewmember told me later that, "While we waited for the tide to change that morning, a little motorboat came alongside with a journalist who came to interview Eric and have a cup of coffee; we just couldn't believe it."

Out in the Atlantic a massive low had been brewing with weather soon to come from the west. The option was to bank on an expected heat low over the Iberian peninsula giving rise to a fresh northerly down the coast

We had learned that for Duran Duran fans, any bit of rubbish from *Drum* was worth something and instead of used, balled-up masking tape, this was a quality piece of garbage indeed.

known as the Portuguese Trades, a situation that four years ago pushed the Swan 57 *Berge Viking* ahead of the fleet down past the Canary Islands.

On October 1st my log invokes the name of sailor-explorer Bill Tilman, that rough-and-ready Arctic explorer: "Major Tilman would have smiled on us this morning: last night's leftover curry to complement a meager ration of powdered scrambled eggs for breakfast." The fare on board looks to be quite Spartan compared to four years ago on *Alaska Eagle*. Like the well-known joke about "hell on earth," our cook, Richard, is English. He uses no refrigeration and makes do with freeze-dried food, three meals a day for 17 people. We had originally planned to divide up the cooking duties with a sophisticated system that had to be scrapped after the capsize as there was no time to test it out. Conscripted at the eleventh hour, Richard was left to his own devices to plan the menu and already short rations of powdered eggs and milk are making the others concerned. Understandably he seems to be panicking a bit, and the bilge water sloshing around his ankles on starboard tack last night almost broke his spirit.

Unlike previous races, navigation today has become a time-consuming if not complicated exercise. In a tight cubicle back aft the Sat Nav ticks off our position while the Brookes & Gatehouse 290 computer gives us basic wind and speed functions. The full comprehension of the Sharp 5000 performance computer, radar, telex, weather fax, Decca, Ham radio and SSB is necessary to be competitive, and while Roger Nilsson and I struggle to become "user friendly" with all these flashing lights and readouts, we are quickly brought back down to base, human reality by a conversation up forward.

"Philthy" Phil Barrett, bowman and rigger, leaves no one in doubt of his *nom de guerre* when he announces in a deep Hampshire accent that his Musto long johns "take on smell, mate! Two farts, especially after that freeze-dried chili, and you have to give 'em the old heave ho!"

Abeam of Cape Finisterre we had decided to play the Portuguese coast, as did *New Zealand Enterprise* and the South African *Portatan*. *UBS Switzerland* and *Lion New Zealand* went west, which by October 3rd had paid handsomely; they were 115 and 95 miles ahead respectively, reaching south while we three wallowed inshore.

With no excuses we had blundered badly. Swedish doctor and navigator Roger Nilsson, a theoretician to almost an annoying degree in these situations, reckoned that unclear thinking was the cause due to the heavy pressure he and I were under before the start. Certainly the tactics were the last thing on my mind back then, and the planning was reduced to a rushed 20-minute breakfast meeting with Jim Allen from the Southampton meteorological center where we largely discussed situations portending the Portuguese Trades. He must now think we are simpletons for ignoring possibly the biggest low pressure center of the season out to the west.

On the evening of the 4th I had taken a round of stars with Roger's sextant. Three days before our Sat Nav blew its display—the same unit that never failed us all the way around four years ago—which made a mockery of the words I had written in an article last summer to the effect that, "Electronics are becoming as basic to navigation as pencil and dividers." We have only one sextant on board—no spare, no plastic job, no nothing, and assuming it is, as crewman cum-comedian Neil Cheston likes to put it, "Reg Bistry," (cockney slang for history, but soon to be incorporated into "*Drum*speak,"), we had better be damn careful with it.

Short-tacking with the shifts is rough work on a Maxi offshore, both on deck and below. Arguably illegal in the IOR, all the sails below must be shifted to the new weather side for proper trim and not least of all to give clear access to the leeward bilges. Of course the off-watch also had to shift to the weather-side bunks, and it was their job to move the sails, aided, it is hoped, by gravity down to the low side before the tack. This was an unpleasant task, but Englishman Lawrie Smith took it in his stride, sleep-walking to weather trailing his sleeping bag—an art well-practiced from sailing a succession of level-rating boats in the Admiral's Cup. On deck, more often than not, it was up to race veteran Bill Biewenga to drive them on with streams of good-natured obscenities that only an inspired American can muster.

What had been an ad hoc interior design of the most simple of concepts had proven superior in shifting gear as it consisted of two symmetrical corridors running full fore and aft divided by a center console of generator, main engine, sewing machine and nav station. Outboard are rows of double-tier pipe berths with block and tackles, and amidships abreast the main hatch is a rudimentary galley with a custom gimballed range top and gimballed microwave. This is opposite the single head, both sited for maximum ventilation. There is no salon table, and our meals are taken on our laps while liquid refreshment (a standard-issue juice concentrate aptly labeled "the backwash") is dispensed at will from a jug suspended from the mast partners.

Almost by virtue of the numbers involved and the space available, the watch system must be complicated. We used a system of four groups of four that stood three four-hour watches at night and two six-hour watches during the day. Two groups were always on deck giving us eight men, and every two hours at night, or four during the day, a new group would come on and another go off. During this switch 12 men could be called upon for a sail change, and they usually were. Imagine incorporating meal times, dogging this system for time changes, and staggering the two groups as well as a roster for cleanup duties, and it is no wonder that few of us could understand it at all. It was up to watch leader Phil Wade, a South African deepwaterman, to tell us all what was happening next, and luckily he looked like a man who could be trusted.

"Philthy" Phil Barrett leaves no one in doubt of his
nom de guerre when he announces that his long johns "take on smell,
mate, especially after the freeze-dried chili."

At 6 degrees north latitude, *Drum* parks in the doldrums. There was much company for her after 16 days of racing as the six Maxis got trapped in the same vacuous weather system. Leg I is traditionally the most tactical section of the Whitbread. Avoiding, or at least quickly escaping, the doldrums can spell success or failure in this contest.

After 10 days out and working our way through the Canary Islands, we seemed to have settled down to old familiar routines on board. Even Richard was coping fine, and on that morning pleasant smells of freshly baked bread reminded the crew of what seems to be his only saving grace. I think most of us have accepted eating more as an act of sustenance, rather than the indulgence—the pleasure—it usually is. Most admit that half the normal intake is leaving us satisfied, and Neil says that he's never felt more mentally alert. On the other hand the workload has been light and the temperature mild and a

few like Phil Wade, a big man, claim starvation is at hand. With flying fish regularly found in the lee scuppers at dawn, he can be seen harvesting his breakfast with a bucket and scuttling off to the galley.

That same morning we raised *Portatan* on the VHF, abeam of us near Las Palmas and stuck in light airs. This Bruce Farr-designed masthead-rigged Maxi was the race favorite for many after her decisive performance last summer. Portatan Ltd. UK is a division of the American company Portasun. If the reason why a company selling portable tanning equipment

Running a Maxi boat and trying to win a popularity contest
are not at all compatible. But as the Arab proverb has it, "The camel
driver has his thoughts, the camel, he has his."

would want to sponsor a Whitbread yacht is not completely clear, the reason why South African skipper "Padda" Kuttel changed the name of his *Atlantic Privateer* to such an unappealing one as *Portatan* certainly is: "Every man has his price."

The portly Kuttel (Padda translates into "bullfrog" in Afrikaans) is a determined man taking his racing seriously, and today with *UBS* 250 miles ahead he is in a state of depression. Earlier we overheard him in conversation with his wife in Cape Town discussing domestic affairs, and for a man with the reputation of running an inordinately tight budget, he easily succumbed to the lady's request for a few thousand Rands worth of new furniture—obviously a man with more pressing things on his mind.

The next day a strong trade wind filled, and we finished the 24-hour run with a 301-mile day, to date *Drum*'s best. This was our first real downwind blast and gave us a good chance to sort out the heavy running gear for the Southern Ocean. In the middle of the night, we blew the 2.2-ounce spinnaker to smithereens, and in spite of a few raised eyebrows *Drum* owner Michael Berrow, who's proved to be one helluva shipmate on a ship that possesses no amenities whatsoever for owner comfort, took his owner's cue and without the slightest hesitation told us, "Don't worry about the money."

Surfing to 20 knots with the storm chute has been a great morale booster for us. With the gear coming under new loads, in spite of some new groans, pings and creaks, everything seems to be up to spec and the boat relatively easy to handle. The first time we cracked 15 knots, the watch hooted and hollered, but quickly settled into the old routine of strolling around on deck balancing coffee cups while the helmsman casually lit a cigarette while careening down the face of a wave. The ambience on board was such that any man would quickly be confident he was sailing with a crack, ocean-going crew that possessed a depth of knowledge from the hundreds of thousands of miles collectively sailed.

Further south the sailing becomes very pleasant, requiring little or no clothing even at night, and although nudity with 17 men on board is handled in different ways by those in different boats, we soon became accustomed to seeing the complete watch stark naked up forward for the headsail changes.

This was not only convenient, but also by doctor's orders. With the rising water temperatures, bathing on deck with the canvas bucket is a daily exercise, unlike farther north where a case could be made for lack of hygiene on board causing an overabundance of stomach infections and pimply posteriors. Anyone who has gone offshore knows the symptoms. Philthy, one of the worst afflicted, has been under Dr. Roger's direct, but (and I can't blame him) unenthusiastic supervision requiring regular washing, plenty of ultraviolet and clean underwear washed in fresh water.

A makeshift clothsline between the radar bracket and the antenna pole bearing a row of men's underwear dangling unaesthetically above the helmsman's head was a regular feature on *Drum* in the tropics.

Typically, *UBS Switzerland*, the one-time fleet leader, had stopped in the doldrums, and we had compressed up to within 50 miles of her by October 13th. At 6 degrees north we had started to slow up ourselves, and the race was practically restarted with the six Maxis choosing east or west options in hopes of breaking through the variable winds first.

For reasons of safety as well as publicity, accurate position reporting and inter-yacht communications were mandatory for the race, but it is no secret that on any given occasion, when you can get away with it, it is a great advantage tactically to conceal your position while knowing where the others are. To prevent a situation that in previous Whitbread Races allowed a competitor almost any excuse for not reporting, and which became a true bone of contention, the race committee supplied each yacht with an Argos transceiver. This little plastic dome attached to the transom was a sealed, battery-powered unit that uses the weather-satellite system to transmit exact positions back to the Argos center in Toulouse, France, which the committee made public twice a day. In addition, from a roster, the "duty yacht" for the day had to attempt to make contact with the fleet on the ship-to-ship frequencies and then via any coast radio station call the race committee to give the daily report. With the main requirement being fulfilled by the Argos, the committee felt that the duty-yacht concept, although strictly enforced, would not necessarily burden anyone as your turn only came up once a week.

Not so for the likes of New Zealand skipper Digby Taylor onboard *NZI*. This outsized Farr-designed fractional rigger was the antithesis of the *Lion New Zealand* campaign as Digby's was a home-built, do-it-yourself effort in the finest Kiwi tradition. *NZI* was bailed out financially by a consortium of farmers down country, and if the project didn't appear downright shaky at times it certainly was (if I may use the word) agricultural. By contrast *Lion* was heavy, conservative and backed by Auckland city money and on appearance very well organized indeed.

This private contest that would polarize the New Zealand population was already in evidence as the fleet broke through the doldrums and out into the southeast trades. For a variety of reasons involving generator problems, insufficient fuel, a radio malfunction and an Argos that mysteriously failed as well, Digby had managed to hide his position from the rest of us for the last two weeks. Only after we lodged a formal protest with the committee did he surface—just over the horizon from his arch rival *Lion* and well to the west for the long beat down the South Atlantic against the trades.

"Honey, this race is so close, it's just like racing around the cans back home." "Then why," she sarcastically replied, "did you have to sail around the world to do an around-the-cans race?"

On October 19th in a fresh beat we broke our first wire-genoa sheet. We exchanged the 11mm wire standard for a 20mm unidirectional polyester sheet and hoped that this would permit some give in the system. With Kevlar sails, wire halyards and wire sheets there is not much chance for the gear to absorb the shock loadings, and in the short seas the effect was showing up in the rig. The head was falling off a bit in a blow and the lee rigging, always on the slack side, seemed to be getting looser.

Watch leader Magnus Olsson, a Swede of many talents, not least of them being the ability to keep a sense of good humor in the most difficult of circumstances, is responsible for the mast and rigging. Last night, he went aloft 80' to retune the "D4" shroud. Today he had to take up one and a half turns on the mainspans. Magnus had the disquieting experience of sailing by the upturned hull of *Drum* (the boat he was about to join after the Fastnet) shortly after the capsize, and needless to say he wasn't smiling then. Contemplating the fatigue in the mast is no less of a *bête noire*.

The other night when the sea came up I bumped heads with our photographer, Rick Tomlinson, in the dark of the forepeak; both of us were furtively listening for odd noises in the structure and sticking our fingers in between the carbon-fiber ring frames and the mast step, a not too scientific method for monitoring what we had been told was an "acceptable" amount of movement. Rick is a soft-spoken, almost retiring man who, as an amateur boatbuilder, helped build the hull when it was *Colt Cars*. I thought to myself, does he know something I don't?

For the others, perhaps less attuned to these potential problems, life on board is a routine of eating, sleeping and watch-keeping at 25 degrees of heel. Micky Olsson, our engineer, and Janne Gustafsson, one of the best point men in the business, are two of a kind: uncomplaining, blond-haired, highly energized Swedes—the breed of men that made the Scandinavian tall ships what they were. Micky uncomplainingly accepted the "dunce cap" he was given for trimming the down puller on the genoa sheet for a solid three hours—a menial task if there ever was one.

A worsening hernia condition found me in poor spirits in the rugged conditions. The inability to heave sails around with much facility left me in the awkward position of an almost total dictatorship. As skipper, I had decided from the beginning to stand a watch and was expected to do my share of the work. It is a fact of life that running a Maxi boat and trying to win a popularity contest are not at all compatible, and I think in these hard times of trying to push the boat and crew, I didn't come off very well. But as the Arab proverb has it, "The camel driver has his thoughts, the camel, he has his."

At least I didn't have to put up with what skipper Peter Blake on *Lion* was expected to do. Spending more and more time in shoreside communications has become a big part of sponsorship in yacht racing, and the *Lion* project,

possibly the most complicated promotional exercise of the race, seemed to be taking it to extremes. While monitoring Portishead Radio one morning I overheard Blake's New Zealand shore contact giving him a short list of 10 or 12 numbers to call back home in a scheme described by Kiwi Chris Barker that, for a $1,000 NZ subscription, the "bloke" in New Zealand would get a *Lion* half model, various other tokens of appreciation, and a personal radio-telephone call from Peter. I must admit it was amusing listening to Blake explain himself as they were not well placed at that stage of the race.

Simon Gundry, the stalwart aide-de-camp from Blake's *Ceramco* days, also placed a call to his wife back home, and with unguarded enthusiasm told her, "Honey, this race is so close, it's just like racing around the cans back home." "Then why," she sarcastically replied, "did you have to sail halfway around the world to do an around-the-cans race?"

On October 24th the wind had eased, and in almost a dead calm the on watch lined the leeward rail, each with his own thoughts while the light No. 1 genoa lazily slatted in the ocean swell.

The sun was setting for the 27th time on this passage. Phil Wade tried to inspire the guys with things to come in South Africa, but was immediately mocked by Micky. Said Phil, "Imagine a white sandy beach, steaks on the grill" ("freeze-dried chili," says Micky) "a bottle of wine," ("bottle of backwash and a dirty cup") "and a beautiful woman" ("a soggy Playboy.").

On the second leg once again, we just made the start in a situation that could only get better. We left the Cape Town docks after having sailed only 10 miles in sea trials in a light westerly. (I actually had to motor in reverse to get the spinnakers to fill.) Dockside pundits shook their heads in disbelief while everyone who had anything to do with *Drum* no doubt had their fingers crossed.

The Southern Ocean literally begins off Cape Town and doesn't end until the North Cape of New Zealand some 7000 miles away. I justified the situation by reckoning the worse case would be a retirement in Perth or Hobart if the repair went wrong. At best we would make it in one piece and, frankly, most of us were not too concerned with the race results.

"Mama," said Phil Holland in a call to New Zealand, "I've got some good news and some bad news for you. The good news is I'm coming home; the bad news is I'm coming on *Drum*."

Due to join us for the second leg, Phil as well as my old mate Brian "Mugsy" Hancock had to think long and hard before committing themselves. Our nucleus of 12 was also rounded out at the last minute by the additions of local yachtsman and boatbuilder (who helped repair *Drum*) J.J. Provoyeur as well as Mugsy's brother "Topher."

While Leg II, from Cape Town to Auckland, is billed as a downhill slide, as seen in the opposite photo, this time it showed more heavy-weather reaching, as seen at left. The start was delayed one month, and for the Whitbread crews what a difference a month made. Beam seas find a Maxi boat a much bigger target than do following seas. It was a cold, wet and almost endless port-tack reach around a South Indian Ocean high.

J.J., however, was not so amused. He asked me one
fine, miserable day what motivates people to do this type of thing
when we are obviously not having a "good time."

Starting the race one month later than we did four years ago was thought to blame for the fact we had little of the expected heavy downwind conditions that all had hoped for. Instead, the majority of our passage to New Zealand was a port-tack reach skirting the South Indian Ocean high.

The conditions in what I described as "reaching around the high" may not sound bad, but were, in a word, miserable. Changing headsails and reefing in the wintry conditions was no fun, what with being burdened by layers of thermals, polar gear and heavy foul-weather suits—the pockets of which were well-weighted with harnesses, flares, strobe lights and other safety paraphernalia. If you were so unlucky as to fall overboard down there, this rig, ballasted by heavy, leather-lined seaboots, was sure to send you to the bottom in a jiffy—no worse a fate than struggling in 40-degree water.

Conditions below were equally appalling with an interior filled to the overhead in places by spare running sails and gear we would never use, the clothing and sleeping bags damp from the condensation and a leaky companionway hatch (the dodger being carried away almost daily by the seas coming aboard). It rained continually on a galley that for a variety of reasons was turning out substandard food. In spite of these hardships, most of the crew found ample time to adorn the head bulkhead with graffiti, an indication that not all humor was lost. These not too subtle, unpublishable messages usually castigated the skipper for leading the crew to the Southern Ocean, and themselves for being so stupid as to follow.

J.J., however, was not so amused, possibly not expecting this kind of treatment from man and the elements. He asked me one fine, miserable day, what motivates people to do this type of thing when we are obviously not having a "good time." Granted, he had had it rough, cutting his hand early in the leg he had received three stitches. Later he was below for a few days with a stomach infection only to surface and have the both of us (probably while discussing the definition of a "good time") washed out of the cockpit down to the leeward rail by one of those silent waves that just lap up over the topside. Score for that one: cracked ribs for me, five stitches in J.J.'s forehead. I can easily understand J.J.'s somewhat hard opinion of us at times.

After a punishing test, the good news was that *Drum* was holding together. Even the fact that the other Maxis had shown they could easily take 20 miles a day out of *Lion* and ourselves in reaching and heavy-running conditions, did not detract from the joy of just arriving in New Zealand. *Atlantic Privateer* (which had lost its Portatan sponsorship in Cape Town) and *NZI* had virtually match-raced from mid-ocean right to the finish with *Privateer* only seven minutes ahead of her hometown rival. That was the big story of Leg II.

Côte d'Or had become the media's whipping boy, finishing sixth in the Maxi division with more delamination up forward, a broken quadrant and a damaged masthead. The heat was off us as we finished without incident on Jan. 3, 1986, four hours ahead of *Lion* for an added bonus.

Pale and a bit flabby, pop-star Simon arrived in town after finishing a demanding recording session up in the northern-hemisphere winter. The press corps followed his every move hoping he would step out of line, and the little girls would devotely perch on the quayside, day after day, waiting for him to make an appearance. Down below, the *Drum* crew, suntanned and hard-bodied, worked quietly away on the gear. If invited on board, these fans would drop off the dock onto the deck like lemmings to see "where Simon slept."

Well-rested and for the first time race-ready, *Drum*'s crew was looking forward to Leg III after six weeks ashore. Even the kids on the dock noticed it. "Smile!" they said, as I refused to sign any more autographs. "Getting to be a pain in the butt," says Philthy, and even Simon seems to have had a gutful of attention. After all, this was an exercise designed to "get away from it all." Half-hearted waves and smug smiles were all he could muster.

Auckland and its environs is without qualification the yachtsman's paradise, with large tracts of protected water for racing and coastal cruising. February 15th left no one in doubt that sailing is also the national pastime as the media and 300,000 spectators watched the start. Above were 22 helicopters and 25 aircraft carrying the world's press. For those who couldn't be there, there was also live television coverage.

After a beautiful day's sail through the Hauraki Gulf past lush islands and headlands, the fleet of 15 reached out into the Pacific on the backside of another anticyclone that was ridging well to the south. The Cape Horn of every sailor's dreams was 4000 miles away, and with most of the leg sailed below the 50th parallel, we were bound to encounter some heavy weather along the way.

In spite of the mild conditions, disaster struck for *NZI* only three days out when a swage fitting on one of her jumper shrouds pulled out, and the rig went over the side. Motoring back to the isolated Chatham Islands off the New Zealand coast they attempted to fly in their spare mast so as to make it in time for the start of Leg IV in Uruguay. They never did make it, but they were then out of the running anyway. One could only speculate about the reaction to this news aboard *Lion*, and it was no surprise that one of the older members of her crew confided to me later that the ebullience of some of the younger guys was, at the time, "sickening."

"Smile!" they said, as I refused to sign any more
autographs. "Getting to be a pain in the butt," says Philthy, and even
Simon seems to have had a gutful of attention.

Above is rock star Simon le Bon, steering *Drum* on the fourth leg of the Whitbread. After the race, le Bon commented that this was one of the greatest experiences of his life.

With *Privateer* well to the south and *Lion* opting for an extreme northerly track, we felt confident taking a conservative course up the middle with *UBS* and *Côte d'Or*. Positioning yourself close to, but on the northern side of the traveling lows was all-important, but the fact was that the farther south you went, the less miles you had to sail along the great circle.

With the crew mentally fresh, the ambience on board was gratifying for those of us who had stuck it out through the hard times. Under the watchful eye of owner Paul Berrow, a gastronome who had no intention of roughing it, Richard's galley also improved immensely. Although using a superior freeze-dried food from Alliance of New Zealand, it was freeze-dried none-the-less as I described in my log one evening: "A tasty meal, the 'Fish Supreme' swimming in the creamy mash sprinkled liberally with a topping of peas and corn; an homogenous mixture that would have done credit to the best of old people's homes where eating usually requires no chewing and a fast, clear passage through furred-up plumbing."

On February 22nd near 55 degrees south, the Maxis sailed into iceberg country in foggy conditions, still under the influence of a northerly airstream over the cold sea. *Privateer* reported two icebergs on radar and a few growlers close aboard. *Lion* sighted a "large tabular berg" about 300 meters long. And there we were, right in the middle.

The reaction to this news on *Drum* was varied and revealing. Chuck Gates, old sailing friend from Chicago and on just for Leg III, was delighted by the prospect of bergs, while others professed reserved enthusiasm. Traveling at speed in the fog lent a certain credibility to one man's abject fear who asked me hopefully: "If we hit a growler, surely it will bounce off?" "No," I assured him calmly, "we would most likely hole the bow and sink in a matter of seconds." While we kept a constant watch by the shrouds in the few hours of darkness I am sad to say we only saw seven bergs on the radar screen and none visually.

For the first time in 10 days, a good westerly blow had filled in on the morning of the 25th, and the crew looked forward with confidence to being able to push her hard. We had the boat rigged for two pole jibes and a remote trip system for the spinnaker guy should a quick takedown be necessary. With pole guys, down-and-out pullers, preventers, trip lines and all the usual rigging, all 19 winches were busy.

One of the great attractions of ocean racing is the unexpected, and given the dynamic conditions in the Southern Ocean, when you think you are well-prepared, things can very quickly go wrong. In the first light at the 0300 watch change *Drum* started to become unstable in 30 knots of true wind with the full-size 2.2-ounce spinnaker. "Bang!" went the tack shackle as we tripped it out, and one watch gathered the spinnaker under the boom

bove is co-owner
Mike Berrow. After seeing
the 2.2-ounce spinnaker
explode, his comment—
"Don't worry about
money"—endeared him to
the crew. Below, *Drum*
crewmen Richard Freeman
and Phil "Philthy" Barrett
pack the .75-ounce
spinnaker. In the sunset

photo to the right, *Drum* is
two days from Cape Horn.
On the opposite page, a
crewmember splices a
Kevlar spinnaker sheet. After
her early troubles, *Drum*, a
Ron Holland design, stood
up tall to the Whitbread test.
The Holland boats, however,
like *Drum* and *Lion New
Zealand*, could not sail with
the much lighter fractional-
rigged Bruce Farr Maxi,
UBS Switzerland.

"If we hit a growler, surely it will bounce off?"
"No," I assured him calmly, "we would most likely hole
to bow and sink in a matter of seconds."

Drum sails home. The boat finished third in class; the winner in the Maxi class was *UBS Switzerland*. The boat, sailed by Pierre Fehlmann, set a new Whitbread record of 117 days, 14 hours. The overall winner of 1985-86 Whitbread was *L'Esprit D'Equipe*. The 58´ French boat posted a corrected time of 111 days, 23 hours.

while the other watch methodically rerigged for the 90 percent flanker. After a quick check of the running gear for chafe we rehoisted, and it was drawing hard—ten minutes hoist to hoist.

It was a cold morning—the air temperature at around 40 degrees—and we were glad to get below for some sleep, secure in the knowledge that the right sail was up. In what must have been no longer than five minutes, *Drum* started to roll dangerously to weather, and although the helmsman recovered from the first, the second oscillation of the spinnaker and maybe one unlucky wave laid *Drum* right on her beam ends pinned well and truly by a full spinnaker kissing the water and a fully backed mainsail. For the second time since Cape Town we had succeeded in jibing her, "all standing." This is decidedly a black mark in any helmsman's book, and you could almost hear the sigh of relief from the only other man who had the distinction of performing this most unpopular of feats on Leg II, with equally disastrous results.

No one down below was left in doubt as to what had happened. Groggy, indignant heads popped out from behind the curtained bunk modules only to be peppered by paperbacks, magazines and all manner of things carelessly stowed. Simon le Bon, in the middle of an SSB conversation with his secretary in London, was upended in the swiveling chair as he calmly told her, "We seem to have a bit of a problem on deck; have to go now." Given the English habit of understatement, we could only guess her reaction.

Making the aft cockpit with some difficulty, I crouched cowardly in its bottom not knowing what would give way first. Down to leeward Philthy was up to his chest in the gentle pool of water in the lee of the upturned deck trying to fire off the tack shackle, but the pole end, now a good 10´ underwater, was probably fouled. The main boom preventers were also jammed and, thinking quickly, Mario let the spinnaker halyard fly to relieve the main load.

Simon le Bon, in the middle of an SSB conversation with his secretary in London, was upended as he calmly told her, "We seem to have a bit of a problem on deck; have to go now."

As the main boom was finally eased amidships, and *Drum* righted, the chute was immediately snatched up out of the water and blown into the aft rigging, quickly taking out the fax antenna and the aft spotlight before self-destructing. In addition to this just dessert we had lost one spinnaker guy, chafed one sheet and broken the topping lift and block aloft. It took all 18 of us to manhandle the flanker up and over the lifelines. I thought we had gotten off easily until I instinctively checked our feathering propeller through the inspection window only to find what was obviously the bright yellow spinnaker turtle streaming merrily like a lure from the opened blade of the prop. A quick check at the rudder window confirmed it was well over 20' long, disappearing astern out of view.

Aware of the speed loss, it was without hesitation that I summoned Micky, our Swedish Navy diver, to prepare the dive gear. Although the water temperature was a bracing 38 degrees, he seemed to take the news well enough, but I suspect he silently regretted all those stories he had told us about dives in the Baltic in midwinter.

Tethered by a line from a winch passed through a snatchblock on the rail and then to his harness, Micky heroically jumped over the side as we lay a-hull in the Southern Ocean waves. He was down for no longer than a few seconds before the roll of the boat knocked his mask and mouthpiece off and shunted him to the other side of the hull aft. His tether, once his lifeline, was now pinning him up under the stern counter, and there was no going back the way he came. Streaming him aft with plenty of slack he had taken a mouthful of water and was clearly losing it. Anxious seconds went by until the tail of the mainsheet was thrown to him and with barely enough strength left to hang on, we landed him like a fish up on the transom. Eager hands passed him below where he soon recovered, but no one had to be reminded we had almost lost a man.

Luckily his efforts were not wasted as he had managed to unwind most of the fouled spinnaker turtle. Phil Wade successfully grappled up the turtle with the small Fisherman anchor and with winch power it pulled clear. After two hours of chaos, we were again up and running with the storm chute, having lost an estimated 16 miles. This sobering exercise was only partially alleviated when Peter Blake reported similar carnage on *Lion*, having lost three chutes in an interesting sequence of rigging failures as well as coming close to losing a man aloft. His tally: 30 miles lost.

Only a day after our last close scrape, the wind had eased and the skies had cleared. Englishman Patrick Banfield was on the wheel as I broke one of my own rules and casually chatted with him. Patrick doesn't panic easily, but the freak wave that caught us both unaware (neither of us was clipped in) gave him uncharacteristic concern because it was immediately obvious that if he didn't hold her straight we could likely capsize in the trough—

that is, if we didn't pitchpole. I must confess I closed my eyes as I gripped the mainsheet pedestal and didn't come to my senses until I floated out of the cockpit, the boat then safely submerged in the backside of the wave. After a few of these experiences, the message on the head wall was clear; "_____ this _____, guys, let's go home."

It was almost a relief then when the wind swung back into the north as we reached around Cape Horn on March 14th. Enough has been written by better men than I about this celebrated piece of land. Leaving some of the mystery intact for the reader who might be inclined to venture in high southern latitudes, it's sufficient to say that for me Cape Horn signaled an end to the Whitbread adventure as well as a great personal milestone.

UBS was well ahead, already beating up the Atlantic to Uruguay almost 1000 miles away, as we rounded into sheltered waters only a handful of miles behind *Côte d'Or* and *Privateer*. *Lion* was safely 200 miles astern, and it was here we realized it was conceivable that after all of our problems we had a shot at second overall. After the rugged tactical beat up the Argentine shore we beat *Lion* by 24 hours and nipped the other two to come in second on Leg III—a minor victory for all of us, especially for Simon le Bon, who admittedly stepped ashore a new man.

The last leg back to England was a tough test of wills between *Lion* and ourselves for second overall. After a seven-day beat side by side with her, we broke free just south of the Equator in hopes of getting a better slant around the Azores high, the last obstacle of the course.

In mid-Atlantic we listened to reports of the bombing of Libya, and soon after we learned about the nuclear-dust cloud from Chernobyl that was threatening northern Europe. But like the sailors in Nevil Shute's *On the Beach*, the boys were ready to go home regardless. We ran up the Channel five hours ahead of *Lion*, thirteen short of a second place. *UBS* had won the Whitbread by a landslide.

The determined looks on the crew's faces as they struggled through those last sail changes—pulling, heaving, slipping and sometimes being carried along by the bale of unruly Kevlar—seemed to epitomize what it takes to go the distance in this race.

In our easy world, "giving up" in the hard times may not be as significant as it used to be. But the *Drum* crew has the reward, if not in victory, then in the personal satisfaction that they fought through and persevered, at least in the world of ocean racing—the toughest project going.

EDITOR'S NOTE: SKIP NOVAK'S WHITBREAD BOOK WILL BE PUBLISHED BY W.W. NORTON IN THE LATE SUMMER OF 1987.

A boyhood fascination with the North Atlantic fishing fleet has served marine artist Tom Hoyne well. He imagines events that might have occurred, scenes he would like to have seen, or just paintings he would like to do, and then backs them up with impeccable historical research. The activities may be routine: men furling sails; or dramatic: men against the sea. But Hoyne's work is always a sound marriage of imagination and historical realism.

In this painting, "Parting the Crest," *Helen G. Wells*, out of Gloucester, and *Evelyn M. Thompson*, a knockabout built in 1908, close in on a coasting schooner on their way to the fishing grounds. While the event is ordinary, the onboard perspective and accuracy of detail make for a compelling image.

D eep blue-greens and strong lighting characterize Tom Hoyne's paintings of the great North Atlantic fishing fleet that sailed out of Gloucester for nearly a century. Each is a visual reconstruction of a particular vessel and its encounter with the elements and the hazardous routine that fishermen faced on every trip. Tom takes us close in, and sometimes aboard, to view life as it was on the banks. Gloucester and the surrounding towns prospered from the 1870s until well into this century, as hundreds of schooners were built and outfitted for the banks. Most came from yards in Essex, MA, with the Story yard accounting for more than half of all the schooners that sailed from Cape Ann. Construction peaked just after the turn of the century, then fewer ships were built each year as the fleet gradually declined. During the 1930s Tom Hoyne spent summers with his grandmother in Ogunquit, Maine. By this time, the Gloucester fleet was well into its decline, but some of the ships still worked the coast nearby. "I was fascinated by them beyond all reason," Tom recalls. "I began to see the beauty and life which were connected with the fishing fleet, particularly the men and vessels of Gloucester." Tom knew he would not be able to share in this life and began to think about recreating scenes of these great vessels and their work.

DRAMA

ON THE BANKS

—THE MARINE PAINTINGS OF THOMAS HOYNE

BY GEORGE P. ROTH

Hoyne's oil-on-panel painting "Five to Port" shows the men of the Gloucester-built sloop Vesta doing a hard day's work in the North Atlantic fishery. The ships and men of Gloucester appear with frequency in Hoyne's work, and that great Massachusetts fishing port occupies a special place in his heart. Hoyne met famous marine artist Gordon Grant in his Gloucester studio, and while visiting Gloucester in 1938 he saw the movie "Captains Courageous." The two events eventually set the impressionable young man on his life's course. Vesta was built in 1899 in Gloucester by Tom Irving and the Bishop brothers. She was 52′ overall and typically fished with from four to eight men. Here Vesta's crew is fishing with a single dory, but they also set trawls and did handlining.

He spent much of his time in Ogunquit and back home in Winnetka, Illinois, drawing pictures of sailing ships. He built models and collected books and clippings, beginning a research library that now includes information on more than 5000 vessels. He collected pictures of paintings by Gordon Grant, Charles Robert Patterson, Anton Otto Fischer and other artists. From these he began to learn how his visions of great days of fishing the banks could be made into paintings of his own.

A friend of Tom's grandmother arranged for him to meet Gordon Grant and visit Grant's Gloucester studio. This meeting had a strong influence on Tom's decision to pursue a career in maritime art. The decision was reinforced when Tom saw the new film "Captains Courageous" in Gloucester in 1938, but was tempered a few years later in the Pacific during long watches as gunnery officer aboard LST-48. "I became nervous about the art business as a career and decided instead to study architecture," Tom recalls.

His apprehension about an art career proved groundless. The architectural schools were full when he returned home, so he took a job as an apprentice in an art studio while waiting to resume his studies. He was successful from the start despite a formal art education limited to art classes while in high school. He opened his own studio soon after and became one of Chicago's top illustrators.

Tom's commercial work included commissions from International Harvester, United Air Lines, Standard Oil, Phillips Petroleum and other multinational corporations. Several paintings for foreign clients of Harza Engineering were later used on postage stamps. Tom had the honor of meeting 16 American winners for the Nobel Prize for Science when he was commissioned to paint portraits of them. But he retained his interest in maritime art while accepting these commercial commissions, and maritime subjects gradually became more dominant in his work. He has pursued maritime art exclusively since the 1970s.

The essence of Tom's paintings is the interrelationship of the men and the ships of the Gloucester fleet. What he could not share, he now recreates through imagination, skill and careful research. The activities in Tom's paintings are real. "I conjure up ideas of paintings I would like to make, scenes that I'd like to see, events that I would like to witness," he says. The activities may be routine work such as furling a sail or putting dories over, or they may involve incidents of peril that men and vessels faced on the fishing grounds.

Tom imagines what action would be taking place on board, what ships would be in the background, what coastline might be evident, what manner of seas would be running. He begins

with several small sketches to solidify an idea and explore different compositional schemes. When he has one or more sketches that satisfy him, he goes back to his research materials to verify details of the scene.

Tom's research materials include the books, photographs, ship's plans and also a collection of large-scale ship models built by Erik A.R. Ronnberg, Jr. Erik is an artist, author, historian and model builder who learned some of his ship-modeling skills from his father, who worked as a ship rigger on schooners in the

Gloucester fleet. Ronnberg draws on the experience and memory of men who built and sailed these schooners to insure accuracy.

The models are big and well-detailed. The blocks run, the windlasses work and the sails and spars can be raised and set with the running rigging. The deck layout and equipment are correct for each vessel at a specific time in its history and for a particular type of fishing. The accuracy of these models is essential to Tom's work. He often places them in sand and sets up the gaffs and booms as they would be under

sail. By doing this, Tom is able to draw the lines and attitude of a vessel working in heavy seas with precision.

Erik Ronnberg is one of several men having firsthand knowledge of the Gloucester fleet with whom Tom developed friendships over the years. Gordon Thomas was another. The son of Captain Jeff Thomas, Gordon grew up playing on the decks and in the rigging of his father's schooners, but he was not allowed to become a fisherman. *Adventure*, Captain Jeff's last schooner and one of three surviving Gloucester

schooners, was named by Gordon and christened by his sister Natalie. Gordon's ties with the fleet were strong, and he made it his life's work to keep the memory of the men and ships of Gloucester alive.

Two other friends who have provided invaluable assistance to Tom are Dana Story and Charlie Sayle. Arthur Dana Story launched 425 ships from his Essex yard between 1880 and 1932. Dana Story continued the tradition established by his father and ran the Story yard until it was sold in 1985. He has compiled information

Hoyne's painting "On the Station," on the opposite page, shows immigrant fishermen at the Boston lightship around 1915. The ship was located six miles east of the Boston Light. Irish and Italian fishermen used their disparagingly called "Paddy boats" for inshore fishing. This " fleet of what were known as "mosquito craft" was largely motorized by 1910. On this page is Hoyne's "Off to the Set." In the 30´ x 24´ oil-on-canvas painting, the dory crew has just finished its "mug-up" and is casting off to under-run the trawl and take the fish.

on 1000 wooden ships launched from Essex yards during the 107-year period. Charlie Sayle, of Nantucket, began fishing out of Gloucester in 1926 at the age of 17. He took pictures, collected the photographs of others, recorded information about ships and the men who sailed them, and he has near-total recall of the details of 50 years at sea. He is recognized as a leading historian and is frequently called on to assist museums and nautical associations. He and Tom consult with each other regularly.

Once Tom is satisfied that his information is correct, he enlarges his compositional sketch to a full-size drawing from which the final painting will be done. This drawing is a critical step in the process Tom uses to develop an idea into a painting. He applies the results of his research here, drawing in all of the details carefully. These full-size drawings are often more detailed than the paintings that are done from them. He takes special care with the water at this stage and sometimes does additional detail drawings of wakes and wave formations. Tom usually does a small color sketch at this time, too, to develop color arrangement. After all that, the painting is begun. And after hard work, hard concentration and certainly some magic, the finished painting is titled and a brief synopsis of the story it tells is written.

Tom Hoyne's paintings have become a standard of excellence in the world of maritime art—

for their accuracy, for their drama, for their wonderful detail—and they have been in demand since Hoyne first began creating them.

Joe DeMers was an artist and print publisher who ran a gallery on Hilton Head Island in South Carolina. He was instrumental in bringing Tom Hoyne's work to the public during the 1970s. He set up a show for Tom at Hilton Head and began publishing limited-edition prints of his paintings. Tom has exhibited regularly throughout the country since. His prints are currently being published by Mystic Maritime Graphics at the Mystic Seaport Museum Stores. His latest print, released last spring, is of the schooner *America* approaching LeHavre in 1851 before her race against the British.

Tom is a fellow of the American Society of Marine Artists, an honor bestowed by the artist members of that society. He received the Rudolph J. Schaefer Award for "Morning Watch" during the 1983 Mystic International exhibition at the Mystic Maritime Gallery. Several of his paintings are in museum collections; many others are part of private and corporate collections.

Through his vision and the mastery of his medium, Tom is providing a new view of life in the Gloucester fleet. Many of the scenes he paints of incidents and activities on the banks have been seen only once before—by the men who lived them.

Hoyne's painting "Running By," seen across the newly built *Shepherd King* passing the schooner *Norumbega*, trailing a Seine boat. To the left is Hoyne's 32´ x 26´ oil-on-canvas painting "Morning Breakout," which shows the 114´ *Arethusa* and the steam tug *Nellie*. *Nellie* has just helped *Arethusa* through slush ice in the Tarr and Wonson Paint factory, a Gloucester landmark at the entrance of the inner harbor.

S·E·A·S·O·N·S

GREETINGS
·FROM CARL AND MARGARET VILAS·

BY deLANCEY FUNSTEN

n an era of fast-paced, high-tech living, some people still prefer slow, traditional methods. For 52 years Carl and Margaret Vilas have delighted their friends and relatives at Christmastime by sending cards they designed and produced themselves. In addition to being lovely, the cards are thoroughly nautical. The Vilases have chosen their chief preoccupation—sailing—as their theme. The painstakingly made cards reflect more than half a century of Carl and Margaret's sailing adventures; they also reflect more effort given to holiday greetings than dashing out to the Hallmark shop for a mass-produced cliché. The Vilases sent their first cards in 1934, two years after their marriage and twelve years before they bought the historic yacht *Direction*. The decision to create Christmas cards nicely combined their interests and abilities. Charles Harrison Vilas II worked in the printing industry as a pressman, printing-ink technician and salesman. He became the associate editor of the Cruising Club of America's Cruising Club News in 1962 and eventually its editor, a position he still holds at age 80. Margaret Van Pelt Vilas graduated Phi Beta Kappa from Vassar, then earned a bachelors degree in Architecture from Columbia, a masters in Architecture from MIT and the honor of being a life member of the American Water Color Society.

The selection of cards shown on these pages represents less than a quarter of the total number of Christmas cards designed and produced by Carl and Margaret Vilas since 1934. Carl masterminded the print run after Margaret drew or painted each year's design. These are some of the Vilas's particular favorites. These eleven cards demonstrate the range of printing achieved—from one- to five-color. They celebrate the Christmas season with a nautical emphasis that makes them especially appropriate for this issue. The historic cutter *Direction*, owned by the Vilases for 39 years, was the subject of most of their cards. *Direction* was the vehicle for Rockwell Kent's voyage to Greenland in 1929, described in his book *N by E*.

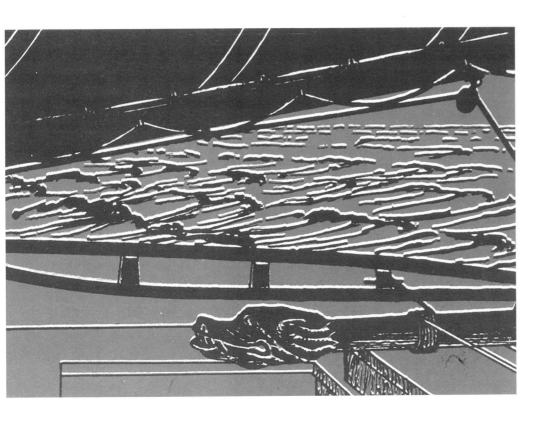

When first married the couple lived in New York City; after their daughter Diana's birth they moved to Johnson's Point in Branford, Connecticut. Their summers have usually been spent cruising Canadian waters, either Newfoundland or Nova Scotia. Their involvement with the cutter *Direction* was written up in Nautical Quarterly 13. Carl says he could not even begin to estimate how many miles were sailed during their 39 years of ownership.

The first Vilas card was cut on a linoleum block and sliced like a pie. Each slice was inked separately with a different color and then fitted with the others on press. In this way a variety of four-color cards were made, with the Christmas message standing out in block letters against spinnaker-like rays of color. The design and printing process grew progressively more sophisticated over the years. The Vilases began printing on a Potter hand proof press at Carl's office in New York City. They started experimenting with lithography in 1940 after Carl brought home a hundred-year-old stone press similar to that used by Currier & Ives. As circulation increased, this method became too slow and cumbersome, and they switched to a precision Vandercook proof press that used zinc engravings, later to a similar press and ultimately to silk screen.

Margaret drew or painted the image to be printed, finding inspiration in any number of sources. Her designs include a dramatic scene of their boat fleeing a bank of fog, a view of *Direction* nestled in a rocky cove and a close-up of her dragon's-head tiller illuminated by the binnacle light. Whatever the decision, Margaret would work up the idea into a series of thumbnail sketches, often as polished as the final product. From this stage she would carefully transfer the outline to a black-and-white sketch to use as a separation key and make single-color proofs to determine how it would all work together. Carl was expert at creating original ink formulas to match the

MERRY CHRISTMAS

shades his wife selected; his printing schemes varied between one- and five-color printing, depending on the design's complexity.

Carl has been an avid sailor as long as he can remember. His catboat *Nancy Lee* appeared in a story Carl wrote for Yachting magazine in 1929. This was the year that the cutter *Direction* was built in Nyack, a vital event for the Vilas family. *Direction* was conceived in a Bronx apartment by a draftsman dreaming of the South Seas. Having no yacht-design training, M. H. Miner took his lines directly from Colin Archer's double-ended Norwegian rescue boat, the famous 47´ *redningskoite*, and scaled them down to 33´. That summer Arthur S. Allen Jr., Lucian Cary Jr. and Rockwell Kent sailed her north by east from Battle Harbour, Labrador, to Godthaab, Greenland, only to be shipwrecked on the Greenland coast just short of their goal. The adventure was lyrically described in Kent's book *N by E*, accompanied by his stark and powerful drawings, and the wrecked *Direction* remained in Greenland where she was eventually repaired.

As a childhood friend of Arthur Allen and lifelong admirer of Rockwell Kent, Carl Vilas was impressed with *Direction*'s glorious past. He bought her sight unseen when the opportunity arose in 1946. From that season on, and until 1983, when she was donated to the Patriot's Point Museum in Charleston, S.C., cruising aboard *Direction* was a significant part of Carl and Margaret's lives. It would be difficult to imagine how anyone could appreciate the historic little ship more than this family. They have proven their love with their devoted care for her, their decades of ambitious cruising and the annual tribute of having her as the subject of their charming Christmas cards.

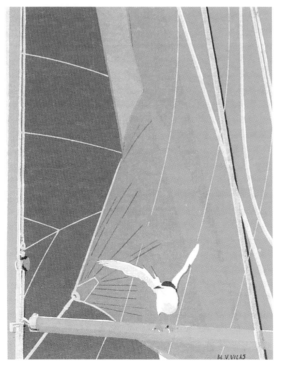

Phil Wade carries the world around with him as he sails the globe on yacht deliveries and occasional cruises and races. After 15 years of distance-cruising experience, a lot of the world is in his head—from the intricacies of a harbor entrance on some out-of-the-way coast to what kinds of free meals might be fished up from particular South-Pacific lagoons. And a lot of the world is in the nautically oriented stamp collection he's been putting together during those years as souvenirs of voyages and accessories of voyaging dreams. On the following few pages we are pleased to present a selection of Phil Wade's exotic stamps and exotic sailing experiences.

PHIL WADE

BY SKIP NOVAK

—COLLECTOR OF STAMPS, COLLECTOR OF DREAMS

Phil Wade delivers boats—all kinds. He has no fixed abode, carries no business cards and doesn't advertise his services. Nor does he have to, because he is one of those enviable, sought-after sailors who work the waterways of the world on behalf of absentee boat owners. His track record is extensive and speaks for itself; but he also possesses a severe physical aspect that unsuccessfully hides a boyish charm—a combination that makes the most doubting of those same boat owners embarrassed to ask for his credentials.

I first met him in Rio back in 1977. He was on his way to the Caribbean, and I was bound for England. We didn't arrange to keep in touch; it was simply one of those unspoken, foregone conclusions that our paths would soon cross again. Indeed, two years later we met again in Sydney, and after that we met again in the Med. He then took a job as the first sailing master on the resurrected J-Class *Velsheda* for her sea trials in England, and I served as his mate. He did the same job for me on board the Maxi yacht *Drum* in the last Whitbread Round-the-World Race.

"How many miles have you done, Phil?" an awestruck, aspiring youngster asked him recently. "I really don't know," he lazily replied. "I've been telling people 250,000 for years. So it must be well over 300,000 by now." (He forgot to count the Whitbread Race, which was good for a quick 30 grand).

Over the years I had heard of many of Phil's maritime adventures and assumed there were many left untold; but out of courtesy I never pressed him for more. Reticence in announcing your own accomplishments (a rarity in today's world of self-promotion) is still common to men whose sense of security and well-being lies not in their bank balances ashore and future prospects for retirement, but rather in their ability to spear and clean a fish for dinner, weather a gale and fix a diesel engine (all in a day).

While we were both packing our seabags before the circumnavigation, Phil casually unzipped a canvas pouch and asked me, "Did I ever show you these?" With weathered and calloused hands, the same kind of hands that Conrad once described as "never having hesitated in the great light of the open sea," Phil carefully thumbed through three books which guarded an incredible nautical stamp collection assembled during his last 15 years of worldwide travel under sail. That revelation inspired what follows—seven Phil Wade adventures accompanied by appropriate stamps from the collection. Only a few of this seagoing philatelist's voyages have been selected, voyages that really represent a lifetime of travel and adventure, and which, we must assume, like many adventures, started out as a dream. The stamps tell this story while the text is merely anecdotal. I will now leave it to the armchair sailor in all of you to conjure up your own voyage, your own dream.

After merchant-marine schooling in his native South Africa, the young and green Phil Wade put to sea as a navigating officer—first stop, Colombia. Says he about that trip: "After two weeks out we got caught in the eye of a hurricane. I somehow got the impression that it would be like that all of the time." Seven years later and after not a few tropical and extra-tropical storms, he gave it up to take a job ashore. As he described it, "I slowly came to realize that there might be more to life than continuing what was then a career surveying the bars and brothels of the world's big-port cities."

What started out as a simple delivery of a Contessa 32 from the U.K. to Brazil also turned out to be fortuitous—not for the Brazilian owner when the boat was seized (he not having paid the 300% import duty), but for Phil and Sue. For the owner's benefit they claimed the boat was theirs, and soon after they bought the boat from him to keep the story straight.

"Those were carefree years on our *Snowflake*. With only the two of us we explored the entire Brazilian coast and then went on to visit all the islands in the Windwards and Leewards. We lived on the fish we caught and avocados purchased or traded for next to nothing from the islanders. For everything else we simply traded more fish, and I can remember buckets of sea water all over the deck trying to keep the lobsters alive . . .

"Hiscock reckoned the Caribbean was a rip-off joint. I lost some faith in him when his Yachting World article I read while still in Brazil misquoted prices in U.S. dollar equivalents of the E.C. dollar. On a tight budget, Sue and I handmade instead of bought the many courtesy flags we would need—the designs described, again, by Hiscock. Many turned out to be completely wrong!"

RIO TO THE **SEYCHELLES**

Two years ashore was enough to satisfy this man that a jacket-and-tie existence was also not the answer. With little experience of sailing other than in dinghies he landed what he thought was a romantic job delivering a 123´ staysail schooner called *Dwyn Wen* from Brazil to the Seychelles.

"It was a very quick education for myself and the five crew. We happily motored out of the harbor in Rio—the motor then packed up and would never work again. There were no winches on deck, only block and tackles. It was really a case of Eric Hiscock's book in one hand and the wheel in the other . . . In Cape Town, I put an ad in the local paper for a cook. Somehow, through the grapevine, word had gotten back to the drydock in Trinidad, the drydock that the previous skipper had left without paying. The police came down and we spent six weeks impounded. Under new ownership and fresh capital we completed the voyage to the Seychelles and spent two months chartering in the Indian Ocean."

Landing a delivery like the 43´ *New Morning* from the U. K. to Sydney with six months to do it is a skipper's dream. The passage was not without its hassles, as Phil explained:

"Transiting the Panama Canal was a nightmare. The pilot we took on was a nervous ex-tugboat captain who had just wrecked another yacht the day before. Between him and the commandante at the other end, who fined us because our courtesy flag was too small, I swore that next time I would go around Cape Horn. But the passage through the Pacific was certainly redeeming. We spent a lot of time in the cruising mode, exploring the islands and doing a lot of diving. In Fiji I speared a 30-pound coral trout and, in what I thought was a friendly gesture, gave the meat to another cruising boat in our anchorage. I had no idea it contained ciguatera, which almost killed the crew while they were at sea later that week. When I found all of this out, I then understood why they were not that pleased to see me on the dock in Sydney."

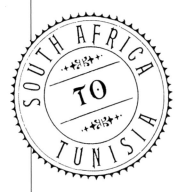

Phil stands a full 6´4´´, and his biggest complaint about the 38-footer he was delivering from South Africa to Tunisia was that it had absolutely no headroom. A custom design, *Argyll* was owned and constructed by a Scotsman, who, as Phil described him, "Was a nice-enough guy but stood five-foot-nothing tall.

"I remember it was Sue's birthday. We were only a day out of St. Helena Island, running with the south-east trades when the rudder fell off. There was no way to turn back so we rigged a sweep with the spinnaker pole and made it in four days to Ascension for repairs. Besides splitting a tank and running out of water up past the Cabo Verdes, it was a great trip. Dolphins followed us all the way up the African coast."

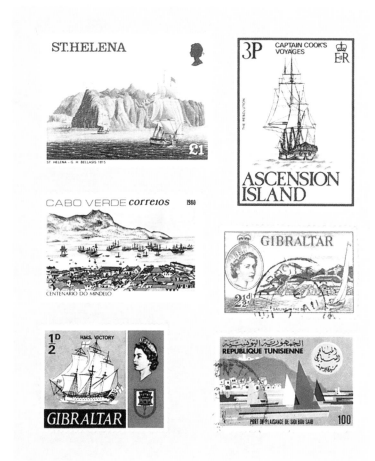

Javelin was a cruising Maxi designed by Germán Frers and built by Palmer Johnson in Sturgeon Bay, Wisconsin, and Phil was hired to make the delivery trip from the Great Lakes to Greece. I asked him how it was to have sailed on fresh water for the first time.

"We couldn't get out of the place quick enough," said he. "It was late October, and it was starting to freeze in Montreal. We were very lucky with the weather—having it downwind all the way out the St. Lawrence—and it continued across the Grand Banks where we averaged over 10 knots. After fueling in Lisbon, we picked up a retired Greek shipping captain who would skipper the boat for the owner, a very common custom in Greece. We scared the shit out of him on that Maxi!"

Back in freezing water again, this time in the Baltic. But the time of year was the same, and with snow on the deck Phil navigated out of the Finnish archipelago on the Deerfoot 61 *Moonshadow* in late October.

"It was a great trip because we had to make a lot of stops due to bad weather, including the Scandinavian ones which I hadn't been to before. But, then again, there was the normal running repairs of a new boat, and the warranty work to do, so in fact we really didn't see that much.

"In December we entered the Atlantic Race for cruising boats from the Canaries to Barbados, an event that saw the biggest armada ever crossing the southern North Atlantic."

It sure was a lot more pleasant than the Whitbread Race, Phil admitted to me. "You know we did that race with just me and six businessmen/yachtsmen from New York, and we were the first monohull to finish . . . Trade winds blowing, T-shirt weather, cocktails at sunset and a bellyfull of flying fish for breakfast. What else does a man need in life?"

Anyone contemplating marine photography should first purchase a pint of alcoholic beverage, hold it delicately but firmly in both hands and motor from England to the Isle of Wight in moderate sea conditions. If, after his trip, he has three-quarters left, then he has possibilities and will need every drop to combat the ups and downs at sea!" These words of Frank Beken's were printed in a guidebook about the Isle of Wight, found in a dusty corner of the Chelsea Library in London. The advice is racy for a turn-of-the-century photographer famed for his precision of image and excellence of composition, founder of the esteemed photographic institution, Beken of Cowes. □ The Beken firm's spectacular black-and-white photographs of big-class yachts are found in nearly any volume of sailing history. The name has been inextricably linked with fine nautical photography since the reign of Queen Victoria, when Frank Beken bought a 14′ dinghy and rowed out to the middle of the Solent to immortalize the racing activities of Britain's Royal Yacht Squadron. Each generation of Bekens has produced a worthy successor to Frank Beken, and this year marks the family's first century in Cowes.

BEKEN OF COWES

THE FIRST 100 YEARS

BY deLANCEY FUNSTEN

t all started in 1888 when Edward Beken moved his family from the cathedral town of Canterbury to Cowes, on the Isle of Wight, to open a chemist's shop. The move was fortuitous in combining an ideal location with Edward's interest in the relatively new technology of the photograph. Cowes had been accepted as the center of yachting in England for most of the 19th century, and it became in the latter decades of the 1800s a watering place much favored by Europe's royals, including the King of Spain, the German Kaiser and Czar Nicholas. Queen Victoria spent each summer on the eastern side of the Medina River in Cowes. The harbor was filled with the most important yachts of the time, representing boats designed by Fife of Scotland and Nicholson of England. Dominating the others in these waters were the Royal Yacht *Victoria and Albert* during Victoria's reign, and the several *Britannias* during her son's and grandson's time.

Helping things along was the Beken & Son window with a spectacular view of the water. Looking out at a glorious assembly of yachts during a regatta, Edward's son Frank decided that he had to preserve such a spectacle on film (or, in his case, glass). Photography was already a Beken hobby. Although most of his time was spent in the pharmacy, Edward was well-known for traveling about the Isle of Wight with his big black box and hood.

"Imagine Cowes Week—that mecca of yachtsmen: the Royal Yacht moored in the Solent surrounded by three hundred yachts of up to 400 tons, anchored and about to raise sail; longboats rowed by crews dressed in white, plying continuously between the yachts and landing-quays; thousands of craftsmen employed in building and repairing; victualling craft sailing in and out of the harbour loaded with wines and food. Cowes Roads, that splendid area of water, starts to come alive, hundreds of yachts tacking and cross-tacking, blue skies and rolling cumulus clouds. . .

"Imagine the big schooners, with a cloud of sail; ketches, yawls and cutters, all with their spinnakers lifting and curling as they sail past the mouth of the river . . . Who could fail to fall in love with this scene and record it for posterity? This is what Frank Beken set out to do ," Keith writes in his history of the family, *The Beken File*.

Achieving the goal was somewhat more difficult than Frank Beken anticipated. Photography was in its infancy in the late 1800s, and cameras were large and cumbersome. Frank bought a dinghy and began to experiment. After many trials, he perfected his own method for taking sharp pictures from a boat oscillating in all directions. He held the twenty-pound camera at arm's length in both hands, using his body as a shock absorber, and released the shutter with a connected rubber ball clenched between his teeth and given one brisk bite at the moment when things settled down. The first camera used produced 12″ x 10″ glass plates that weighed close to ten pounds. Each plate represented two negatives, and Beken carried 30 for a day's shooting. Because reloading plates was time-consuming and only a limited number could be carried, there were no second chances for a missed shot. It was necessary to develop a swift, accurate, well-informed eye.

> Photography was already a Beken hobby. Although most of his time was spent in the pharmacy, Edward was well-known for traveling about the Isle of Wight with his big black box and hood.

Frank pursued photography for nearly 80 years, recording more than 20,000 yachting scenes and becoming one of the great pioneers in his field. By the turn of the century, the firm was granted the Royal Warrant, one of three it was to receive. The first was given by Queen Victoria, the second by George V (who always enjoyed seeing Cowes Week again in print form and annually summoned Frank aboard the Royal Yacht *Britannia*) and the third by Prince Philip. The warrants neatly cover a wall in the back of the shop. They are large, colorfully-painted examples of English heraldry, suitably impressive documents of the firm's eminence. The association with the royal family is longstanding; the Bekens have hobnobbed with British royalty from the start, when Frank was appointed chemist to Queen Victoria during her summer sojourns on the Isle of Wight. They remain in good graces; Prince Philip wrote the foreword to several of their books and appointed Beken & Son "Marine Photographer to Prince Philip" in 1957.

Despite the advice quoted in the beginning of this piece, Frank Beken must have spoken well of his craft, for each successive generation of Bekens has produced a gifted photographer. Frank's middle son, Keith, joined him in the mid-1930s after qualifying as a chemist in London. The two shared pharmacy and photography and worked well together. After Keith's return from the war, the decision was made to make the photographic business pay its own way rather than relying on the chemist's shop's support. Keith recalled, "My father, in his innate wisdom and kindness to people, had determined at an early age to make his photographs available at a price accessible not only to wealthy yachtsmen but also to all the enthusiastic youngsters taking to the sea in small boats. They could be bought by everybody, and as a result they came to be seen all over the world. I was determined to carry on this principle; but with one difference: the chemist business had always financed the photographic section, and I was determined that our marine photography should stand on its own two feet." By concentrating energies in this direction, business flourished, and the chemist's shop was eventually sold.

Keith Beken is the current patriarch of the family firm, working contentedly alongside his younger son, Kenneth. Keith's appearance is not unlike his father Frank's at a similar age—very much the distinguished, well-groomed Englishman. Keith remembers his boyhood delightfully in his book. "Inevitably, any young fellow who lived by the sea had a natural inclination to sail on it; when the dinghy was not being used for photography, we three brothers rowed all over Cowes Harbour, exploring the Medina River and generally turning into water-rats. The dinghy had an iron centreboard, and it was not long before we fitted a mast with a gaff mainsail and a jib; the world was now our oyster, and we foraged 'abroad' to England across the Solent, westwards to the Needles and eastwards to Spithead. Evening races were held by the Island Sailing Club and of course we had the urge to compete: I asked Uffa Fox, who was then a young man living on a ferry-bridge in the river, and well-known for his enthusiasm for sailing, if he could find the time to give me a few lessons. He immediately jumped into the dinghy and gave me a first lesson. One evening a few weeks later, out in the Solent, he suddenly said, 'Well, Keith, you know all about it now.' With that, he dived over the side in shirt and shorts and swam ashore—half a mile away. This was my introduction to the inimitable Uffa."

Today the old chemist's shop retains the name Beken & Son, standing practically across the street from the Beken of Cowes photographic studio at 16 Birmingham Road. A well-kept, glossy façade displays their name in bright gold lettering. The sale of the pharmacy business in 1970 does not seem to disturb the now-photographic

On page 118: 1905 portrait of the schooner yacht *White Heather*, with the stack of her steam auxiliary poking up between the two masts. On the top right of page 119, Frank Beken, the founder of Beken of Cowes, holds the bulb connected to the shutter of his twenty-pound Mark I camera between his teeth; elsewhere on page 119, a quartet of 6-Meters vies for one another's wind. On page 121 the great British racing schooner *Rainbow* sweeps past in sweeping seas. On page 122 is a four-masted, four-man windsurfer sponsored by J&B Rare Scotch Whisky. On page 123 is an aerial of the high-tech Maxi racer *Il Moro di Venezia*. On page 124 a hat-and-suited pair of ladies race *Broadglance* and *Coot* in 1895. On page 126 the Olin-Stephens-designed *Stormy Weather* heels to port. The final photograph, on page 126 was taken in Antiqua in 1981 and titled "Seahorse."

Bekens, but a nostalgic memory of the connection between that business and the "good old days" of sailing is contained in Keith's book. "In Frank Beken's chemist shop, lined up and ready for collection, are a row of medicine chests all made of solid oak, finely varnished, with such famous names as H.M.Y. *Britannia, Sonia, Margharita, Waterwitch, Nyria* and *Hispania* printed in gold-leaf on the top. These chests were constantly being refilled, for in those days many limbs were damaged, fingers split and bones broken . . . *Britannia*'s medicine chest is still kept in Beken's shop to this day."

Beken of Cowes is a unique institution. The firm can boast immediate access to every picture that has ever been taken by a Beken. This is a near-miracle for magazines and newspapers. To order a photograph from most photographic archives or museums often requires a lengthy wait. The Beken firm operates so efficiently that a phone call or letter will deliver a package of black-and-white prints or original color transparencies virtually by return mail. And the Bekens are renowned for being faultlessly courteous as well as prompt, which makes dealing with them a pleasure rather than a chore.

"Our paramount purpose is to try and collect photographs of as many different boats as possible and to have a library of them that is virtually unequaled anywhere in the world. That's our main aim, to formulate this vast collection of boats of every regatta, every race. To have these available for anybody to take advantage of," Keith explained.

The Bekens have done just that. They have every (acceptable) negative they have ever taken. Asked about their inventory size Keith replied, "too many," with a laugh. Kenneth later told me that their inventory contained an estimated 75,000 black-and-white images and close to as many in color. That may not sound like so many for 100 years, but consider it reduced by editing out what Keith refers to as "the ordinary stuff" and it represents a vast quantity of "superb, classical photographs." They willingly pulled pictures out of the files to demonstrate this—breathtaking sepia prints of the J boats in their racing days, the last photograph ever taken of the *Titanic*, tall ships, small ships, King Edward VII and King Alfonso XIII aboard *Britannia*, Prince Philip at the helm of an Uffa-Fox-designed Flying Fifteen . . . The list is practically limitless.

The quantity of photographs is a marine rival to the great Rosenfeld Collection, considered to be the largest group of photographs in the world devoted to a single subject. The Bekens are a sort of British parallel to the Rosenfelds. They acknowledge a sense of kinship, saying that the families share many of the same attitudes and enthusiasms towards their profession.

> "Our paramount purpose is to try and collect photographs of as many different boats as possible and to have a library of them that is virtually unequaled anywhere in the world."

Another Beken goal is excellence. "Every picture must be perfect," said Keith. "There is no time to change, fool around." The Bekens have two main principles: a sufficient quantity of original material to send out to whatever magazines request them and absolute quality of detail. "We insist on absolute detail . . . so that you can practically see the color of the person's eyes," he elaborated. "If we don't get it, we throw the bad shots out immediately. That's really the basis on which we work. The other details are technical."

The photographic work continues to be done primarily from a small boat, although helicopters are rented when necessary. "A powerboat goes by at 50 knots, so you've got to do it by helicopter," Keith said. "Otherwise we're yachtsmen—we think that a yacht should be seen from sea level."

Father and son are continually busy with everyday chores while maintaining a string of extracurricular projects. The day I visited, the telephone rang nearly as frequently as the shop bell, and Keith and Kenneth devoted as much time as they could to a visiting journalist (and fan), in between answering their four assistants' queries, speaking definitively to people on the phone. ("If he can't meet our terms then we'll just call the deal off."), and arranging meetings with their publishers. The Bekens produce a book every few years. *A Century of Tall Ships* and *One Hundred Years of Sail* are in the bookstores, and they recently completed *The*

New Big Thoroughbreds, a look at the Maxi boats. Keith wrote his history of the family's photography, *The Beken File*, in 1979, which was first published in French and later by the Channel Press in Aylesbury, Buckinghamshire. There are now less than half a dozen copies left in the studio. Eight versions of calendars are produced each year, selling more than 250,000 copies.

Keith has enjoyed inheriting the Beken tradition and was joined by his son Kenneth in 1969. Both men continue to be active photographers, continually adding to the overwhelming amount of stock in the archive. There is an air of glory about them, an earned pride of accomplishment. Keith exhibits a stereotypical English humility by his simple and evident pleasure at what he is, who he is, and the fact that his son Kenneth has not only chosen to carry on the Beken tradition but agrees fully with his own ideas on how pictures should be taken. "I feel very fortunate that I have a son who follows the business because it's not often that an artist will follow his father," Keith asserted. "Ken's got exactly the same technique—unless we knew it, we couldn't tell which of us took the pictures."

The Bekens are pleased with their business and proud of their heritage. "We get nothing but compliments," said Keith. "We think our prices are nice and everyone else agrees." Chances are good that everyone will continue to agree and that the Beken tradition will continue for another century. Keith related, with obvious pleasure, that a camera already hangs about the neck of Jason, Kenneth's four-year-old son.

Cowes remains a significant place in the world of sailing. Cowes Week draws a lively crowd to the town that appears as lovely and unspoiled as it was a century ago, when European royalty could walk unguarded through its tiny streets. The J-Class sloop *Velsheda* still sails Cowes waters; I watched her elegant shape glide past from a hydrofoil window on my way from Southampton. Keith smiled when I told him of this, saying that it might well be my only sight of a J-boat under sail. Certainly the world may never see enormous yachts racing in the Cowes Roads as they did in the 1930s; but thanks to the Beken family such visions have been preserved. We present a few of them on these pages, part of a retrospective of a hundred years of great photography.

BASE CAMP
PELAGIC

BY SKIP NOVAK

Traveling to Antarctica can evoke thoughts of either self-imposed privation or indulgent tourism, depending on your bent and pocketbook. Scientists, of course, have coveted the austerity of the place for more meaningful pursuits. Long ago, a famous Arctic explorer clarified the mystique of Polar travel when he said, " The great majority of men who visit the Arctic do so because they want to, a large number do so for publicity, while it is possible that one or two have gone there for purely scientific purposes." □ We ventured to the Antarctic Peninsula during the austral summer of 1988 for a combined sailing/ mountaineering/filming expedition with no loftier goals than what could be reached by ice axe and crampon. The yacht *Pelagic*, which according to the dictionary means "of, or performed on the open sea," was our mobile mountain refuge.

129

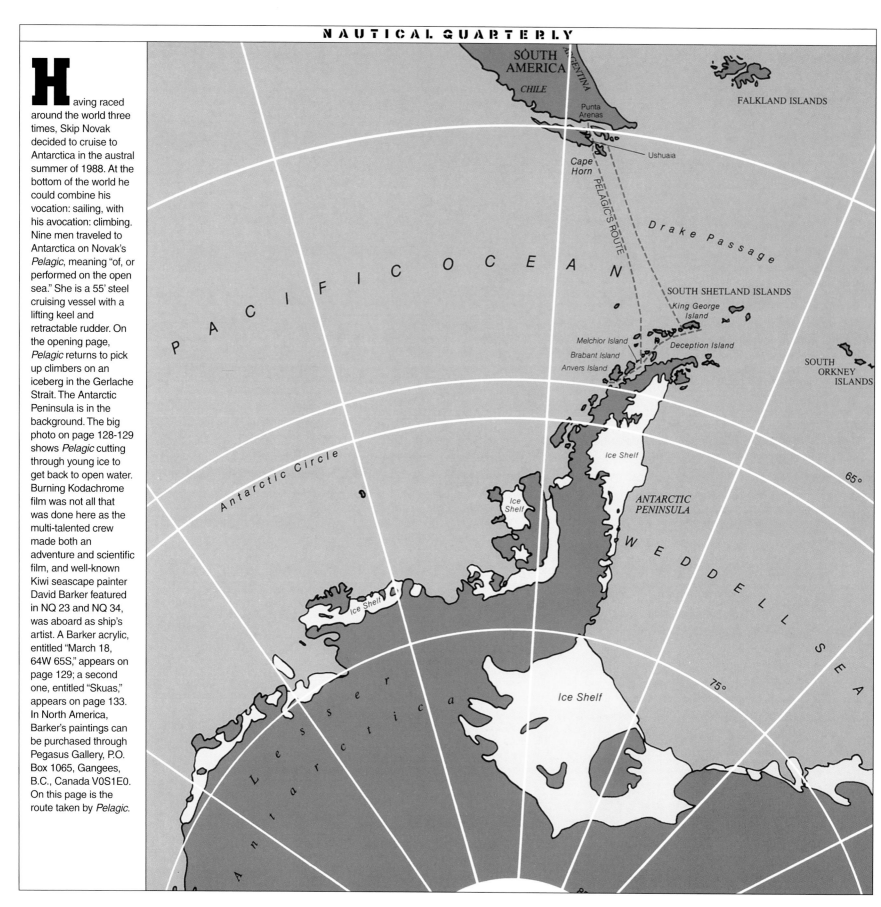

Having raced around the world three times, Skip Novak decided to cruise to Antarctica in the austral summer of 1988. At the bottom of the world he could combine his vocation: sailing, with his avocation: climbing. Nine men traveled to Antarctica on Novak's *Pelagic*, meaning "of, or performed on the open sea." She is a 55' steel cruising vessel with a lifting keel and retractable rudder. On the opening page, *Pelagic* returns to pick up climbers on an iceberg in the Gerlache Strait. The Antarctic Peninsula is in the background. The big photo on page 128-129 shows *Pelagic* cutting through young ice to get back to open water. Burning Kodachrome film was not all that was done here as the multi-talented crew made both an adventure and scientific film, and well-known Kiwi seascape painter David Barker featured in NQ 23 and NQ 34, was aboard as ship's artist. A Barker acrylic, entitled "March 18, 64W 65S," appears on page 129; a second one, entitled "Skuas," appears on page 133. In North America, Barker's paintings can be purchased through Pegasus Gallery, P.O. Box 1065, Gangees, B.C., Canada V0S1E0. On this page is the route taken by *Pelagic*.

Sailing is my job, and mountaineering is my hobby; and while my racing sailor friends were somewhat mystified by my plans, my few climbing friends marveled.

People can be confused about adventure travel by its myriad forms of advertisement and subsequent reality, and this really boils down to terminology or abuse of it. For example, the popular catch phrase "expedition" is used liberally today to identify the exploits of long-haul stuntmen on sailboards, anything smelling of science in the field or an adventure in assessing the quality of the cuisine on a 500´ cruise ship. Purists (from all of the above) would probably define the word as a self-contained unit in a remote area operating for some specific purpose. It can be argued than that the cruise ship qualifies as does any solo boardsailor. The fact of the matter is that adventure aficionados love to denigrate the more pampered and catered traveler, and that the pampered don't really give a damn. For the sake of taking a stand, and by way of explaining what we were doing in the Antarctic, I feel the line needs to be drawn somewhere so I will offer a very simple definition: If you cook your own food, do your own dishes and clean your own head (if you have one), you are on an expedition—all else is tourism.

We were an eclectic group of nine professional climbers and professional sailors, including a non-practicing doctor from France, a casual biochemist from Italy, a New Zealand artist and a Swiss TV film crew of two, out on speculation. We came not to discover or explore anything (it has all been done before), and we did not try to justify ourselves with science (I lie: the biochemist did, in fact, collect lichens for a long-term study of world pollution). We were not stuntmen (in spite of the photographs) aiming to climb the highest mountain or sail the furthest south in hopes of spectacular publicity. We were not *cruising* in the classic sense, either, for that implies itinerant wandering and dependence on shipboard life. Our simple goals were to spend as much time as possible ashore in mountain travel, while the more difficult challenges were in fulfilling commitments to make two films for Italian and Swiss television.

For me, sailing to the Antarctic was a logical extension of a professional sailing career. The experience of having raced three times around the world in the Whitbread Race via the Southern Ocean, daring as close as possible to the ice for the beauty of it and resisting the temptation to make an unexpected call at one of those subantarctic islands just for the hell of it, surely encouraged the strongest aspirations of an amateur mountaineer. Sailing is my job, and mountaineering is my hobby; and while my racing sailor friends were somewhat mystified by my plans, my few climbing friends marveled. Not at the difficulty—because we were not out to do anything epic—but rather at the remoteness and difficulty of access that implies quality in mountain travel.

This marriage of sailing and climbing is not a new concept. When that indefatigable mountain explorer Major Bill Tilman was too old to climb the tallest peaks he took up sailing late in his fifth decade in order to get to some remote areas with lower but no less demanding terrain. For almost 30 years, he sailed a succession of three Bristol Channel pilot cutters to East and West Greenland, Spitzbergen and the islands of the Southern Ocean, including one ill-fated expedition to the Antarctic Peninsula back in 1966/67. Tilman was lost at sea in 1977, again on his way to the Antarctic to celebrate his 80th year. Although the French (who always seem to be years ahead of everyone in adventure pursuits) followed in his footsteps with purpose-built expedition yachts and popularized the area, Tilman's seven mountaineering/sailing books, written in his typically understated but profound style, remain the classics. "But sir," Tilman was once asked by a young man at one of his lectures, "how does one get to go on an expedition?" "Son," he replied, "just put on your boots and go."

It is no doubt apocryphal that Tilman and his long-standing Himalayan-climbing companion, Eric Shipton, used to plan their expeditions on the back of an envelope. "If it needs more planning than that it is probably not worth doing," one of them said. These are complicated times, however, and despite our best attempts to keep things simple—just put on our boots and go—things got terribly complicated out of circumstance. For a start, we needed a vehicle to get us down there. Unlike Steinbeck's character Henri, the painter of Cannery Row, who was already 10 years in the building of his boat and never intended to finish it, I quickly formed a three-man partnership back in the summer of 1986 to build a 54´ steel cruising boat with a lifting keel and retractable rudder (especially suited for ice, tight anchorages and careening) that would be ready for the Antarctic season of 1987/88. Each partner was to have a year on board.

Before construction began in September I met several times with Dr. Luc Frejacques in Paris, a sailing friend from two Whitbread Races. He had been to the Antarctic twice before in 1983 and 1985 on small yachts and did not hesitate to entertain plans for another visit. He suggested I contact Marco Morosini in Milan, who had been successful in securing sponsorship contracts from Italian companies in using a project like this for their advertising campaigns. I arranged to see Morosini later in the year, and the "Italian Connection" eventually led to Swiss cameraman/director Fulvio Mariani and film editor Gianluigi Quarti Trevano (Giangi) who got consent from their employer, RTS1 (Swiss State TV) to shoot two films for television while in the Antarctic. This, in turn, would provide the necessary carrot for Morosini's sponsorship search in Italy.

Meanwhile, I had little trouble convincing New Zealand artist and yachtsman David Barker to come along. Today it is very difficult to better the best of Antarctic photography, so our idea was for David to document the expedition in a series of paintings sketched on site—again not a new idea, but a neglected one post-Kodachrome. I had met David six years before while he was building a 60´ catamaran of his own design in an old cow shed on New Zealand's North Island's east coast (see NQ23). Living

"But sir," Tilman was once asked by a young man,
"how does one get to go on an expedition?" "Son," he
replied, "just put on your boots and go."

in a broken-down trailer next door, he was also building a reputation as New Zealand's foremost marinescape artist. He was one of those "do-it-yerself" Kiwis who could run his hand to whatever needed doing and, if he was standing over me now, no doubt he would remind me about the mast he helped me repair and the rudder he reshaped for *Pelagic*. Like most good things from new Zealand, he now exports his talents to the rest of us and divides his time between New Zealand, London and Vancouver.

Back on the construction site, British ski instructor and computer dropout Hamish Laird joined Luc on the building team with Luc's girlfriend Lillian, my girlfriend De and later André Mechelynck, a Belgian sailor and engineer I knew from the Whitbread. They all worked for no compensation for four to five months before the boat left the UK. On the eve of departure, we also signed on professional climber Marco Pretti, and he brought us some sponsorship funds, equipment and an incredible enthusiasm. All on board could climb except David, all on board could sail except Marco Pretti. Everyone put a lot of time, effort and money into making it all happen, although at times it was frustrating, complicated and financially debilitating.

In our way, we had put on our boots and gone. After months of inevitable delays in the 7000-mile delivery from the UK with repairs to the boat—which had never been sea-trialed except on passage—we got ourselves and our gear to the high latitudes. The prospect of arriving too late in the austral summer was always looming. Without further incident *Pelagic* finally crossed the Drake Passage late in February of 1988 and moored safely for her first night in the Antarctic at the abandoned Argentine base on Gamma Island in the Melchior archipelago, latitude 64 degrees South. Immediately the angst was forgotten as easily as the first summer's snow hid the odd bits of unfinished rusty deck fittings. We had nine on board representing seven nationalities, a ship's cat, food for three months, 1200 liters of fuel, a quarter ton of wine (the Italian Connection) and the prospect of three months in the triangle between Tierra del Fuego, the Antarctic Peninsula and South Georgia.

Most activity in the Antarctic goes on either in the Ross Sea (south of New Zealand) or on the Antarctic Peninsula due south of Cape Horn. The New Zealand side, like the rest of the coastline of the continent, is open with few good shelters and fringed with pack ice all of the year; it is thus tenuous for any sort of vessel, let alone a small sailboat. The west coast of the Peninsula is quite a different area in that offshore islands, deep fjords and relatively deep channels protect shipping from the seas of westerly winds that also bring in the pack from the Bellingshausen Sea at an alarming rate. Most of the time lighter winds prevail from the east blowing offshore, and this gets to be more typical the further south you go closer to the Polar high. For these same reasons the east side of the Peninsula is closely compacted by drift and glacial ice.

Referring to the "Peninsula" is certainly the safest political thing to do because the area is up for grabs, and this becomes immediately apparent when clearing out of or into either Stanley in the Falklands (British), Ushuaia (Argentina) or Punta Arenas (Chile). Since this part of the continent is centrally located and easily accessible to these three nations, they have all claimed a sector as their "Antarctic Territory," which they have temporarily agreed by the Antarctic Treaty of 1959 to relinquish. Nevertheless, it pays dividends when in Punta Arenas, Chile, to know that Bernardo O'Higgins was the liberator of Chile and to speak of Tierra O'Higgins. But never refer to Tierra O'Higgins in Argentina where San Martin is the recognized liberator with the same piece of terra firma named after him. Even the British and the Americans had such a disagreement years ago, and in 1963 reserved the British Graham Land as that part of the Peninsula north of roughly 69 degrees South, and the American Palmer Land (named for a yankee sealer who claims the first sighting of the continent) as the part to the south.

There is no authority to prevent or contest anyone sailing directly to the continent from elsewhere, but since we were using Chilean hospitality in Punta Arenas as a terminus for airfreight shipments, overseas arrivals and for bunkering and provisioning, we shamelessly played the O'Higgins card. Punta Arenas is an austere workingman's town and seaport up on the Straits of Magellan, backed by a flat, dry landscape, and is relatively efficient in modern communications (they have a Fax!). Ushuaia, in the Argentine sector of Tierra del Fuego, where we finished our journey, is mountainous, lush and pleasantly South American. That is another way of saying that it's impossible to make an overseas telephone call.

It's only a three-day sail from Punta Arenas through the canals of Tierra del Fuego before you can enter the Drake Passage, but that is in fine weather. It would be foolhardy to try to stand against winds in these canals that frequently top out at 50 knots in driven spray. But we were lucky in that a good northwesterly was blowing that first day, and we had dropped the hook 80 miles down the track in the heart of "Fireland." We spent the night at the head of an icefall in Seno Chico, a fingerlike fjord off the head of the Cockburn Channel. The next morning we were off for a short run to one of Luc's favorite places where some crab fishermen occupy a rude shack. It was idyllic; we tied to the shore with the keel up, cooked an asado (BBQ'd mutton) with the fishermen in the afternoon, and some of us went duck hunting and harvested mussels and sea urchins.

How deceiving this tranquility. Next day, after a six-hour struggle against all of 50 knots, we turned tail in the Cockburn Channel with the afternoon fading fast. Earlier Hamish and Luc, tethered to the lifelines by only strong arms, had inconveniently gone over the side while saving a headsail back aft. It was also getting incredibly cold. We anchored not far from the place we had been the night before and spent three relaxing days hunting and fishing in an almost windless cove while the southwesterly

Above, Hamish Laird pauses to enjoy the view of Dorian Cove on Wiencke Island. In the upper-right photo, the crew unloads equipment in the same cove. It was here that *Pelagic* ran aground. The bottom photo on that page shows equipment for the expedition in a rented garage in Punta Arenas. On page 137 are ice "sculptures" in the Argentine Archipelago. The birds are Antarctic skuas.

gale, at times reinforced by williwaws, and visible as white water kicking up in the Cockburn only a mile away, eventually blew itself out. The original projected three days turned into a week, but no one was complaining, not least of all "Cat-so," the ship's cat that joined us the day before we left Punta Arenas. Found as a stray in an alley and only four or five weeks old, she was then dining on mussels and steamer duck and had immediately gained our undivided affection. Finally the wind turned in our favor, and we made an easy day of it down the Cockburn Channel. Although the mouth of the Cockburn is a recognized entrance into the convoluted hinterland of Tierra del Fuego 200 miles northwest of Cape Horn, its seaward approaches are foul with rocks and islets in heavy swell up to 10 miles offshore. Instead we hooked southeast into the narrow reach of Paso Brecknock before bailing out of Paso Pratt, a clear channel dividing Isla London and Isla Sidney. Isla London also has a good anchorage on its eastern end that can serve as a last-minute shelter. But by early evening a light northerly was still blowing, and David Barker remarked, "Let's get going and get across this thing!"

We had no dramas to report when crossing the Drake Passage other than that the fresh mussels stored in buckets on the side deck ran out on day three of the four-day voyage. At around 60 degrees South, halfway across,

life changes very abruptly when you transit the Antarctic Convergence. This is the dividing line between the warmer northern water and the colder water to the south diving beneath it. It affects the way in which you live. Whereas before we ran our diesel heater intermittently, now we had to run it 24 hours a day, not so much for the cold—that was only just above freezing—but to control the condensation below. Water tanks and fresh-water plumbing need to be drained down here as sea water near freezing is below the temperature of fresh-water ice. In anticipation of that, four of our five water tanks had been stocked with canned goods and liter boxes of wine that could handle a few extra degrees before going solid. The wine was also more cheering than the water could ever have been!

North of the convergence it usually rained and sometimes snowed; south it usually snowed and sometimes rained. Icing could also be a problem under sail, and luckily we spent very little time battling against the wind and sea. When you want to move on the Peninsula you have to wait for the right conditions not only for security in making the next anchorage but then surely for comfort. Frankly speaking, the Antarctic is a terrible place to go sailing, but a lovely place to be in harbor. And that was our intention on *Pelagic*.

Melchior Island is a good first stop well down the Peninsula. An open approach from the northwest leads into a gap between the towering heights of Anvers and Brabant Islands. Here the Palmer Archipelago and the old abandoned Argentine Base at Gamma Island provide first shelter for small craft. Early that morning we slid into a narrow cut in the rocks and ran four lines ashore with the inflatable dinghies. Galleries of fur seals who occupy the island seemed unimpressed by our arrival, and we spent the day rummaging through the base and hiking around the glacier. "Established in 1947, inspected in 1963," said the Antarctic Pilot. The long wooden barracks, painted a fading bright orange, were well preserved like everything in the Antarctic's cold, dry air. Sadly, pharmaceuticals, food stores, books, magazines and record albums, no doubt left intact and stored neatly the day the place was abandoned, had been pilfered by vandals, and what remained was scattered carelessly about the rooms. This can only be because Melchior is more accessible than the bases further south, which as a rule have been left in their original state. The striking thing was that even delicate foods like pastas and tea leaves in thin cellophane bags were still intact after decades because there are no rats or other pests in Antarctica—except, of course, man.

We left Melchior early the next morning for the 45-mile run to Dorian Cove on Wiencke Island, which passes through the Gerlache Strait that separates the Peninsula proper from the outlying islands and later into the Neumeyers Channel between Wiencke and Anvers Island. On this passage we had our first real sense of Antarctica. Motorsailing in flat water, running the gauntlet of ice sculptures as big as buildings, we wondered in silence what lay behind and above the low layer of cloud that cast a gray shadow over us all.

One of the biggest advantages to sailing in the Antarctic is that there is rarely anyone around to witness your blunders. The entrance to Dorian Cove is restricted to small craft, which means that a 50-footer with a fixed keel would probably not risk it. An object lesson at no cost to anyone, we promptly ran aground in the channel that couldn't have been wider than twice our beam. The rule of thumb with a lifting keel is to leave it down as a veritable depth sounder unless you know it must be raised to make an entrance. Since this was a known entrance we did not bother to sound it, and consequently the dinghy was not overboard and ready to go. This was our first mistake. To complicate matters we lifted the keel with no lines ashore to hold us in place. We then drifted with the wind further on the rocky ledge and had to take the rudder blade out of the sleeve. If the two Weddell seals lying on those rocks had been sunbathers instead, they would have been more than amused—and perhaps they were. While we bounced up and down virtually on the shore, Fulvio and Marco Pretti ran out the

Frankly speaking, the Antarctic is a terrible
place to go sailing, but a lovely place to be in harbor.
And that was our intention on *Pelagic*.

spools of floating polypropylene warps with the dinghy to the opposite beach, and we winched our bow and stern back into deeper water before motoring ahead into the bay. Looking back at that insignificant episode it was as if all the justification for the *Pelagic* concept had been vindicated: steel boat, shallow bottom, lifting keel and rudder.

And inside the cove—the reward! In eight feet of water we ran four lines ashore belayed to chain and wire-cable slings to rock bollards or pitons. Crowded with Gentoo penguins, the barrier rocks protecting the bay kept the large bergs out, and in any case in the shallow water large bergs would have grounded out before they could do us any damage. We would spend more than two weeks on two separate occasions in Dorian Cove because Wiencke Island had something for everyone. This was where we shot most of the climbing scenes for the fantasy film we had begun while in Punta Arenas. *Pelagic* and her crew had become the cast, the technicians and the props, and the film crew filming itself became an incredibly interesting but time-consuming exercise.

The gist of this feature, which mixed fantasy with reality, centered around Marco Pretti, professional climber, who joins *Pelagic* in Chile for the Antarctic expedition. He is a climbing cult figure, lean and muscular with reptilian splayed fingers. He sports a punk hairdo, wears a walkman continuously, and while sailing for the first time across the Drake Passage begins to fantasize about being the hero of the voyage. Since he eventually presses us further south we inevitably get trapped in the ice; he and I have a big argument and I send him off to effect the rescue with Luc, therefore providing him with his heroic scenario. Ironically, we on board manage to extricate ourselves while they are busy falling into crevasses, living in ice caves and trekking across the Peninsula to the nearest British scientific base. Exhausted, Marco finally enters the base pub and discovers us casually sipping pints of bitter. His dream is shattered. The End.

Meanwhile, sometime supporting actor Marco Morosini was busy collecting samples of lichens on Wiencke Island, one of the few types of vegetation found in the Antarctic. Like Pretti, Marco is a northern Italian, punctual and precise with a questioning personality. He speaks fluent French, English, Spanish, Portuguese and some Greek and German. He studied in Milan and has a degree in chemistry and pharmaceutical technologies. Wavering between science and journalism, he has been doing an on-going study of world pollution that theorizes that certain kinds of pollutants (primarily DDT and heavy metals) migrate in the atmosphere to Polar regions and high-mountain areas. This has enabled him to collect samples in Antarctica, the Himalayas and Africa.

Dorian Cove, like all good anchorages in the Antarctic (of which there are very few) has a supply depot and refuge, this one owned and maintained by the British Antarctic Survey (BAS). Only the Americans and the British do any real science south on the Peninsula. The Americans maintain

their Palmer Station around the corner on Anvers Island, and the two countries cooperate quite willingly in supply and projects. But while the Americans are serviced by first-class icebreakers like the utilitarian *Polar Duke*, and lead a lifestyle not too different from home with packaged food, too many videos and even women personnel(!), the British have a more basic existence here that, although maybe more typical of the British in general, is in my opinion more fulfilling given the time and place.

The Damoy hut book includes visits by the odd yacht or two every season, but is mainly a running dialogue of the complaints of FIDS (an acronym for the Falkland Islands Dependency Survey, predecessor to the BAS and now a set of letters that applies to new recruits). The weather, the food, BAS, the problems of being hut-bound and escape are the main topics, and an extract is worth repeating. The parentheses are mine: 2nd December 1983, after 20 days: "Another dingle (fine) day here at Billy Butlin's Holiday Retreat for the Mentally Unstable, or at least you soon will be! Unfortunately, as so often is the case, the 0500 radio sched with Bucket Mouth (Rothera) dispelled all fears that we might be departing our paradise island, and enabled everyone to relax into their now only too familiar, bloody monotonous routines—once around the penguin colony and back for more scradge (food)—will it ever end?"

Indeed, on a dingle day in the Antarctic your optimism soars about what you can do. After three days of blustery weather we woke up to eight inches of snow on deck, and saw that pancake ice had formed throughout the bay and that the sky was pale blue and cloudless. Although we were still in the shadow of the Fief Mountains on Wiencke, Mt. Français on Anvers Island across the channel was already a blinding pyramid in the morning sun rising to well over 9000´. In the cold, clear air it looked "just there" close enough to go and climb in a day. Distances in these conditions are incredibly deceiving as the top of the mountain was well over 10 miles away and would require a major assault with camps.

While the film crew set up shop in a hut and began shooting climbing scenes on and around a rock face above the bay, Hamish and I set out for an assault of our own on Mt. Luigi, 4700´ and only four hours on skis to the base of the climb. We failed in that first attempt (late breakfast, ominous-looking weather), and after 10 hours hitched up to skis and rucksack we had the pleasure of schussing five miles back to Dorian Cove and our base camp. It is an expected and well-earned privilege for those who have been on a mountain to be welcomed by a hot cup of tea and a meal by companions back at the refuge. This was wishful thinking, however. Surprisingly we found cold tea and a colder reception when we learned that De De (Andre), who had slept in the hut for some strange reason, didn't get up until 1300. That accounted for one dinghy, and we accounted for the other. Thus, the others on board were marooned for half of a fine day. Granted, we were partly to blame for not bringing a dinghy back in the early hours of the

For the reader who takes the parochial two-week
holiday per year and leads a relatively structured life, months
of Antarctic bliss may seem irresponsible.

morning, so we guiltily prepared the evening meal of beans, potatoes and cabbage casserole followed by crêpes flambé. This seemed to cheer everyone's hearts, and the ambiance was restored by the second liter of wine.

Evenings were a great pleasure on board. The cooking was handled at random, and we never went without an imperial feast. Luc, who excelled in the culinary department, sometimes would insist on doing everything himself and was almost obstinate at times in this regard. Other times it seemed as if the whole crew was in the galley. De De would be chopping onions and garlic on the main saloon table, Morosini grating the Parmesan that accompanied everything, Fulvio inspecting his bread in the oven with a headtorch, and Luc and I debating the seasoning of a monumental stew on the stove while the pressure cooker above the diesel heater, buried in amongst ripening socks, underwear and gloves on the drying line, hissed and splurted the familiar tune that began the countdown to gluttony.

This was a bad anchorage at the best of times — and
the best of times could never be confused with a wind from
the east. We had to motor out at panic stations.

Because we lived by the long daylight hours on the mountain, dinners were late and conversation (in mixed French, English and Italian) usually lasted well into the early hours of the morning discussing previous expeditions, future projects and most of all just plain nonsense. I slept aft in an athwartships harbor berth behind the saloon table. This was very convenient as when I got drowsy I just slipped aft from the table into my sleeping bag while the guys served me coffee and sometimes dessert in bed. At any time I could quit the conversation by lowering my head away unnoticed around the bulkhead corner. Morosini, by comparison, invariably fell asleep immediately after dinner and woke up in odd postures later to saunter off forward to the starboard cabin he shared with David. Cat-so was much in demand during those winter days of summer. She didn't mind whom she slept with, and it was always a great delight when you found her (Hamish described her as "hot-water-bottle-sized") burrowed in your sleeping bag purring away.

It would be hard to have enjoyed an evening like that anchored in an open bay with the boat tugging at the cable. Instead, tucked away safely in shallow water, we regularly indulged heavily in food and drink and were disturbed only infrequently during the night by the odd growler banging the hull and fouling in our bow and stern ropes.

Only about half the days we spent down there were good and clear; but there was a lot to do when it wasn't. Fulvio would be taking his camera gear to pieces, cleaning, adjusting and reassembling—his concentration as intense as a Swiss watchmaker, while his older partner, Giangi, looked on sipping some Grappa, obviously very content with the situation. Giangi had taught Fulvio to climb when he was 15, and since then they have climbed and filmed all over the world. They spent four weeks together on the north face of Everest in a succession of blizzards. It was clear they had no secrets from each other but that didn't stop them from arguing—something they did almost constantly. While Luc and I speculated on the next meal the others read. David took over the chart table as a cramped studio and colored in his sketches of the day with pastels. Morosini, the most scholarly of the group, filled notebook after notebook from his readings and experiences, intending to write the first broad-spectrum book on the Antarctic in Italian.

De De, our engineer, never had an idle moment ripping into the plumbing, wiring and mechanics on a regular basis. De De is probably the most persistent guy I know this side of sanity. With scant regard for his appearance or his own welfare, he always took comfort in doing things for other people. We all regularly came to him with all kinds of problems: charging the film-equipment batteries, fixing an oven burner or the engine alternator. Walkman stereos were his specialty, and he jury-rigged some incredible contraptions with wire, solder and duct tape. If you needed a certain size bolt or clevis pin and we didn't have one, he would disappear into the forepeak and be heard filing away for hours until the job was done. This persistence equally applied to chopping onions, carrots or anything involving repetition. If you didn't stop him he would eventually disappear from view behind a mound of grated Parmesan cheese.

For the reader who takes the parochial two-week holiday per year and leads a relatively structured life, weeks and even months of Antarctic bliss may seem irresponsible. Let me assure you, however, that there is no greater pleasure than blending this so-called irresponsibility with the intense dedication of jobs at hand like climbing, filming, eating and sleeping.

Sadly, even we were bound by a schedule, which meant that we had to leave the solitude of Dorian Cove for the suburban atmosphere of Faraday Base (British) in the Argentine Islands 35 miles further south. We arrived in the Argentine Archipelago just before dark the next evening, having spent too much time motoring up through the Le Maire Channel, which is reputed to be the most picturesque passage on the west coast. Cruise ships advertise the Le Maire "when possible," meaning when it is ice-free. Nicknamed "Kodak Valley," the narrow gut is flanked by steep cliffs rising to icy pinnacles guaranteed to make the most jaded tourist reach for his photographic armory. We logged over 2000 images during our two passages, and the jockeying for position on the deck became aggressive enough to be ridiculous at times.

Peter Starkey, the bearded base commander at Faraday, greeted us pleasantly but without enthusiasm. He agreed to let us charge the equipment batteries and to use the base and pub for filming, including doing a few interviews for Morosini's scientific film. But this was from a political sense of protocol and not because he really wanted us around. Unfortunately, the base was very busy in preparing for the arrival of the *Bransfield* to discharge cargo and to change personnel. Starkey, having spent several full terms (three summers and two winters) was now only the summer commander in charge of a staff of 30 scientists, technicians and regular personnel. In winter this number dwindled to 12. We questioned Starkey very openly about BAS policy regarding yachts and cruise ships. "We have no official policy for yachts, and as far as I'm concerned they don't have a bad reputation; but, in fact, we do know of one instance where a French yacht pilfered one of our supply depots."

D. W. H. Walton, British Antarctic Survey and co-author of the book *Antarctic Key Environments*, stated his opinion with a little more conviction when he wrote "The proliferation of private yachts in the Southern Ocean has added a new, and largely unwelcome element to the tourist problem. The activities of these yachts seem, at the moment, to be beyond any general control." Reading this certainly didn't inspire confidence, but inspecting the base register of visiting yachts in comparison to the number of tour ships I would have to say that the problem is exaggerated by Walton. Starkey agreed that tour ships are the real problem; in fact, BAS has had to limit their visits to only four per summer season as they were too disruptive for the scientific activities of the base. Imagine 300 tourists overrunning a base fit for 30; everyone wants Antarctic stamps franked at Faraday, a Faraday patch, souvenirs—all dispensed by the base commander. Of course this is revenue and public relations, but at what price? "We spend an inordinate amount of time with them when they are in. And for what they are getting out of it, I think they are getting ripped off," says Starkey. "But they don't seem to mind because the important thing is to go back home and be able to say that they've been to Antarctica. South Georgia can work for tourists because they can get ashore and wander around in safety, but here there is very little you can do without some mountaineering experience, plus there's a lot more wildlife in SG."

It was clear that the folks at Faraday resented the tourists coming down and intruding for a day on the place they call home for two and a half years. We were slightly more acceptable because we had made a bigger effort and were willing to spend some time to get to know the area. Most people find it hard to imagine stable, normal individuals committing themselves to a celibate exile for that length of time. But when you are in your early twenties what better way is there to gain self confidence by working to stay alive and by surrounding yourself with wildlife and the sights and sounds of a rugged environment instead of daily doses of television and the confusion of city life? What better way to spend those precious years and gather your thoughts to formulate a plan for a lifetime? The Faraday visitor's book was excellent evidence that in the Antarctic you must expend some energy in getting there to appreciate what it's all about. This can be seen by comparing the simple unadorned signatures of 90 passengers from the *Lingblad Explorer*, like Mr. Joe Blogs, Peoria, Illinois, with the elaborate artwork, prose and poetry left by the very few yachts that had fought to get there and had the opportunity to spend some time.

Certainly David Barker left his artistic mark, He made the point that the Antarctic landscape is both an incredible visual opportunity for an artist and probably one of the most challenging to capture on canvas. Although the glacial landscape often lacks contrast, the moods are anything but subtle. A featureless flat shoreline comes alive in seconds with a hole in the clouds, and the ever-changing light scintillates through and around the ice in a full spectrum of colors—and more often than not just for a precious instant. David is a gentle, patient person of 46 who spent hours ensconced on bouldery beaches or drifting about in the dinghy letting those moments take hold in his memory. Later, on board, he would quickly color in his pencil sketches. These sketches would be the basis for bigger canvases in acrylic that he would do in his studios in either London, New Zealand or Vancouver during the following year.

After five days of hospitality we bid farewell to Faraday and made once again for Dorian Cove for more climbing. Hamish and I finally had the pleasure of seeing Base Camp *Pelagic* from the summit of Luigi on our third attempt from a bivouac at the base of the climb. That was a glorious day. A week later we were bound for King George Island back up in the South Shetland islands. Another rare day in the Gerlache Strait made all schedules seem ridiculous. Windless and sunny we motored through fields

of diamond icebergs on an ink-black sea. We spent the afternoon tied to one small platform with an ice mushroom sprouting from the center that Marco Pretti was destined to climb as soon as he saw it. For a devoted climber an iceberg must be the quintessential climb, never to be repeated because it will soon capsize, break up or vanish forever—a first and last ascent.

While he was "front-pointing" up the sheer face of the mushroom with no rope, I remembered some of our late-night conversations. Marco is not really a mystic, but a thinking-man's romantic in the way he leads his life. Now, at 32 years old, he is one of the top climbers in Europe but admits to having been eclipsed years ago by younger tigers. Looking beyond the days of scaling big walls, which are his specialty, he studied cinematography and wrote a thesis on filming big-wall climbing. *Rockman* is the beautifully

illustrated book he wrote documenting 10 years of climbing around the world, using each situation or expedition to explain his philosophy of life and his thoughts on the future of climbing. In the book, he concludes that big expeditions (like Everest) are the antithesis of his interest in climbing for himself or with a small group of friends, which is really how the whole sport started. He wants to follow an adventure-film career because his climbing provides the vehicle to create fantasy situations, and the film we were making then was really the pilot for this idea. It was clear that we will be doing things together in the future.

Going to King George Island was not on our original itinerary, but David was already late in getting back to New Zealand because of our late departure date some six weeks previous. The Chilean Base Marsh is the transit hub of the Peninsula for all countries and is serviced by regular flights from Punta Arenas in C-130 Hercules aircraft. There is a postal

On the left-hand page, Marco Pretti, leading, and writer/adventurer Skip Novak, belaying him from the foredeck of *Pelagic*, climb the 45-meter iceberg that came to be known affectionately as "Frank." Frank would provide shelter when the wind blew 60 knots one night in a blizzard. On this page Pretti solo-climbs an ice mushroom in the Gerlache Strait. Because of the ephemeral nature of an iceberg, Novak describes this feat as a "quintessential climb—a first and last ascent." Pretti is the author of *Rockman*, a lavishly illustrated book documenting 10 years of climbing and his philosophy of climbing and of life.

service, a weather center and a radio station, but that is where base life ends and a community begins. In the scramble for turf the Chileans have established themselves as the de facto authority and clearing house down here. They boast a working community with women and children. The married couples come down to Marsh for a two-year contract to have a

> "In climbing, the penalty for a mistake is sometimes
> exacted instantaneously, so that on the whole there are fewer
> foolish climbers than foolish sailors."

child—which, of course, is an Antarctic citizen. There is a hotel, and tourist groups from all over the world are billeted for five days and nights at the base to be entertained not only by the Chileans but also by the other bases as well. The Russians are just next door across the frozen stream that flows into the open bay; the Chinese are just down the bulldozed road a piece; and the Koreans, Argentineans, Brazilians and hosts of others are scattered across the bay and along the coast. Each claims to be busy with science, but as one sarcastic observer noted, "There is only one positive aspect of all of those bases taking wind speeds and directions, and that is that the wind is an inexhaustible resource."

When the Antarctic Treaty comes up for review in 1991/92, Chile is probably best positioned to lay claim to that disputable sector by virtue of the fact that the Chileans have put the most effort into developing the area for whatever eventual purpose. They certainly aim to please any visitors, but are sensitive about giving the wrong impression. We did not intend to stay longer than it took to disembark David and his portfolio. While this was being organized it was a fine day, and we took *Pelagic* out into Maxwell Bay where an enormous tabular iceberg had grounded out. Marco and I climbed the 45-meter pitch up the face directly from the foredeck and spent a rare hour on the top living in a dream while strolling around in the sunshine. We then free-rappeled back into the dinghy, which was a fine ending to a well-executed bit of stuntwork. Should someone point out the frequency with which icebergs collapse, cleave off or capsize, I have no excuse for this lunatic behavior other than to say that, if your number's up, what a way to go!

By this time we had had no close shaves in the Antarctic, and our attitude toward the obvious dangers was understandably relaxed at times. It was during one of those times that the easterly blew in right in the middle of an intense cake-baking session early of an evening. This was a bad anchorage at the best of times—and the best of times could never be confused with a wind from the east. We had to motor out of the bay at panic stations, nearly beaching the boat when steering, and we found our headway marginal in 50 to 60 knots of wind and zero visibility in a blizzard. Only Luc, Pretti, De De, Fulvio and I were on board, while others were marooned at the base working on Morosini's scientific film. Unknown to them we spent the whole night motoring back and forth in the lee of that same tabular iceberg we had affectionately named "Frank" that afternoon. Without the radar, finding Frank would have been a much tougher proposition than it was. First light revealed every rope, block and piece of rigging on *Pelagic* frozen solid from sea spray and snow, and we thankfully were able to amble back into our anchorage while shedding our survival suits.

There is no doubt we took risks while in the Antarctic, and it should be made clear that the right equipment and people with ability both on land and sea makes the concept of "sailing to climb" seem like a reasonable endeavor and not foolhardy behavior. But the two activities should be put into perspective for what they are. As Bill Tilman once observed, "The perils of the sea are less apparent than the perils of climbing, and have to be carefully assessed. In climbing, the penalty for a mistake is obvious and is sometimes exacted instantaneously, so that on the whole there are fewer foolish climbers than foolish amateur sailors."

Our last stop before recrossing the Drake would be Deception Island, southwest down the South Shetland chain. It was a calm foggy night with zero visibility when radar led us through the gap in the crater known as Neptune's Bellows. Deception is famous, and its name becomes obvious once you're inside. Port Foster is the lagoon that stretches five miles across to the other side of what is a perfect circular crater and a true haven for any size of ship. The Chileans, the Argentineans and the English all had bases around the lagoon years ago. That was before an act of God blew the lid off a corner of the crater in 1969 and covered most of the exposed land with a heavy layer of ash. The Chilean base was the worst hit, being buried; the BAS base at Whalers Bay survived with some damage, and the Argentinean base on the other side was left completely intact. All personnel were relieved by Chilean and British ships that ran the risk of being trapped in the lagoon if the cliffs above Neptune's Bellows had collapsed, a real concern at the time. We visited all three and found garrisons of fur and elephant seals still on duty.

The expedition was coming to an end. When Antarctic explorer Ernest Shackleton recorded his thoughts in his famous book *South*, he spoke kindly of his ordeal while in the Antarctic in spite of the loss of his "well-found ship, full equipment, and high hopes." "That was all of tangible things," he wrote, "but in memories we were rich. We had pierced the veneer of outside things . . . . We had seen God in his splendours, heard the text that nature renders. We had reached the naked soul of man."

There is a safe small-boat anchorage in the north of the Port Foster lagoon named Telefon Bay, a double cove formed by a fumarole during the last eruption. It still does not appear on the Admiralty chart. We spent six days there getting more and more anxious for the window of weather we needed to fetch safely across the Drake Passage to Ushuaia. It was nearly April and winter was in the air. On a fine day we hiked up the ash and scree to the ridge above the lagoon and saw the ocean sparkling with ice all around. And during the last storm at Deception, before we woke to new-fallen snow on the mountains, we huddled below at the saloon table and talked of future projects together. The planning had already begun. The back of a new envelope was filling up.

The old button factory in Portsmouth, New Hampshire, is remote from the bright commotion of Market Square and the ancient tugboats on the adjacent waterfront. The Morley Company still produces a few buttons, but most of the structure has been converted into studios where a variety of things from advertisements to armoires are created. There is a graphic design firm, a photographer, a furniture maker, a potter, even a theatre group in the rambling brick building. In a sunny and spacious studio amidst this assortment of creative talent, Don Demers, marine artist, stands at a large easel and paints for ten hours a day. □ The artist's rooms are sparsely furnished, the walls bare of everything but his own dramatic paintings. These are vivid representations of schooners working through heavy seas, renowned old whaling ships sailing past glaciers, a derelict lobsterboat and its reflection. The importance of preserving such things is deeply felt by Demers. "It's leaving evidence—a sort of legacy—of our civilization," he says.

DON DEMERS
—TRANSCENDING TIME

BY deLANCEY FUNSTEN

ON PAGE 142, TOPSAIL TRADERS

ABOVE: CROSSING TACKS

TIME TRANSCENDING

These paintings both document the past and meet the artist's need to justify his own existence. They aren't splashes of oil laid on at the artist's whim but carefully thought-out compositions intended to add beauty and meaning to a rapidly changing world. "As I became more serious and interested, I realized that the things I'm most fascinated with are days gone by. The things that motivate human beings now are no different than they were a hundred years ago," says Demers. "I consider myself more of a historian all the time. And I like that about what I do."

It started for him about 27 years ago. "Art has been an interest of mine since I was four or five years old. The minute I could hold a pencil I drew, much to the dismay of most of my teachers!" says Demers with an unrepentant grin. He grew up in Lunenburg, a small town in Massachusetts 50 miles from the Atlantic Ocean. "When the summer months hit I was just miserable there; I was much happier being along the coast," Demers says. His family would often stay with his

> "AS I BECAME MORE SERIOUS AND INTERESTED, I REALIZED THAT THE THINGS THAT I'M MOST FASCINATED WITH ARE DAYS GONE BY."

grandparents in Boothbay Harbor, Maine. These visits aroused powerful responses within Demers. "For some instinctive reason I was just more prone to being around the water than I was the land," he says.

For Demers to combine the inclination to draw with his love for the nautical world was only natural. A friend of his grandfather's, Judge Chet Marden, provided the beginning. "I was just a small boy, and he would come down with these big, big books of sailing ships and old books of seamanship, and I would just sit and devour the stuff," recalls Demers. "By the time I was about 13 I knew pretty much all of the rigging on quite a

few different types of traditional sailing craft—old schooners and square-riggers and stuff like that." Demers meticulously drew these ships over and over again, accurately representing every line. His grandmother preserved the drawings carefully. "She's got a trunk full of them. And each one is exactly the same—just a profile view of a boat—but I was just fascinated with the ships. I literally couldn't wait to get my next book from the judge. I would just consume it . . ."

Demers concentrated on art in high school and enrolled at the Worcester Museum School after graduation, later transferring to Massachusetts College of Art. He found it difficult to choose a medium or a style, of the many in which he was competent, to focus on. Narrowing down to traditional watercolors and oils took a few years. "I had so much ambition and yet so little focus; I had a great tendency to want to be able to do everything. When I worked as an illustrator in and around Boston I did everything from gouache to casein to air brush to pen and ink . . . I was never getting very good at any of it. I used to have this running joke with an illustrator friend of mine. He'd call me up and say 'So what's the technique of the week, Don?' Because I'd have a new one. 'This week it's going to be paraffin and permanent dyes mixed together and floated over fabric.' I used to do all these crazy techniques. I guess it was a good learning process," Demers admits.

Demers did not lose his affinity for the sea during his years in art school, but for a while he was absorbed by a variety of other interests. Then a vessel right out of one of Judge Marden's books came into his life. When he was asked to paint the old Grand Banks fishing schooner *Sherman Zwicker*, Demers received a jolt. "We went on a delivery from Boothbay to Lunenburg, Nova Scotia," Demers remembers. "That really hit me. It was only about a five-day trip, but being on that schooner changed my mentality, changed my attitudes. I really began to focus on who and what I was."

Demers was then a student at Mass Art, and when he came back from the schooner trip he wanted to place as much emphasis as possible on marine art. The faculty didn't agree, and the resultant controversy meant that Demers received

AT LEFT, REPRIEVE/ABOVE, MAIL TO MONHEGAN

very little training in what he wanted to study: traditional oil and watercolor painting. "I got tired of having teachers tell me what I had to be interested in to find integrity. I kept wanting to do a painting of a sailing ship, and they kept wanting me to do an abstract interpretation of the social order. Or something less than that. Some colorfield painting of how two reds responded against each other." This academic difficulty did not hinder Demers; rather, it allowed him more freedom to develop his own style.

The following summer Demers discovered the two-masted, square-rigged training ship *Unicorn* tied up across from the Boston Aquarium. He applied for a place, took a week off from his summer job and climbed on board. "It was literally a dream come true. I knew practically every line on that boat. I'd studied them before—I'd just never be able to get my hands on them." He asked the first mate if he could continue to sail on the boat as a volunteer. "He said I could, so I sublet my apartment, quit my summer job, withdrew from school; I just dumped everything and went sailing." When monetary considerations began to interfere, Demers found a freelance job as an illustrator for a greeting card company that specialized in nautical subjects. "If sailing on the

Sherman Zwicker was the seed that was planted, then the *Unicorn* was really the harvest because I was completely entrenched in maritime history. I loved it," he says. "I knew that that was where my interests, my attitudes, my philosophies lay. It was a real period of self-realization because it confirmed all these vague notions I'd had prior to that and gave me something tangible to sink all of my feelings into."

There is a philosophical quality about Demers, a realization that there are more important things to consider than meeting his mortgage payments on time. This seems to have developed from his fascination with the past, with old vessels, old adventures, old ways of doing things, "I think you can learn so many lessons by looking back at the way things were. And you also have a realization that things really haven't changed that much as far as the human experience is concerned, even since the 1700s and 1800s. The way we got here, from way back then, was a thing that happened day-to-day. It was from yesterday to the day before—a change that none of us notice on a day-to-day basis. The past is tied in with the present and I'm particularly fascinated by that," he says. "It was reflected in a lot of the old-timers in Ireland who spoke about the potato famine back in the 1800s like it happened ten days ago. They've really got that sense of the unity of time . . . The painting that I'm working on now is going to be titled 'Time Transcending' or something to that effect, because even though it's a present-day scene in Mystic, there isn't anything in that image that really can place it in this century."

After leaving school Demers worked as an illustrator in the Boston area. He painted traditional vessels at every opportunity but was only averaging four or five marine paintings per year. He found this increasingly frustrating. In 1984 he sailed from Jamaica to the west coast aboard *Fair Sarae*, a 110´ staysail schooner. The three-month trip gave him an opportunity to examine his life, which resulted in a decision to leave Boston. The next year he moved to Kittery, Maine, where he lives with his wife, graphic designer Francesca Mastrangelo.

The move coincided with, or perhaps triggered, what Demers feels was a surge of improvement in

> "MY SOLITUDE IS IMPORTANT TO ME. THE MORE THOUGHTFUL I CAN BE, I FIND THE MORE EMOTIONAL AND EFFECTIVE MY PAINTINGS ARE."

his maritime work. "I went through a catapulting of development," Demers says. "Every painting gets better." He seems somewhat astounded by this. "I've actually done some paintings that I never thought I'd be able to do." The catapulting of development, he thinks, might also have something to do with the work ethic that his father instilled in him from an early age. "Just simply by putting in that much time and loving something, it was bound to evolve. I'm not even

sure how much of a role talent plays in it. Other people are a lot quicker to make those claims than I am."

Some of Demers's clients include Sail Magazine, Yankee Magazine, Reader's Digest and Down East Magazine. He is a member of the American Society of Marine Artists, which he feels has helped his career immeasurably in terms of exposure to other marine artists. In addition, Demers has been accepted twice into the Society of Illustrators' annual show and twice selected for the Communication Arts annual publication. One patron with no doubts about Demers's talent is Elizabeth Meyer, owner of the J-boat *Endeavour* and publisher of a lavish new book on the Concordia yawls. "Don is extraordinary," Meyer says. "When we began to plan the Concordia book I thought of him immediately. He's very good, extremely versatile, in addition to being a really personable guy. It's just such an unusual

AT LEFT, HADDOCK CHASERS/ABOVE, RESTING HER BONES

combination." One of the artist's illustrations for the Concordia book appears in these pages. Meyer's one concern for Demers is geographic. "The only thing is, he's sort of off in a corner; he really isn't getting the publicity he should," she explains. This lack of exposure is being remedied. Demers's first one-man show was held in November at the Mystic Maritime Gallery, part of Mystic Seaport in Connecticut.

Demers still sails traditional vessels at every chance, and values the friendships made aboard *Unicorn*. He owns a 16´ Whitehall and an Alden Ocean Shell, and when he's not frenetically preparing for a show he rows for about an hour every day. "My solitude is important to me," he says. "The more thoughtful I can be, I find the more emotional and effective my paintings are. So

> "FOR ME THE MOST IMPORTANT THING IS NOT TO KNOW WHETHER I'M GOOD OR NOT, IT'S TO KNOW THAT I'M GETTING BETTER."

besides the physical-exercise aspects of rowing in my shell, the mental process involved in it is at least if not more important to me. I come out of that thing just bursting with goodwill and a sense of my environment."

Demers supports himself by doing what he likes, which is quite an accomplishment for any

person, particularly an artist in his early thirties. "I could never be a lot happier than I am now," he says. "The great thing is—if I had a week off, I'd paint. I do honestly feel as though I'll be doing the same thing when I'm 65 or 70, God willing. And I hope to be doing it at a more developed level.

"To me a painting or developing a career is like a horse race," says Demers. "You've got to look over each shoulder and see what the other guy is doing, but your primary objective is to keep moving forward. It's sort of a dual awareness. For me the most important thing is not to know whether I'm good or not, it's to know that I'm getting better. As long as I can keep making those relative comparisons against my own work that's what's going to satisfy me."

PERSPECTIVE

WHO ARE THESE PEOPLE?

BY REESE PALLEY

There were three of us in the room wearing sweaters. Two had ties under their blue V-necks and I had an open collar under my orange crew. The rest of the 150 men wore blue blazers, double-breasted and with golden buttons engraved with anchors and intertwined line and other marine devices. Some of the buttons were, I am sure, of real gold, as were the majority of the folk in the room. Neckties were scattered with flags and flying fish, and trousers were of varying shades of unobtrusive colors save for one gent, saltier than the rest, who sported a pair of bright red slacks. The men were well-fed and over 50. Their women were handsome and tough-looking, managing to meld beauty, money and respectability into an ageless sexuality. A successful, homogeneous, tailored gathering of cookie-cut people on whose politics and attitudes you could bet the ranch and never lose. Or so I thought.

The occasion was a Mystic Seaport meeting of a sailing club of unassailable respectability. I squirmed some in my sweater, and it was with relief that the house lights dimmed and Mr. R. tickled our history bone with an erudite and amusing tale of the origins and growth of our "pastime," as he called sailing. I settled back secure that I knew these folk. No surprises here—and if I was a bit *outré* for their tastes it was better that I should attract the small smiles than the poor saps in the blue sweaters who, unlike myself, should have known better.

The first crack in the façade almost swept past me. The podium was dealing with the recent history of the America's Cup and, in that heavy ambience of the New York Yacht Club dragged north, I knew with certainty what was coming. And then, without warning and out of context, the speaker announced that, "as a Calvinist I view the recent defense of the Cup much as I would a *mugging* on the streets of

> The cruising types I have met fit no mold but share one clear characteristic —all have come to know that real freedom exists only at sea.

New York." I thought that he had misspoke or that I had misheard the speaker, so secure was I in my pre-judgments. But as he went on to reduce the Cup defense to an arrogant farce, I had to reconsider my opinions—first of the speaker and later, on other evidence, of the sea of blue about me.

Afterwards the meeting settled back with genteel chit chat and good (and uniform) fellowship. The mugging mystery behind me I was once again secure in the regularity of these blue-jacketed and Laura-Ashleyed folk until, as we passed from meeting to cocktails, one of the ladies greeted a friend with, "My dear, I hardly recognized you with your clothes on!"

This one remark, so out of phase with the seeming proprieties of the meeting, instantly evoked the strange sailorly folk with whom I, and I hope you, have been consorting for some decades. All of the cruising types I have met fit no mold but share one clear characteristic—all have come to know that real freedom from our too-much-with-us world exists only at sea. We are all, with a wink at the blue jackets who understand anyway, anarchists and revolutionaries. While we carry no bombs, and indeed some will not even carry a pop gun, some countries consider us freedom-seekers as dangerous as the old-time Bolsheviks.

No matter from what class of money or background, we are all strangely equal in one anothers' eyes. We are all immigrants to the sea. Each of us starts from ground zero and gains sailorly respect not from what we bring to the sea but from what we learn from the sea. We are the only real democracy left on earth.

So here are a few of the cruising types that good fortune has found for me. Unregenerate, uncontrolled and undisciplined (except for sea sense and a seaman's prudence), they sail to an unheard rhythm the words of which are something like "goodbye to things that bore me, life is waiting for me."

Most of us go to sea to please ourselves. This South African sailor was old-fashioned enough to go to sea to please his God. I first met him in Israel at the marina in Tel Aviv. His boat was home-built with a poop deck as high as a mizzen all hung about with the debris of family. When I asked an Israeli friend about the strange boat he raised an irreverent eyebrow, lowered the other, pursed his lips in mordant disdain and said, "Oh, that's the Christian sailor who talks to God every day." It is easy to spoof believers, especially these days when we are surfeit with religious boobies who clutter up our tubal Sundays and preempt the Late Late Show. When the genuine article comes along we are so confused by the phonies that we tend to hold it with tweezers at arms length.

Bob Schaafsma, the sailor who talks to God, is the real thing. In Bob's lovely world God talks back, and one day in conversation God reminded Bob that the Bible had predicted that Judgment Day could only occur when His Chosen People were once more all returned to Israel. God assigned to Bob the task of return. Bob was to arrange, in the face of locked borders and reluctant governments, the transportation of the Hebrews to the Holy Land.

How simple and obvious was Bob's scheme. He would build 50′ sailboats, wide and deep, rigged

PERSPECTIVE

below to accept a small car and a house trailer so that the escapees might have transportation and a place to live on arrival. He would load the boats with families and all of their worldly goods and sail them, free of borders, free of police and customs officials, to Israel. I hid a snicker as Bob, wide-eyed and serious, revealed to me his grand plan of salvation. The snicker died as I thought of how many victims of the Holocaust might have been saved by small boats lifting harried souls from the coasts of Hitler's Germany. Bob Schaafsma had tapped into the central fact of the small sailor's world. He knew that sailors in small yachts are more free than any other folks on earth and can do quietly what armies fail. He knew that sailors may not be the shakers of the world, but, on a tiny scale, they can be the movers.

Like all the other cruising types I have met, Bob Schaafsma knew in his soul that the roads to freedom lie only across the deep oceans.

Captain Peter was pushing a clownish little tramp containership around the dingier ports of hopeless East Africa when I met him. He sat with me in his little cabin and worried at his absence from the good fight like a baby worries at a new tooth. He is a young man, at least by my ken if not by his. He is tall, Lincolnesque and troubled.

For occasional visitors he relives his glory days of Greenpeace, the great battles in Iceland and the Antarctic between the small sailing vessel he skippered and the whale factories he challenged. He spoke of adrenaline and Zodiacs, an unconscious alpha and omega of the perfect life. He spoke of the substitution of guts for guns and brains for the brute swoosh of the harpoon. He spoke of giggly, exalting glee, over a pod of whales rescued from the flensers' knives or a single animal saved by a man in a rubber boat offering his own breast, as he had, to the harpooner's gun. Peter had reached for, and found, the reason for his existence. He was at the front lines between the children of light and the children of darkness.

> Ziggy was a dream
> in any emergency. He was
> frighteningly strong,
> and would put his strength
> at any risk without
> a thought to himself.

But Greenpeace was over for Peter. He now had a new project. He had discovered a new Greenpeace. He and his vessel would stand not between whales and harpoons but between the helpless, hopeless folk of East Africa and poverty, disease and starvation. "We call it Devon Sail and it's about building a sailing ship," he said, and here his voice speeded into a rush of explanation as if I might not stay to listen. "And we will take kids from England in trouble with the law and make sailors out of them and sail down the coasts of Sudan and Ethiopia and Somalia and set up artisan workshops and teach agriculture and water technology and carry native goods back to England to sell and use the money for other trips, and we will be only the first seed of many sailing ships that will copy and imitate us until we have a nation of little boats curing the cultural emptiness of our own young while filling the bellies of East Africa."

A sailor's vision. A looming hope for a sailor in need of a cause. Peter's adrenaline was up and, as it sped him to his saintly goal, some poor folk in poor East Africa, not many but some, would die later rather than sooner.

Hooray for Captain Peter.

I never knew a less admirable human being nor, at the same time, a more admirable shipmate. When I met him, Ziggy was on the run from the Spanish government for desertion from the Spanish Foreign Legion. He had joined that curious unit to escape from the German government to whom he admitted

owing a very large sum of taxes. I suspect that the tax problem was only the tip of an iceberg of fiscal and civil offenses because Ziggy, the eeliest of types, would easily have slithered out of so small a *contretemps* as taxation.

Ziggy was primal. His every instinct, his every response, was a manning of the ramparts. He was a survivor in a game he was not destined to win. He had been dealt lousy cards which, it must be admitted, he played badly. Ziggy could read—about a page a day—but only from sappy love and adventure novels printed in large type. In the time I knew him he never read, or even glanced at, a newspaper. The world about him was tactile—what he could touch he knew. All else beyond the reach of his senses was a fog that held neither threat nor promise for him. Politics, art, literature and history were not even words in his vocabulary.

Ziggy was blond and his judgment of folk was on a descending scale of whiteness. Anyone less blond was suspect. Dark skins were "monkeys"; Italians were dismissible as Europeans; the English made goods that were "rubbish"; the French were lousy engineers. Women were an unmentionable word and existed solely for his pleasure and use. He must have been a creative lover because despite his despicable nature his retinue of obedient females was impressive.

Ziggy gave no one his loyalty. For short periods he would rent his loyalty out but the lease was easily and frequently canceled. He was a liar, a cheat, a scoundrel, a thief and, if the truth be known, probably a murderer, a pedophile and a pederast.

But that was Ziggy ashore. The moment Ziggy stepped aboard a sailboat he was the best shipmate I have ever known. He became intensely loyal to the boat and the skipper and would fight off attacks, both financial and physical, with the intensity of a doberman. He was gentle with crew and refrained from the more obscene four-letter words while untied from dock. And Ziggy was a dream in an emergency. He was frighteningly strong, and would put his strength at risk without a thought to self. He was instinctive as a sailor and

PERSPECTIVE

brutally creative as a mechanic. Engines did not last long around Ziggy but when needed they ran—cowered a bit, but ran.

His touch on a tiller was as gentle as his view of the world was fierce. Ziggy, stateless and without a passport, knew that the one place in the world in which he could be free was in a sailboat. Ziggy came to me in Djibouti, rowing over from a boat on which he had just arrived. He was in trouble with his skipper and, without papers, he could not even go ashore. Ziggy needed passage to the Med on a small sailboat free of the close scrutiny of officialdom. I was his only hope, the only small boat in Djibouti going north.

I took him on and he restepped my broken 55´ mast almost with his own strength alone. He kept my reluctant engine going in the turbulence of the Red Sea and he cadged free fuel and supplies from beer buddies on oil rigs on the way north. Ziggy saved my life and my boat more than once and served with cheerful selflessness all the time he was aboard.

I agreed to take him to Israel where the Israelis, with their deep knowledge of statelessness, let him ashore. Someone gave him an engineless, mastless, sail-less wreck of a wooden 21´ sloop for which Ziggy promised to pay a huge sum when he had it in shape. I pointed out that he was being cheated, but Ziggy shrugged and went on rebuilding his frail craft with whatever inadequate materials and equipment he could beg, borrow, or as it proved, steal. Ziggy, who had always held the world at ransom, was getting his comeuppance.

One dawn we awoke to find Ziggy, his latest female serf and the little engineless boat gone. In the night he had slipped his lines and drifted quietly in a most seamanlike fashion though the tight noose of security that the Israelis have thrown around their beleaguered nation. He left behind him innocent folk who, secure in Ziggy's lack of a passport, thought that their property was safe with him. Ziggy had found a way, the only way, to survive in a world where people *sans* passports were fair game for any petty policeman. Ziggy knew, as those of us who, in

Landlubbers would label
him an "invalid" while sailors
would applaud his
ranging spirit and label him
"valid," or, more to
the point, not label him at all.

other contexts, take to the sea know, that only at sea, needing only the winds, would he ever be able to be his own man.

I sailed from Israel and made port in Larnaca on Cyprus. As I pulled in, a familiar blond sailor waved to me from the dock. Ziggy in his impossible little boat had made the first leg of his passage to freedom. I was delighted.

I leaned across the bow and called out, "Hey Ziggy—terrific—glad to see you." Ziggy smiled, cupped his hands and in a stentorian stage whisper called back, "Don't . . . call . . . me . . . Ziggy!"

One day in Rhodes I met the Standing Sailor. He is a Scandinavian who had run afoul of his orthopedic surgeon. Having contracted an arcane condition which necessitated a fused spinal column, his doctor offered him Hobson's Choice—either he could spend the rest of his days on his back (unthinkable!) or on his feet. He chose his feet and instead of opting for the steadying reassurance of solid land he chose to build himself a lurchabout boat and go to sea. A strange choice for a man who could neither sit nor lie down; but no one ever accused the Standing Sailor of not being strange.

The Standing Sailor needed special accommodations not to be found at any boat show. He designed and built his own, a boat both weird and ugly which he dubbed *Plato* for reasons that I never understood. It consists of a tall box (for standing up in) mounted on a pair of hulls. The box is lined with chest-high shelves for eating at and for writing

on and a place to lean for sleep. The catamaran, for so it is, sports a rigid wing sail so much like its creator's fused back that it could hardly have been accidental. His head is a slit-trench built down into one of the hulls—a particularly clever solution to a tough problem.

The Standing Sailor is less interesting for his physical solutions than for his instinctual grasp that the landlubbers would label him an "invalid" while sailors would applaud his ranging spirit and label him "valid," or, more to the point, not label him at all. The Standing Sailor is out there now, somewhere in the Med, potting along very slowly with his inefficient sail and even less efficient back.

But he is doing it, on his own, and he is free.

Thomas had an appointment in Phuket, and come hell or high water he was going to keep it. Thomas was a beautiful, very young man who was hiding his South African origins and accent behind a German passport when I met him in Djibouti. He had accepted the job of delivering a lightly built French sloop from the Med to Thailand. In Djibouti he was halfway there, and both he and his vessel were displaying their sailorly inadequacies. Thomas had never been to sea before, knew no celestial, had no electronics or safety gear aboard. His crew deserted him, as I would have, and he picked up an Ethiopian refugee with no sailing experience. His other crew was a young drug dealer who was desperate to get out of town ahead of the police. He said he had experience but, in truth, he had no more than the Ethiopian and was a damn sight less dependable.

Despite our pleas, Thomas set off for Phuket at the wrong season, in the wrong boat, with the wrong crew and with himself as a dangerous and deficient skipper. There was no way he could make it across the nasty Indian Ocean.

But he did. He kept his appointment in Phuket. I received a card some months later from Thomas that told me he was delighted with his accomplishment, delighted with Thailand and delighted with himself.

PERSPECTIVE

A week later a call came from his parents in South Africa. Thomas had kept his appointment in Phuket. He had been killed in a dumb motorcycle accident after bravely crossing one of the worst oceans.

The 25´ Vertue came in under full sail, no engine and no one on the foredeck. Only the helmsman could be seen. The little boat sailed quietly through the cluttered anchorage, picked her way among the clumsy big charter yachts, and swung around sharply into the wind in a small clear area far from the crowd. She stopped dead as a sailboat must when brought into the wind. The helmsman crawled creakily out of the cockpit and, in an old man's hobble, limped to the bow where his rode had already been flaked out. He silently paid out and put his hook into the harbor bottom. He slowly (for he was a very old man and could do little quickly) took down his main and bagged his jib while the Vertue was finding her natural lay. He then went aft and disappeared below, from which he reappeared eight hours later refreshed, as he told me the next day, by a sound nap. The whole process took about ten minutes and was accomplished without a sound.

From this little dance, a soft-shoe shuffle by an old man approaching his eighties, I learned that an entrance into a harbor need not be, nay must not be, accompanied by the shrill business of panic and dismay. The old man knew his boat, knew her habits, knew the harbor and had carefully prepared for anchoring. All went as well for him as it usually went badly for me, and I decided to stop charging full ahead and to start learning. The elegant ancient was Humphrey Barton, Admiral of the Ocean Cruising Club, Crosser of Big Oceans in Small Vertues. The Admiral had something I wanted.

I didn't know who he was that day in the harbor of Tortola but I went acalling anyway. He and his lady welcomed me graciously aboard a tiny boat (this was his 17th Atlantic crossing) that was neat as a pin and salty as a herring. It was all warm, dark wood and laden with books where, today, we

> I learned that an entrance into harbor need not be, nay must not be, accompanied by the shrill business of panic and dismay.

might be overladen with electronics. We talked about the elegance of his entrance and the disasters of mine. He assured me that it was no disgrace to be a beginner—the only disgrace was to *stay* a beginner.

From Humphrey Barton I ultimately learned that a good entrance into any port is no accident. It is a product of thought, judgment and experience. "An elegant entrance," the Admiral told me, "is when you arrive with the least possible effort and," he added with a wry smile, "a *perfectly* elegant entrance is when you do it with no effort at all."

Ed was no sailor. He became 65 and developed an unscratchable itch to put the world behind him. Ed was not locked in by outside forces. He had been imprisoned by an unstoppable urge for more and bigger businesses. Everything he touched grew, expanded. Money became merely a way to keep score. There was nothing left that Ed could not buy, and this, in a way, made him less free and more dependent on using the endless sums he was generating. For if he could not use money in a manner that would calm his ambition, his aggression, then why was he working so hard at accumulation? And if accumulation ceased to have a goal and became the meaningless goal itself, Ed sensed that he would be cheated—richly cheated but cheated nevertheless.

So one day at the Annapolis Boat Show, in Henry Wagner's booth where I was signing books, this tall, spare and elegant man introduced himself. He had known my dad, which instantly endeared

him to me. As a favor, he asked with an appealing diffidence whether I would give an opinion on a boat he wanted to buy. I hated the boat. Ed loved it—and, then and there, he bought his first-ever sailboat at a million dollars, never having so much as sailed across a lake.

Ed had no idea of the delights of sailing. He knew nothing of the climactic thrill of a landfall or the quiet self-confident delight that suffuses a sailor after a bout with a squall. But Ed knew something. He seemed to have a deep conviction that this boat would give meaning and stretch to his life. The boat, he confessed to me later, was acquired on instinct alone. This most unpoetic man said that his heart told him to do it.

Three months later we gathered a crew and crossed the big pond. Ed was never to be the same again. In the three weeks of passage he saw the shape of his future. His businesses became annoying intervals between passages. His family became crew. He stretched his no-longer-young-muscles on the foredeck; he took his turn in the galley; he shot the sun each day and the stars at dusk. He stowed stores, worried about the depleting fresh water and, sitting astride the lurching bowsprit, he mended a jib when a seam opened. These tasks, unthinkable burdens at home, became joyous celebrations of the sea.

Ed made himself into a sailor and took back his life. His beloved boat had created meaning not only for Ed but for Ed's money—without a boat to buy, his money was dross.

Gray beard trimmed precisely, feet shod in sandals crafted by the small hands of the East, dressed in Thai silk pants full in the stern like a third leg and draped loosely to the waist, he wafted about the lobby of the Pera Palas in Istanbul perfectly at home. It was the hotel and the city that seemed displaced, not Kung.

If Kung said life was a fountain then life was a fountain. You could bet the ranch on it. Like everyone else at the hotel I was in his thrall. I itched to meet him, to learn from him.

PERSPECTIVE

Later that morning he wandered to my table and asked, over his shoulder as he passed, a curious question.

"I am told," a distant look, a long sigh, "but perhaps I am wrong . . . sorry." He turned away and then back "Ah, yes . . . that you are . . . hmmm . . . that you have a sailing vessel. Is that true? To what destination do you go?"

I had him on my ground.

"West toward Greece."

"And . . . but perhaps I should not ask . . . well." Long pause. "How many individuals do you sail with on your boat?"

"Five—my wife, my brother, two cousins and myself," I answered, wanting to tell him more.

"And," he asked as he danced lightly toward and away from me, his voice a mere whisper, rising and falling with the distance, "how many more persons could your boat . . . accommodate?"

A very curious question. But from Kung one came quickly to expect the curious. And an even more stunning followup.

"Perhaps . . . ," the longest pause yet, almost as if the conversation were over, "perhaps, oh, hmm, hmm, yes, yes . . . perhaps I shall accompany you for a day or two."

My voice failed and all I could do was nod with such vigor that my glasses slid down my nose.

"Oh, yes. You would be so welcome. It would be an honor, an honor." I wanted to kiss his sandled feet.

"Hm, yes, it might be . . . ," pause, pause, shuffle and smile and a short walk away then back, "nice. We shall see . . . won't we?" His smile crinkled his eyes behind his Ben Franklin glasses and calmed me, made me feel . . . nice.

I could hardly wait. For some hours to take from Kung a bit of his quiet, his otherworldliness, his contentment. To have him with me on my boat was perhaps the reason why I owned the boat at all. Kung drifted away, his feet barely touching the floor. Mine did not at all.

That evening Kung took us out to dinner. He talked of sailing. He had never sailed and apologized,

> If Kung said life
> was a fountain then life
> was a fountain. You
> could bet the ranch on it. Like
> everyone else at the hotel
> I was in his thrall.

painfully, for imposing himself upon us. His auto-invitation he explained, was part of his search for knowledge and experience. He had, he told us, listened to many sailors and had often wondered what the charm of the sea could be. Our appearance was serendipitous (Kung actually used the word), a gift from the gods, "which would have been hubristic to ignore." His shyness, the hesitancy, the approach-avoidance, the pleasing expression of unsureness of self, spread out and covered us with good feelings.

The next morning, in company with a forlorn and about to be bereft retinue of acolytes, Kung appeared at the dock. Thirty people saw him off, many in tears. Kung offered a farewell blessing to the abandoned ones and stepped aboard. His sense of how to act on a sailboat was intuitively correct. His luggage was small and soft. His sandals came off before his feet touched the deck. He failed to wrench at the Loran antenna at the stern as he mounted the rail. He touched no line as he came aboard and, once on deck, he magically reduced himself in size by half and, for the rest of the voyage, never once was in anyone's way. Had he never really been sailing before? Kung assured us that he had not. Kung had raised to a high level the East's ability to conform to circumstances. He had an innate knowledge of how a sailor should be.

During the two days of the passage from Istanbul, Kung, already a wraith, became less and less substantial. Like the Cheshire cat, at times he seemed little more than a smile as he let himself

sink into the spirit and texture of passing over a sea in a sailing vessel. The pace and tempo, the speed, or lack of it, intensified Kung's essentially meditative personality.

With painful embarrassment he ventured a peculiar plaint, "This passage . . . it is perhaps too pleasant. The winds are mild and the sun is clear and the air is pure. It is, a thousand, thousand pardons . . . it could be just a bit . . . grittier?" We explained that things on a sailing passage were often worse to the point of incapacitation. Kung liked that word. "Incapacitation as a way to truth? Yes, that is very Eastern. Perhaps you sailors lean closer to Zen than you might like to admit." He smiled quietly, looking inward for a dozen moments, and then said, "Thank you. I have learned something about sailing. I have learned something about the West. I have filled in a small gap." When we pressed him to share his discovery with us he said, "A teacher urges, never directs, hints never explains, asks questions, never gives answers . . . patience, patience."

It was on notes like these, scarce on most sailboats, that we passed a day and two nights on a quiet passage. All tensions of the crew disappeared in the soothe of Kung's quiet delight in the sea. He reminded us, sailors whose first tastes of the sea were decades old and whose capacities for wonder a bit dulled by time, of the jubilate moments of our own first passages. He required us to become childlike—to smell, to look, to hear and to feel the sea as a new experience. Most tyros aboard a sailboat require teaching. This tyro taught.

Editor's Note: Free from business (or almost), Reese Palley voyages in the Med and other seas accompanied by friends, family and a variety of "cruising types" aboard his 50´ cutter *Unlikely*. He is himself one of the liberated, eccentric cruising types he describes so charmingly here. Reese and *Unlikely* are in Odessa, U.S.S.R., this summer, and his article on the Russian yachting scene will appear in NQ49.

GETTING THE ESSENCE

BY deLANCEY FUNSTEN

ON PAGE 155, *MATADOR* OFFSHORE/ABOVE, SETTING THE CHUTE

rank Hartman Wagner walked into our office one afternoon last spring and pulled a handful of 8x10″ transparencies of his work from an envelope. Unsolicited paintings, photographs and articles, and casual visits by their creators, are not uncommon at Nautical Quarterly—but this was different. What was unusual was the vitality of Wagner's paintings and the impact that they had on all of us. There was no debate this time about whether or not to publish the work of this newcomer to marine art—editor, publisher and designer agreed that these were wonderful paintings. □ Like many artists, Frank Wagner's ability emerged when he was very young. In a way the vocation chose him. "As a five-year-old I was painting pictures," he recalls. "We had a high-school art teacher that roomed with us in Bay Shore, Long Island. I just loved the pictures coming out of his pencil. He used to put me on his knee and draw pictures, and I've kept making pictures like that ever since." Wagner says he never really felt that he had to work for a living. "I just kept making pictures and it became my livelihood, so I'm very fortunate."

POWER REACH

FRIESLAND SOLILOQUY

He never wavered in his desire to paint, and he was blessed with parents who may have questioned their son's ability to support himself with art but still appreciated and encouraged his talent. "I don't think they thought there was a possibility that I could earn a living with it. The 'strange people' in Greenwich Village in the thirties were what my parents had in their minds as art types, and they didn't see me in that kind of environment." Their confidence was soon justified. Wagner achieved recognition early, winning national poster competitions in grade school, and this earned him the kind of attention that led to art-school scholarships and a year's study in Europe.

Wagner's sense of composition and sure touch in several mediums reveal what years of training and studying the masters at a variety of schools taught him. His family moved to Florida during World War II, and Frank began studying at the Norton School of Art in West Palm Beach. Back in New York he attended the Stony Brook School on Long Island and subsequently the University of Pennsylvania and the renowned Pennsylvania Academy of Fine Arts. When he decided to pursue commercial art rather than fine art, Wagner transferred to Pratt Institute in Brooklyn. After graduating in '54, he was granted a European Fellowship by the Leopold Schepp Foundation, a New York organization established to assist art students financially. The year was divided between classes at the Royal Academy in London and the Rijksakademie in Amsterdam, along with independent study at the Louvre and in the galleries of Florence. Wagner still talks of that year in Europe with a sense of wonder. "It was a year that put me back as far as starting off work in New York, but it was a year that was very important for my development at that point," he says. "I was not ready to go into the art market. It was a good year. I met very supportive friends—the people that I lived with in Holland were just the right kind of people for me to be with as a young man."

Someone Wagner also found to be the right sort of person for him was Elizabeth Bray. He had a bit of trouble getting to know the young Englishwoman he'd met while playing ping pong at a student hostel outside London. "She wouldn't go out with me because she'd been warned by her dad not to go out with strange Americans," explains Wagner. "She came from a seaport town, Portsmouth, and there were American ships there—a lot of sailors. I suppose they might have been regarded by the conservative English in those days as strange company." Despite these reservations, Elizabeth became Wagner's friend and ten years later his persistence paid off when she agreed to marry him.

The young artist accumulated more than 1800 photographs in the course of the year, giving him a wonderful permanent record of the Continent during the mid-fifties. When he returned home, Wagner found work in New York City. There were ample painting assignments from advertising agencies and publishing houses, and his early clients included Reader's Digest, Time-Life and Woolworth's. Manhattan has traditionally been a good place to begin a career, and Wagner reasonably expected to live in his Riverside Drive apartment for some time to come. Then the owner of a large studio in Detroit came to New York to recruit artists. The automobile industry had a great need for high-quality commercial art in those days when illustration was preferred over photography in car advertising. "He took a room in the Waldorf and a classified directory and called every artist in New York City, I think," remembers Wagner. "I went up to see him and as a result of that went out to Detroit not expecting to stay for any length of time." To his surprise, Wagner wound up living in Detroit for 19 years. "It provided a climate in which I was able to be very productive," he says. Literally thousands of paintings were ordered to meet the needs of the car industry. I developed a way

INTREPID

of painting that was very direct, because I had time constraints and deadlines and had to produce an awful lot. So it helped me to really get into a picture and do away with the extraneous stuff. To get to the guts of the painting quickly and go after a feeling and effect that would solve the problem and meet the need of the advertiser. It was a good training ground. When you have to produce a lot, it gets the juices going. When you have one or two jobs, you tend to fret over them—you take a long, long time, and it just gets ponderous—it slows down the process of arriving at who you are. If you have a lot of work it tends to open up an awareness of what your style really comes down to because you're not self-conscious about it—you're not trying to decide what your style is and to make an independent statement. It just happens because you have to get there fast and what you are just comes. And then that gets refined over the years and some things that were there in the beginning have a tendency to drop away. You become a little more facile."

Wagner's long sojourn in Detroit was interspersed with frequent trips to Europe and a romantic year in Switzerland. In 1975, he and his wife and two children, Hartman and Sarah, moved to Cape Cod. He was confident there was sufficient work to be found in Boston or Providence. This was the case, and he began working for ad agencies in both cities. After a while the advertising business proved to be a shrinking market for illustration, and Wagner decided that the time was right to go into fine arts. He'd done some marine work for Sperry Topsider and took it to New York in search of a gallery. There was considerable interest in his portfolio, and he had some immediate successes. He is now on permanent exhibit at the Smith Gallery in New York, a firm that specializes in marine art. He also exhibits regularly at the Mystic Maritime Gallery of Mystic Seaport, where he received an Award of Excellence at the International Exhibition in 1988.

The first public display of Wagner's work was at the New York Armory Show in January, 1988, a stimulating experience. "It was an enormous show

ON PAGE 160, SUNDAY SENIOR RACES ON WEST BAY/ ABOVE, *VIM* AND *MOUETTE*

with galleries represented from all over the world—Florence, Rome, Paris and London—and dealers came with work by Degas, Monet, Cézanne . . . Major American galleries were there also, from all over the country. And lo and behold I was hanging there in such company. Three of my paintings were purchased by a leading American collector, all in one day—fantastic! Two of them were of *American Eagle*, a 12-Meter several friends and I are fortunate enough to own. So that was real encouragement right at the start."

Since his entry into the fine-art world only a few years ago, Wagner has produced about 30 marine paintings. His attitude towards this work is straightforward. He doesn't complicate it with fussiness and second-guessing. "I paint quickly. I aim to achieve an atmosphere and an environment in my painting in one day, so it's there. Then all there is left to do is polish. I know if I have a winner after only one day. If it's not going to be any good I don't bother with it. I begin something else. Many times it's good to have more than one painting going at once, because

there is a tendency to get into something and become absorbed with the delicacies and the nuances of the detail—texture and loving little areas that may or may not contribute to the picture as a whole. So being away from a picture for a day or two tends to help. When you come back to it, you see it fresh."

Some of Frank Wagner's paintings are moody and still and romantic—a skûtsje (Dutch sloop-rigged barge) anchored in a canal near a windmill; a family watching boats pass by from their Wianno Senior in the fading light of late afternoon. These combine memory with some of the hundreds of shots Wagner took with his little Voigtlander camera when he lived in Holland. Others are full of drama—two 12-Meters on a run with their spinnakers flying; *American Eagle* driving for the mark; the Maxi *Matador* plowing into rollers. Wagner claims that he is not really a marine painter. "I enjoy the sea; I've always lived around the sea; it's always held a fascination for me. But I like painting anything, and I find that I can get just as lost in the petal of a flower

JIBING THE SKÛTSJES

ENDEAVOUR AND FAST COMPANY

as in a wave . . ." (Some of his other paintings are spectacular enlarged images of flowers.)

Wagner works in a studio adjacent to his house in Barnstable, Massachusetts. Having worked in association with other artists in a studio environment early in his career, at this stage he really enjoys the clarity of focus that he finds in painting by himself. Long hours pass quickly, unconsciously, a phenomenon experienced by many other painters. "Isolation is not, as some would have us believe, a recipe for dryness; it doesn't have to be that way at all. One could argue that monasticism is a useless activity, but you couldn't prove that to a monk." He continues to be prolific and has begun publishing limited-edition prints of his work, sharing the job of distribution with Janus Lithographs of Hilton Head, S.C. The publishing company is Longfleet House, for which the principal outlet on Cape Cod is Yankee Accent in Osterville. The advantage of discipline in refining natural talent is readily acknowledged by Wagner. "The guts of what I am now was there in the beginning, just unpolished. I think it's that way with every artist. There is an evolution in their style, but what the person was as a young man or woman is what they are later, only more fine-tuned. That points to a process, a development, a gift, rather than a self-made progression of talent. Talent is more a gift that it is self-generated. It's the development of what is given. Some people do a lot with what they are given, others do a little, and some do nothing at all." As the paintings in these pages witness, Frank Wagner has done a lot with what he, an art teacher and his parents first noticed and encouraged when he was five.

he Chinese have an ancient curse: "May you live in interesting times." There have been no more interesting times in the course of my vagrancies about the world than the summer I sailed my 46´ cutter *Unlikely* to the U.S.S.R.—the summer of 1989, the second season of the interesting confusions of *Glasnost* and *Perestroika*. My time was spent deep among the Russians. The city was Odessa. The place was a yacht club, founded a hundred years ago by the French. In this busy, sunny port it is the marina, actually the Odessa Yacht Club, that bridges past and present. The Odessa Yacht Club was a place of liberty and leisure in the forgotten days of Czars and serfs and has become a focal point for 1980s sailors seeking some freedom from 60 years of repression. The sea allowed them

some escape, if even for half a day, and the best of the Russians, sensing the liberation of the sea, gravitated toward Odessa and the only marina in the Black Sea. The club lies on a stretch of littoral that reaches from Odessa port and the famous Potemkin steps till just before the industrial port of Il'chevsk ten miles southward. The shoreline is in the process of being given back to the people. Industrial areas are melting away as beaches and parks and hotels and marinas struggle out of the shell of carelessness created by two generations of official disdain for the common needs of common people.

DEEP AMONG THE
RUSSIANS

ARTICLES AND PHOTOGRAPHS
BY REESE PALLEY

The hour just before sundown, as it is in marinas the world over, is the best time. The Odessa Yacht Club begins to empty out for the night. Here and there some of the more dedicated Comrades work on into the darkness, burnishing, under bare bulbs, a fleet of wooden boats that we would long since have abandoned. Boats younger and more handsome than these dot the tidal flats of the West, biodegrading back into the sea. But here nothing is allowed to biodegrade; old boats and old cars are kept alive, as was a 1938 handmade BMW, still rakish after half a century, that we saw on the rutted streets of this once-beautiful city, a city that still evokes its Frenchy origins.

Odessa is the Russian correlative of Miami Beach. It lies on the empty Black Sea, its climate moderated by that big southern body of water into something like the climate of Annapolis, and it has become the eastern center for yachting in the Soviet Union. The city, which curls protectively around the marina, is only a short climb up a hundred steps through a wooded park. Tram lines at the top of the steps take you anywhere for two cents and the people, the delicious Russian people, apparently untouched by years of virulent anti-American propaganda, would, if you would let them, lift you in their arms and carry you across the streets. Should you complain that an American can cross the street on his own feet, they might well answer, yearningly, "Yes, but thanks to God, *you* don't have to."

Should you come into the U.S.S.R. on a jet as a tourist, cosseted and insulated by hotels and English-speaking waiters, you will get only what you pay for. A bit of museum culture, a chat with a cab driver seeking a tip, some geography viewed through the quarantine of a tourist-bus window. But sail into a port on a small sailboat, tie your stern to Mother Russia, be thwart to thwart with the sailors of the place, and you will be thrust immediately and integrally into the culture. There is no better way to be a stranger nor any quicker way to lose your strangeness. A soft and quiet and unexpected appearance in a strange harbor, especially after a long passage, causes the place to open and readjust to your presence. You are one of the gang. You are foreign and accepted. You are Comrade and, without contradiction, Capitalist. You are enemy and friend. Thus

O ld yachts and old ships characterize the Odessa Yacht Club, although there are some new fiberglass yachts in residence, two of them shown here. The wooden yachts are well-loved, and as well-maintained as is possible given shortages of supplies and parts, and the Odessa Yacht Club is a busy place in season, with old men fishing, young women sunbathing, children in the water, and sailors daysailing or working on their boats. Odessa is the eastern center for yachting in the U.S.S.R., and for the past two seasons officials of the yacht club and the port have been interested in having more visiting yachts from Europe and the U.S. Reese Palley, author of this report on Odessa, advises: "Should you want to summer in the Black Sea, write to me at the following addresses with the name of your yacht, the birthdates and nationalities of all your crew, and I will send you an invitation issued by the Odessa Yacht Club that will be honored by any Soviet Consulate—Reese Palley, c/o Yacht *Unlikely*, Odessa Yacht Club, Odessa, U.S.S.R.—and send a copy to—Reese Palley, 1912 Wilcox St., Philadelphia, PA 19130."

did I come into Odessa, back to a city a few hours from where my father was born, to the place my father left in 1917 "to wait out the revolution." I was completing a circle.

Three days out of Istanbul we coasted along the shore looking for the two big ships tied up inside the marina. One was used as offices by the marina administration and by cats as a pissoir. The other, an ancient Victory Ship built in the U.S. during WWII, was as neat as a thousand merchant-marine cadets can make a ship. Nothing much else gleamed in the marina, all else was purely utilitarian; but the training vessel, white and sparkly, was a daily reminder to the Russians how things should be, could be, if the government ever got its act together.

After a bit of grumbling that we were taking the berth of a Soviet sailboat, we tied up with the help of a hundred hands. There was not much English spoken here but the sailors among them needed no directions. The welcome was warm and, as the months passed (we were there for six months), things got warmer. There were some moments of unpleasant warmth when, for example, the captains of the resident yachts called a meeting instigated by a couple of the more territorial skippers. The intent was to have us evicted as a disturbing influence, which we were, and sent along to Odessa Port a mile north. But curiosity in the majority overcame the xenophobia of the few. We had already become part of the fabric of the place, "part of the furniture," as our friend Tristan Jones likes to say. We had been quick to offer help and advice and to share the enormous wealth (in their eyes) of the stores and spares which any western yacht will have aboard.

Gulfstreamer needed a main. We had an old spare Hood that we had never hoisted, and our sense of being part of their world swelled as the graceful Newick trimaran, brought here thirteen years ago on the deck of an Odessa vessel that had found her abandoned in the Atlantic, sailed out under *our* old sail. *Fortuna*, one of only half a dozen privately owned yachts (all the rest were factory or club boats, but more later) needed everything. She was lying port to starboard with us and the owner, who worked 18 hours a day on her to get her ready for Greece where he dreamed of sailing and hiring himself out, became a close friend. Whatever he asked for we gave, and the gifts were not unreturned. Sergei studied our needs and appointed himself supplier of gasoline to

> Odessa is the Russian correlative of Miami Beach. It lies on the empty Black Sea, its climate moderated into something like the climate of Annapolis . . .

Unlikely. We had acquired one of only a few Mercedes automobiles in the whole city (we were there on business and wanted to make an impression) and gasoline had to be obtained by standing in line for five hours and hoping that the tanks would not run dry. I do not know where Sergei got the gas (I refrained from asking), but for the whole time we were there our gas tanks overfloweth. That was pretty much the way it was in all things and with all friends. The need to reciprocate for the slightest favor led to our extreme embarrassment when one sailor, to whom we had given a few stainless rivets (and our rivet gun over which he almost cried) showed up with a small vial of *French* perfume. In a society where the least western product can cost a month's wages, a bottle of French perfume was a Czar's ransom. I can't remember how we wriggled out of that one.

It was the arcane organization of authority and subtle power that most puzzled us in the beginning and took all the time we were there to unravel. This is a society in which money is not the measure of either success or power, and the rules of the game are the same in the sailorly microcosm of the Odessa Yacht Club as they are in all of Soviet society. The yacht club itself is owned, as is so much else in Odessa, by the Black Sea Shipping Company. This behemoth inherited the club because any activity that looks seaward from the city is in their grasp. There is no logic for an institution concerned with merchant ships to be the authority over yachting; but, since any activity in the Soviet Union means important jobs and even more important privileges, the system honors the ancient principle that them what has gets. Not unlike our own pecking order.

The basic illogicality of the system was made plain when a few western yachts showed up at the Odessa Yacht Club in 1989. The officials of the Black Sea Shipping Company could only think in terms of big boats so they applied the same measurement formula to yachts that would apply to a supertanker. This spawned the "$500-for-even-one-day-entrance" disaster that stopped cold the beginning flow of yachts cruising to the U.S.S.R. from Istanbul. Thirty yachts had been converging on Odessa, and when this piece of stupidity spread out over the Mediterranean via Ham radio all but a few made other plans.

Among the 12 U.S. and European yachts that visited Odessa in the summer of '89 was the U.S. motor yacht *Astraea*, which cruised in from the Med and attracted attention as an example of the lifestyles of the rich if not the famous. Ashore, meanwhile, a keelboat in need of cosmetics got some attention from a group of young Russians while the girlfriend of one of them took some sun on the bow.

A big stink ensued. The newspapers picked up the story and, thanks to *Glasnost*, the matter was reversed. But reversed completely, with more panicky illogic. Now there were no fees. No one wanted to be accused of backward inhospitable foolishness at a moment when Gorbachev had his arms wide out to the West. There are rumors that a fee structure is being worked out; but the insularity of Customs and Immigration makes it probable that the fees charged at Odessa, likely to be $100 or so per month, will not extend to the other fascinating ports of the Black Sea such as Yalta and Sochi. Lord knows what they will charge.

But the damage was done and the international cruising community, so efficient in matters of

> It was the arcane organization of authority and subtle power that most puzzled us in the beginning and took all the time we were there to unravel.

communication and rumor, is now mostly convinced that they will be wildly overcharged or, failing to pay, that skippers and possibly crews will be bundled off to Siberia. Forget it. It will

never happen. No Soviet official will make the same mistake that led to such deep embarrassment, The simple fact, if there is a simple fact in this Gothic country, is that the Soviets have zero experience in dealing with the rest of the world. Their gaffe with the yachts is just a microcosm of their plight in learning to deal with the West in larger matters. The discouragement of western yachts this season was a pity for the Russian sailors who gobbled up every bit of information and experience that we aboard *Unlikely* could pass along. And it was a pity for the westerners denied the experience and the warmth and the passion of the real Russia—not at all the Russia that, for a generation, has been characterized as (to coin a phrase) the Evil Empire.

In the midst of all this is the schitzy business of Soviet daysailing and racing. The boats at the O.Y.C. are mostly owned by factories, clubs and other Soviet (read "government") institutions. The privilege of crewing on one of these boats, a more or less permanent privilege, is fought and schemed for. The captaincy of a boat usually goes to an old-time sailor who, in the dim past, won one or another of the few sailing honors available to the U.S.S.R. in its darker days. These captains rule their ships with the passion of a Bligh. The boats are sailed by the numbers. The crew does what it is told. A bit of sailorly enterprise can dump a crewman on the strand, his chance of sailing again forever gone. The wonderful and subtle interplay between skipper and crew that has raised western racing from rote to art, especially in the postwar years when yachting in the U.S. and Europe became less elite, does not yet exist in the U.S.S.R. That they suffer for this rigidity, in a sport that should be loose and fluid, was brought home when People to People Sports brought over three amateur U.S. teams during the surprising summer of '89 to race the Russians in their own boats using Russian sails and gear. In spite of the knee-jerk attempt by referees to keep the silver for the home team, the brilliant interplay of the American skippers and crews prevailed. The Black Sea Regatta was won by a pickup bunch of dedicated amateurs from below the Mason-Dixon line. The Russian sailors were delighted to be beaten. It was a first opportunity for most of them to observe western sailors at work. They competed. They watched. They learned. The officials, old-guard and mostly non-sailors, still acted as if their jobs were on the line if the Russians lost. And maybe, in all fairness, they were.

There are about a hundred boats in the Odessa Yacht Club. A few are new 35-footers in glass. Most are ancient wooden boats still sailing because of the passionate labors of their crews. There are a slew of 1/4-tonners, most of them made in Poland and some just now coming out of Soviet yards. The new boats, to one of which I was Godfather (*Arizona*, see photos) are as good as the best of the West and can be bought for half the price. In a similar boat, but slower and older, the "Charleston team" from the U.S. took the Black Sea Regatta. These boats so impressed Squeaky James, Teddy Turner, Rick

Henniger, Brian Swan, Richard Spellman and George Puckharber that they bought a couple for racing in Charleston against U.S. counterparts.

It's not that the Russians cannot make things as well as equivalents are made in the West. The 1/4-tonners are an example that they can. It is that, for the most part, throughout the whole complicated industrial structure of the U.S.S.R., Russian workers and designers have lost the aesthetic. Give them a couple of years to learn some of the things they missed during the past few decades, and give them a couple of years more to get the dinosaurs off

The sailboats of the O.Y.C. were objects of love so intense that it rivaled the love for the extraordinarily beautiful women of Odessa. The sailors wooed their boats, not their ladies, and expended labor on boats of such age and decrepitude that we in the West would find incomprehensible. No vessel, let alone anything that might float, is thrown away. Indeed, there are a couple of converted ships' lifeboats with stuck-on keels that can be seen in the waters of the bay. They don't tack too good but they float, and that is enough. Meanwhile, there is much brave talk of building boats for themselves. The spirit is willing but the technology is weak. A few are being built. The aluminum 84-footer that came out of Sochi for the Whitbread Race placed sixth at the first leg, a stunning performance that Skip Novak will tell you more about elsewhere in this issue of Nautical Quarterly. And, although the Russian America's Cup Challenge has not yet laid a keel, it is becoming a matter of national pride for this Socialist nation to enter that quintessential joust of Capitalist ego and exchequer.

But back to the East-West sailing of the summer of '89. Every night the U.S. teams went to the "Red Hotel" to party on champagne and caviar. The rubles for these festivities came from anonymous Russian donors who wanted only that the Americans take back with them a good feeling for Odessa. The Americans were treated like visiting royalty and had to fend off gifts and hide from the stunning women of this town of sunbathing beauties (who also wanted simply that the Americans take back with them a good feeling for Odessa).

Something must be said about the young women of Odessa. As an old sailor, I have to say that it is not that sailors arrive here too long away from home and that the females of the port look better than they are. It is that these women have legs as long as whisker poles and carriages as erect and stately as a three-master running down the Trades. Their eyes have that slight upward leap that reminds us how close we are to Asia, and in this old crossroads of so many tribes and nations, from Vikings to Tartars to Greeks, there is an Elysian variety to unjade the most dedicated rake. Sailor, should you be bored with politics, have had your fill of exotic and cantankerous cultures, and have seen as many Pacific sunsets as are allowed, then hie yourself to Odessa for no other reason than to

Summer activity on the Odessa waterfront includes rowing, daysailing, swimming in the Black Sea and sunbathing. The lapstrake boats—here a slim dory-shaped rowing skiff and a huskier type reminiscent of a ship's boat and with a divided squaresail—have a Baltic heritage. The waters and the beaches are crowded in this Russian equivalent of South Florida, and the young women of Odessa, as Reese Palley tells us, are very beautiful.

their backs, and we western sailors will have a whole new nifty bunch of kids to play with.

A quick look at the boats of Odessa (except for the competitive 1/4-tonners) was enough to convince us that the level of technology was so low and the level of scarcity so high that there was

little likelihood that the U.S.S.R. could get anything as complicated as a nuclear strike together. Their boats are mostly handmade, their gear cobbled together from any old thing, their sails a disgrace and their electronics non-existent. But for all that they are objects of freedom and leisure and definitely ardor.

lie in your cockpit and, as the endless procession sensates along the waterfront, to regain the wonder in the Lord that He could do so good.

Squeaky James of the visitors from Charleston had the worst time with the ladies. Six-foot, smart, hunky, and as sexy as a Playgirl centerfold, he was on leave from his fiancée, and soon to be married. Squeaky was true to Anne, drawling a polite and repeated demurrance to bevies of ladies with grace of which only a southern boy, a product of The Citadel, is capable. Rick Henniger for his size was an unmissable target and Brian Swan, who could silence a room full of drunken partying Russians

with his remarkable whistled rendition of "The International," was stalked but, from all appearances, remained uncaught. Squeaky, the Skipper, had laid down immutable rules. "We are here to race. We will eat race, think race and sleep race. We party only when it is sensible. And as for dalliance with the ladies, never forget that we are watched and judged. We *are* the US of A in Odessa and we will damn well leave a good impression."

Even when the U.S. sailors were being mercilessly persecuted by officials, Squeaky's team and the two teams from St. Mary's College in Maryland to a man refrained from complaints or recriminations.

They remained gentlemen. Congratulations, gentlemen. Our diplomatic corps should only be filled with folk half so sensitive.

Odessa is a tale of two cities. It sits at the edge of an ancient polyglot land and a recent state poised on the knife edge of history, a state as likely to fall back into dark Stalinist repression as it is to beat forward into the Gorbachevian promise of better things. Odessa is, these days, a place of paranoid caution contradicted by the wild Tartar abandon of its sailors as they throw their ancient wooden sloops about in maneuvers that would test the mettle of carbon fiber. Odessa is a conundrum, as is the enormous U.S.S.R. ranged beyond this sunny port from the nearby wheatlands of the Ukraine to the frozen towns you can almost see from Alaska. My frequent thought during the six months we were in Odessa was that perhaps only during the French Revolution has there been a conjunction of place and time so ripe with hope and so full of despair. But Odessa's sailors, like sailors all over the world, inured to risk-taking by a cantankerous Black Sea, present the western cruising sailor with a braver microcosm of this bewildering land. Bound up as they are in an unworkable political system, they have managed to retain a sailorly need for personal freedom, a thing rare among the landbound folk.

As good as it is, though, they cannot entirely rise above the fear of freedom that is felt in every decision and in every move. While the Odessa Yacht Club appears, on the surface, much like any other in the world, scratch it and all sorts of bureaucratic worms may be seen in a grope for power and privilege. As noted, this is a system in which money has, ostensibly, been removed as a measure of privilege or success. It has been replaced by the coinage of petty permissions granted or withheld. As a result, the Soviet yachtsmen in Odessa live in constant fear of official refusal of rights guaranteed them by their constitution and spend inordinate energy, time, and the promise of returned favors to get even the simplest nautical matter resolved. Should a Soviet sailor want to paint his bottom, move his boat, pick a crew, invite friends aboard or even just go out for a daysail, it might well take weeks to fix the arrangements and a precise balance of promised favors in return for the required permissions.

Yet with all the problems Russians sailors may face they have recently chosen an unlikely way to expend their energies and slim resources. The sailors of the Black Sea have created a life-size approximation of the *Argo*, Jason's legendary rowing ship that is said to have visited ports of the Black Sea some thousands of years ago. This is a vessel with no conceivable practical application that requires 70—count 'em, 70—strong Soviet backs to move. They rowed it to Istanbul and are planning to row to Greece in the spring. This romantic gesture, so much better than a Palace of Culture, a nuclear missile or another damn tractor

> This is a system in which money has, ostensibly, been removed as a measure of privilege or success. It has been replaced by the coinage of petty permissions . . .

factory, is a clear signal that the cold and inclement socialist rationalism is melting in the resurgent glow of old Russian passions.

Those few of us who squeezed through the squeaking political gates before the fears of reactionary, anti-*Perestroika* officials threw up new barriers (soon, I hope, to come down again) all agreed that being in Odessa as a sailor at this moment of change and confusion is the largest experience in our cruising life. At no other place and at no other time could we better experience the grinding mesh of politics and people and philosophies than here in Odessa in the interesting summer just past. And it was good to be an American in this time and place. When an American sailor comes in at sea level—at freedom level—and ties up scupper to scupper with Russian sailors, the chemistry is heartwarming. It takes about ten seconds for 50 years of official hatred to melt away. There is nothing in the complicated

Russian soul that is negative toward Americans. Most of the suspicion comes from the American side. When our sailors realize, and they do very quickly, that something very akin to yearning and love flows unreservedly, the suspicions of two generations are smoke in a gale.

Rarely in the West do you see a boat named something like *Lenin's Lady* or *Communist Dream* (although I did once see a boat named *Rosa Luxemburg*), but in Odessa as further evidence of the emotional incline toward the West I saw boats named *Robin Hood* and *Arizona* and, my all-time favorite, *Old Saltov*. How can you hate a people who have the temerity to Sovietize colloquial English?

There is a reaction that occurs among the citizens of Odessa when they first realize that the stranger they are talking to is American. So few of us have ever come here, and so distant America seems, that the moment of recognition is electric. A new acquaintance, met on the street perhaps, will ask if you are German or English or anything but what you are. When the truth gets through the language and expectation barriers, the consistent and universal response is a deep indrawn breath and a soft and delighted "*HaMERica!*" spoken as of some distant and unbelievable Camelot. All Russians dream of America. They do not dream of Italy or Germany or France. What a pleasure it is to meet them and to hear them say it—*HaMERica*, breathed out with such a dreamy affection that is makes you want to pledge allegiance to the flag.

At left is part of the group of foreign yachties that sailed to Odessa—representing the U.S., France, Germany and New Zealand. The Russians, meanwhile, have their own floating ambassador in a rowing/sailing approximation of Jason's *Argo*, the vessel that classical legend tells us cruised into the Black Sea and retrieved the Golden Fleece from King Aeëtes of Colchis.

THERE'S NOTHING LIKE SCHOONERS

BY JOSEPH DITLER
PHOTOGRAPHS BY BOB GRIESER

Every spring in San Diego the schooners sail in from as far away as Canada to race, to host parties, to take visitors for daysails, to fill the seascape with topsails and golly wobblers, to give the old town a dose of schooner fever. The sponsors, charities and dates change almost yearly, but with each year's racing and carousing the ranks grow with new schooners from old plans and old schooners with new owners. One year a sailor with schooner envy rigged his sport submarine with a fore-and-aft sailplan just to be allowed in the schooner dress parade with boats he'd admired since he was a boy. There have been schooners on the U.S. west coast ever since Gold-Rush days, and schooner yachts here and there for most of this century, all willing to race at the sight of another on the horizon. But organized schooner racing began here in 1984 when a San Diego yachting write put two old schooners together in what he called the "Mayday Race of Schooners." Com-peting were the three-masted shrimper *Resolution*, which couldn't find speed if it was running twin diesel engines, and the Dutch topsail schooner *La Violante*, with gaff-headed sails, Panamanian registry and HAM call signs borrowed from a soul-surfer in Hawaii.

The racing wasn't much. *La Violante* pulled a horizon job on *Resolution*, and the crew of the latter sailed a shorter course by a mile or so to keep the finish close. But the publicity the event generated, and the number of schooner fans that turned out to watch, demonstrated a latent lust for schooners that today manifests itself in several schooner races in San Diego as well as schooner fervor in other old-boat races and gatherings up the coast.

Other match races followed, and the America's Schooner Cup was created soon enough. Now in its fourth year, the Schooner Cup has grown from a two-boat race in 1986 to a gathering of 29 schooners in 1989—the largest schooner race on the west coast in this century, and only half a dozen vessels off the record of 35 schooners set in New York in the past two years by the Mayor's Cup Schooner Race hosted by the South Street Seaport Museum. Last spring's fleet ranged from the 15′ *Lime in the Coconut* to the 145′ *Californian*, flagship of the Nautical Heritage Museum at Dana Point. The Billy Bones Schooner Race, held each year since 1986 along the coast off San Diego, is the town's other springtime schooner race, a contest-cum-clambake that has been called the antithesis of the Schooner Cup. The Schooner Cup charges a $100 entry fee, hosts big parties and dinners along with auctions and a dance, gives elaborate trophies and races in the bay. It is a showcase for the host yacht club and for area politicians as well as a gathering of schooners, and it is—well—a little fancier than the Billy Bones.

The Billy Bones Race is free, hosts a large raft-up and barbecue on the beach (also free), gives bottles of Pusser's Rum for prizes, and races a reaching course along the coast, a schooner's best and most exciting point of sail. The promoter, San Diego restaurateur Paul Plotts, owns a schooner and spends thousands of his own dollars each year to perpetuate and celebrate the type. The host/schoonerman also makes a cash donation to a local charity following each Bones Race.

In the spring of 1990, the Bones Race will team up with the brand-new Downwind Coastal Race from Los Angeles to San Diego for a three-day, two-race schooner extravaganza March 23-25 complete with nautical film festival, schooner museum exhibit, rides on the schooners and raft-ups. The America's Schooner Cup, sponsored by the Kona Kai International Yacht Club, is scheduled for the following weekend, March 31 and April 1.

The three races and other diversions will be called the San Diego Spring Schooner Festival, and will raise money for the Maritime Museum of San Diego. The Festival is expected to draw wooden schooners from as far north as Seattle and Canada, and it may be the most ambitious week of schooner racing ever attempted in this country. All the while, schooner entries continue to grow in such established west-coast races and as the San Francisco Master Mariner's Regatta, the Doctor Daniels Race in Catalina, the Anacapa Race, the Long Beach Ancient Mariner Race and the Newport-to-Ensenada Race. And over the years particular schooners have earned reputations, legends and fans.

There is *Kelpie*, for example, winner of the past two America's Schooner Cup races. She has been billed as the fastest schooner on the west coast, and no other boat has been able to prove otherwise. Designed by the

On these two pages and the two previous we see some of the windy, sunlit schooning that enlivens the San Diego waterfront every springtime. On this page is *Alcyone* chasing *Dauntless*. Seen from above on pages 174-175 is *Spike Africa*. A Pacific-trading-schooner type built by Bob Sloan in his backyard over a seven-year period, and named for the legendary schooner sailor and President of the Pacific Ocean, *Spike* is owned, skippered and campaigned now in West-Coast schooner races by Bob's widow Monika. *Alcyone* is Sugar and Leslie Flanagan's lovely topsail schooner from Port Townsend, WA. *Dauntless* is a classic Alden racing schooner, built in 1930 and now owned and campaigned by San Diego restaurateur Paul Plotts.

Ford, Payne and Swiesguth partnership in Boston, *Kelpie* was built in 1928 of longleaf yellow pine. An 82′ racing schooner with the staysail sailplan that was state-of-the-art in the ocean racing of her time, she served as a submarine patrol vessel for the Coast Guard off Nantucket in World War II. *Kelpie* charters out of Newport Beach.

Where *Kelpie* goes, *Astor* follows. *Astor* is a William Fife design, built in 1924 in Scotland, that was the flagship of the Sydney Yacht Club for 20 years. Another staysail type, *Astor* is 86′ overall and a serious threat to *Kelpie* in heavy winds. Last year the winds were 12 knots for the Schooner Cup, getting favorable for *Astor* and borderline for *Kelpie*. Her owners took no chances. They tied their anchor chain to a float, then

Yes, she's a barkentine, not an orthodox schooner. But who cares? The lovely, theatrical vessel above is *HMS Dolphin*, a perfect piece of sailing romance— gunports, ratlines, great cabin and all.

dropped several hundred pounds of ballast before the race to give her an edge. A line formed from the dock to the parking lot, and crew members passed over everything including the galley sink to lighten the load.

Some schooner owners are as famous as the schooners they sail. *Alcyone*, a beautiful topsail schooner from Port Townsend, Washington, is owned by Sugar and Leslie Flanagan. They gained unwanted fame as survivors of the 1986 sinking of *Pride of Baltimore*. While drifting around in a patched liferaft, they decided they would get married if survival were in their future. They survived, got married, and now sail one of the prettiest schooners on the west coast. No one who was there will forget the sight of *Alcyone* sailing into San Diego Bay last year for the

Schooner Cup. Her towering sailplan, topsails and all, was gasping for air as she barely made headway in the fading daylight and evening breeze. She was a poem by John Masefield come to life.

A schooner with as much charm and legend as any other in the fleet is *Spike Africa*, a 70´ topsail schooner built by Bob Sloan in his backyard over a seven-year period and completed in 1977. Sloan used her to haul cargo, for occasional towing jobs, and for bit parts in movies and TV. She was one of the Merit cigarette boats, and most recently joined Tom Hanks for a movie being shot in Catalina. Sloan named the schooner after his friend Spike Africa, self-proclaimed "President of the Pacific Ocean." Spike was a legendary schoonerman and first mate for Sterling Hayden in

Above, the crew wraps up a headsail aboard Rose of Sharon, a pretty 60´ schooner from Newport Beach that holds the record for the Ancient Mariner's Race from Southern California to Hawaii.

his schooner *Wanderer* on the passage to Tahiti that was a major event in Sterling's autobiographical book—also *Wanderer*.

Bob Sloan's widow, Monika, now operates *Spike Africa* as a full-time charter boat. She has the respect of every schoonerman on the coast for the job she undertook in the wake of her husband. She has made chartering successful in this highly competitive market, and handles the schooner better than any schoonerman or schoonerwoman on the Pacific Coast.

The personalities continue among west-coast schooners. The mother of the fleet, and the oldest schooner to race in San Diego, is the 88´ *Lady Ada*. She was built in 1903 for the Crown-Zellerbach family as a wedding gift for their daughter Ada. She is now a charter schooner, running passengers from

San Pedro to Catalina Island, a thing she does with zest. You might not expect much speed or rail-down sailing from an 87-year-old, but once *Lady Ada* clears the headlands of Catalina she acts like a rental horse headed back to the stable. She charges the distance between Catalina and San Pedro, and brings even experienced schooner sailors a rush of adrenaline.

Many of these schooners are chartered to pay for their expensive upkeep, while others are operated out of pocket for the sheer thrill of sailing a boat that spreads the most romantic rig in sailing history. One of the most visible and vigorously-campaigned schooners in Southern California is *Dauntless*, a 1930 John Alden design owned by Paul Plotts of San Diego. Plotts, owner of the Billy Bones Tavern, is the generous man who hosts the annual Billy Bones Schooner Race. If schooner racing is the question, *Dauntless* is the answer. This quick 71´ schooner has seen many owners, including Bob Sloan, who saved her from a slow death in east-coast mud. But none have been as faithful as Plotts. He is known for his starts across the line and the respect he is given by his crew. He has sailed *Dauntless* to a string of victories, including the Newport-Ensenada Race, the Oceanside Harbor Days Race, the Schooner Shootout—a match between *Dauntless* and *Bagheera*, and the America's Schooner Cup. One year he won his own race, but refused to take the trophy, instead awarding it to second-place *Astor*.

For most of the charter schooners, things like harbor excursions, whale watching, weddings, funerals and trips to Catalina are the bread and butter of the business. The 1928 schooner *Valkyrien*, however, has brought something nude to the west-coast charter trade. In addition to standard charters, she hauls a group of nudists each week to the deserted beaches north of Long Beach where they play pirates and mistresses of Tortuga. *Valkyrien* is built of Kauri wood, a wood so hard it has been called bulletproof. Today, Kauri forests are protected by the government of New Zealand, and it seems likely that there will never be another vessel built from it. The 78´ *Valkyrien* was built at Bailey and Sons Ltd.—the same boatyard that built Michael Fay's America's Cup challenger.

Valkyrien's owner, Lee Kitchen, says that he sails a schooner because "it's the only legitimate sailboat built." She needs serious wind to reach her speed, but Kitchen campaigns her every year. When asked about her higher-end size and lower-end results, he wrinkles his face, puts on his best Long-John-Silver voice and says, "I have this old trading schooner that wants to be a Swan." One eyebrow raises, and then he walks away.

There are many reasons for a schooner to travel hundreds of miles to be part of a schooner race. Publicity is one reason, the potential for victory another. But most admit that they come because it's a gathering of the tribe, an opportunity to share with others of their kind the fortunes and misfortunes of owning an old schooner in the closing years of the 20th century. It is also festive, and one of the things to be celebrated is the vitality—in fact, the bright future—of the schooner movement.

Mirror images of schooner sailing at its best—sails filled, flags flying, decks full of folks tending lines with big smiles on their faces—are *Kelpie* on starboard tack and *Dauntless* on port tack. Paul Plotts has sailed *Dauntless* to a string of victories in West-Coast schooner contests—the America's Schooner Cup, the Oceanside Harbor Days Race, even the Newport-Ensenada Race. But *Kelpie* has the reputation of the fastest schooner out there. Designed by Frank Payne's renowned Boston design office, and built in 1928 of longleaf yellow pine, this 82-footer has been a racing schooner—a staysail schooner— since the heyday of Class-A ocean racing in schooners during the late 1920s and early 1930s.

"There's a real schooner renaissance going on," says Monika Sloan of *Spike Africa*. "I like to support the west-coast events, and even though my chartering keeps me from racing in every race, I try to attend as many as possible." There are a lot of rewards to it, maybe especially the subtle ones. "It's fun to see all the schooners, and people all along the coast recognize *Spike*. She has a lot of fans. To hear someone yell, 'Hey, there's *Spike Africa*,' makes it all worth the effort." One tends to believe her. Monika Sloan gave up successful careers as a model and a registered nurse to become a schoonerman. (Make that schoonerwoman.)

Some schooners refuse to race, but wouldn't miss being a part of the spectacle. *Lady Ada* doesn't race, despite her runaway-horse behavior on charter passages in Southern California. Another non-racer is John Baxter and his Pinky schooner *Attu*. He doesn't like crowds, and fears mark roundings. But *Attu*, one of Howard Chapelle's inspired replicas of a traditional type, can always be seen in the distance, skirting the course with her raked masts, gaff sails and bright red-and-white paint job. With her pinched ends and other colorful characteristics from a hundred years ago *Attu* effectively adds to the ambience of west-coast schooner racing, despite her owner's aversion to competition and taste for privacy.

The "jewel of the Pacific" is the 1939 schooner *Mistral*. This L. Francis Herreshoff design is said to have been one of L.F.H.'s own favorites (although he must have had more than a few). She was a Naval Academy sailing ship, and the first of the Academy's yachts ever given over to female command (see NQ6). *Mistral* is also the only sailing vessel known to have had direct communication with a German U-Boat in World War II. Painted gray and sailing as a submarine patrol boat off Martha's Vineyard, her skipper heard the German untersee-motorboote captain come onto the radio and say, "Hey yachtie . . . don't you know there's a war on?"

Many of these old schooners received decorations for service in World War II. Some, like *Valkyrien* (under previous owners), were caught up in espionage and weapons smuggling, and were on the run from the military in several countries throughout the war. The fleet is full of history—in racing, in war, in a lot of activity nobody ever talked much about.

Not all the schooners have memorable histories or larger-than-life skippers; but we may say with confidence that their histories are happening now. The tiny fore-gaffed *Crystal Sea* is barely noticeable in the fleet, but she is tough on the mark roundings and doesn't back down in a strong breeze. Her owner, Don Ljungblad, lost a foot from a land mine in Vietnam, but buries the rail of his schooner alongside the *Spikes*, *Kelpies* and *Astors* out on the course. They are all making some kind of history these days in a fleet that may number 30 schooners in the spring of 1990 and seems destined to grow in fervor and in number into the 1990s. There's nothing like schooners.

navigational errors Castelli 7/13/87

CROSS-COUNTRY SAILING

Marc Castelli is a professional artist who takes his watercolor work pretty seriously. "I'm a very serious watercolor painter," he says, and goes on to explain that he has been drawing and painting for most of his 39 years, an obsession and a talent that took him to the University of Colorado for a degree in Fine Arts and has kept him busy for the past 15 years painting bright, precise portraits of boats, details of boats, and images of sailboats racing. Castelli belongs to the National Watercolor Society, the Philadelphia Watercolor Club, has petitioned for painting status as a member of the American Society of Marine Artists, and currently has work on exhibit in the Mystic Maritime Gallery at Mystic Seaport. □ But that's the serious stuff. The drawings on these pages are something else: outlandish—or, in this case, in-landish—images that Castelli started putting on paper for

Esther's Bridge   Castelli © 3/12/87

fun in 1987 and keeps fooling around with. "They are visual puns—some of them—and impossible situations, and what I guess I would call illogical leaps in logic," he says. The artist spent a dozen years up in Michigan racing E Scows, C Scows and doing distance races as crew on a Peterson 43—"always racing—I'd be bored to go cruising." He knows how to draw a racing sailboat, and more to the point he knows how to draw a racing sailboat hard on the wind in an orchard. There are intimations of M. C. Escher's brilliant plays on perception, René Magritte's spooky combinations of objects out of place, and even Gary Larson's Far Side cartoons in these drawings. But comparisons are odious. Castelli's images of cross-country sailing are not. They are droll and wonderful.

man overboard

Castelli · 5/8/87

racing in the mountains is interesting; starts are everything—

uncharted waters — first day

Costello © 5/15/87

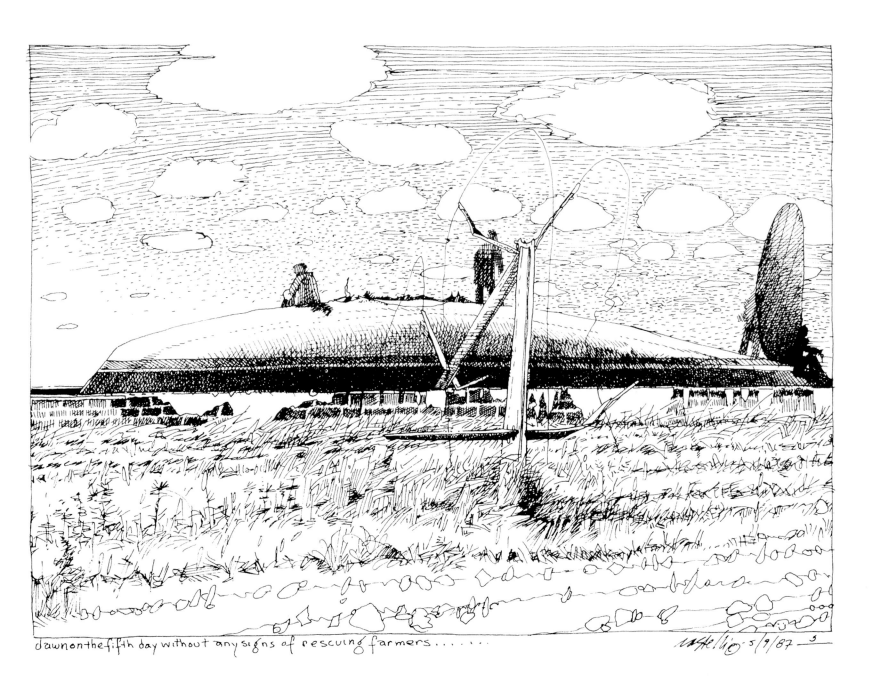

dawn on the fifth day without any signs of rescuing farmers . . . . . .

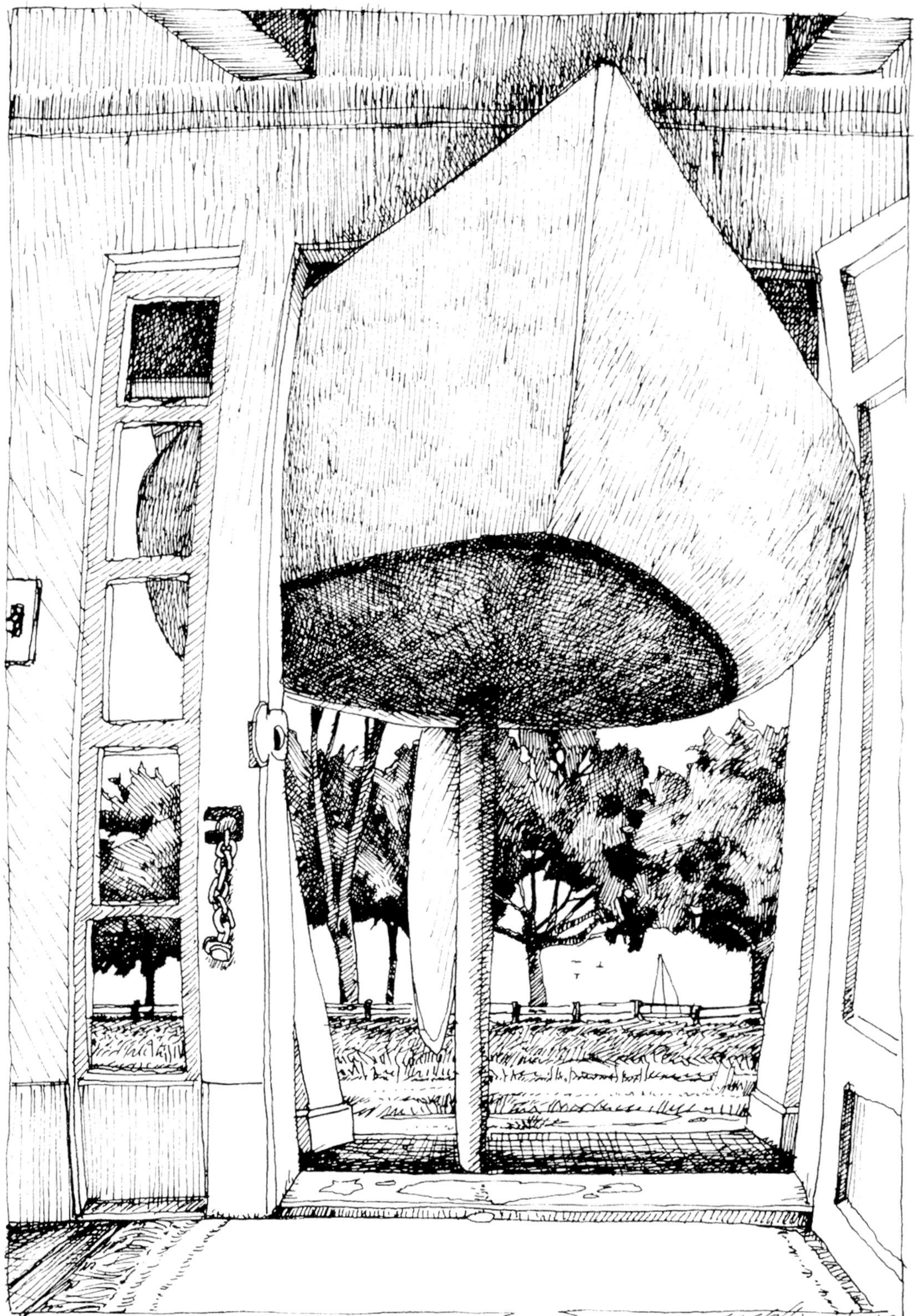

home from the sea

site of ancient regatta.

ACKNOWLEDGMENTS

Preparing *The Best of Nautical Quarterly, Volume I: The Lure of Sail* has been a labor of sheer pleasure. We have been fortunate in, once again, being able to read each and every article in all 50 volumes of the original *Nautical Quarterly* magazine in order to aid our selection process for this book. In researching the history of *Nautical Quarterly* we are deeply indebted to the following for their willing assistance: Paul Adamthwaite of the Archives & Collections Society, Picton, Ontario; Bill Burt, Clare Cunningham, Richard Curtis, Joseph Ditler, Jonathan Eaton, Jim Gilbert, Stan Grayson, Ethel Gribbins, Karen Kavin, Karen Kratzer, C. S. Lovelace, Donald C. McGraw Jr., Elizabeth Meyer, Marilyn Palley, Martin Pederson, Bill Reed, and John Rousmaniere; and anyone we have inadvertently forgotten.

Also, we thank Peggy Tate Smith and head librarian Paul O'Pecko at The Museum of America and the Sea at Mystic Seaport. Mystic Seaport has long been a central player in preserving ships and the lore of ships. Preserving the lore, it can be argued, is perhaps more important than the difficult and very expensive preservation of vessels. To keep a history alive requires dedication and a place to keep important materials. Mystic Seaport has provided that dedication and the space, and both with the highest level of professional care.

The history of sailing and boating is at the core of the development of America during the centuries when she was finding her sea legs as a great nation. Much of that history is today in the careful and dedicated hands of the Mystic Seaport Museum. As Joe Gribbins was an exemplary custodian of other authors' words, so Mystic Seaport is the finest caretaker of a grateful nation's nautical heritage.

Without Mystic Seaport, this tale of the exquisite work of Joe Gribbins could not have been adequately told. During the 13 years *Nautical Quarterly* was published, Joe Gribbins went back repeatedly to the deep well of Mystic for photos and references not available elsewhere. Most important, however, was the support that the museum extended to Joe Gribbins after the magazine ceased publication in the summer of 1990. As soon as space became available they took him in and made a place for his special and rare talents. For some years before his death, Joe was safely ensconced as the publications director of the museum, where he continued to administer his special brand of literary magic on manuscripts by other writers.

When we started to think about a memorial to Joe in the form of republishing the best of his efforts, a file of the 50 volumes of *Nautical Quarterly* was needed. It took only a single phone call to Mystic. In due time two great boxes of the precious books appeared with the comment, "Please use as you see fit."

Many thanks to Dennis Pernu of MBI Publishing Company for having the courage to take this project on board, and for putting up with two demanding authors. In addition, our gratitude goes to the wonderful writers who have allowed their work to be reproduced here and to the photographers and illustrators whose artistic talents are showcased in this book.

In addition I, Anthony Dalton, would like to publicly express my deepest gratitude to my friend and fellow author, Reese Palley, who suggested this project and invited me to help bring it to fruition. Thanks, Old Reese. It has been an exciting voyage.

— Reese Palley and Anthony Dalton

INDEX

CREDITS

Front Cover:	*Parting the Crest* by Thomas Hoyne	**23–25:**	Brian Dowley
Back Cover:	Painting by David Barker	**27:**	Brian Dowley
Frontispiece:	*The Schooner Yacht America* By Frank Wagner	**28&29:**	Brian Dowley photos Drawings by John G. Alden & Co.
Title Page:	Skip Novak	**31:**	Brian Dowley
Contents Page:	Painting by Don Demers	**33–35:**	Brian Dowley
12:	Charles Gregory, Courtesy of Rudolph J. Schaefer and Mystic Seaport	**36–45:**	Courtesy of the U.S. Coast Guard
14:	*American Superiority at the World's Greatest Fair*, 1851, Collections of the NYPL, Astor, Lenox and Tilden Foundations New York Public Library	**46–48:**	Illustrations by Daniel Maffia
		49:	Drawings courtesy of Bill Elliott, Bay Ship and Yacht Co., Novato, CA
15:	The Old Print Shop, New York	**52–55:**	Photos courtesy of the Jack London Bookstore, Glen Ellen, CA, with permission of the Jack London Estate
16:	James E. Butters-Worth, Courtesy of Mystic Seaport	**56–63:**	Farrell Grehan
20–22:	Brian Dowley	**64–73:**	Thomas Andreas Nicolai Ettenhuber
22:	Drawing by John G. Alden & Co.	**75–92:**	Skip Novak
		94–101:	Paintings by Thomas Hoyne

102–109:	Courtesy of Carl and Margaret Vilas
110:	Courtesy of Phil Wade
11–117:	Phil Wade stamps photographed by Bill Burt
118–126:	Beken of Cowes
127&128:	Skip Novak
129&133:	Paintings by David Barker
130:	Map drawn by deLancey Funsten
134&135:	Skip Novak
137:	André Mechelynck
139&140:	Skip Novak
142–149:	Paintings by Don Demers
155–163:	Paintings by Frank Wagner
164–173:	Reese Palley
174–180:	Bob Grieser
182–189:	Drawings by Marc Castelli